lonely planet

ITALY

Angela Corrias, E................................edetta Geddo,
Paula Hardy, Stephanie Ong, Margherita Ragg,
Kevin Raub, Eva Sandoval, Nicola Williams

Contents

ANIBAL TREJO/SHUTTERSTOCK ©

Ionian
Sea

Naples & the
South 182

Lecce
4hr 30m

Bari

Brindisi

Lecce

Taranto

Cosenza

Reggio di
Calabria

Messina

Catania

Syracuse

Aeolian
Islands

Mt Etna

SICILY

Palermo

Agrigento

Marsala

Pantelleria

MALTA

1hr15m

Mt Vesuvius

Naples

Ischia

Tyrrhenian Sea

Olbia

Sassari

Sardinia 218

Rome
1hr

Cagliari

Oristano

Mediterranean
Sea

TUNISIA

ALGERIA

Experience
Italy online

200 km

100 miles

0

0

N

Gaze upon countless museum masterpieces and imaginative street art. Explore dramatic Roman ruins and conquer fire-spitting volcanoes. Indulge in delightful regional delicacies and sip liquid perfection in postcard-perfect vineyards. Rekindle love on romantic weekend escapes. Shred powder on majestic mountains and zip across idyllic lakes to baroque palaces. Carouse with merrymakers at exuberant local festivals. Traverse cinematic landscapes and forage for truffles. Laze about sun-toasted sands in island paradises.

This is Italy.

TURN THE PAGE AND START PLANNING YOUR NEXT BEST TRIP →

Vernazza, Cinque Terre (p72)

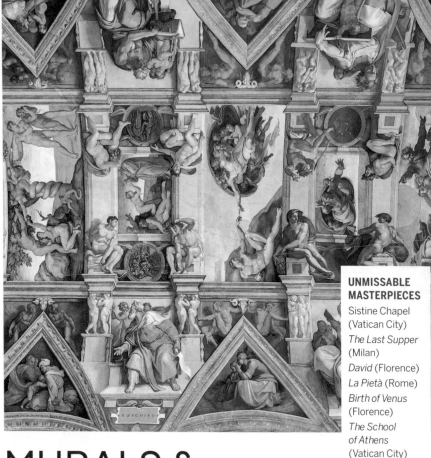

UNMISSABLE MASTERPIECES

Sistine Chapel (Vatican City)

The Last Supper (Milan)

David (Florence)

La Pietà (Rome)

Birth of Venus (Florence)

The School of Athens (Vatican City)

MURALS &
MASTERPIECES

Leonardo da Vinci. Michelangelo. Raphael. Giotto. Caravaggio. Italy's immeasurable trove of artistic masters is so profound it would take more than a lifetime to meet them all, but art lovers happily die trying. For every Uffizi Gallery or Vatican Museum, there's an unremarkable hamlet with a priceless piece or two – and that's just the paintings, sculptures and artefacts. Churches, universities, historic buildings – even streets – teem with treasures as well.

TICKETS

Always buy tickets in advance for Italy's most popular museums. Not only will this ensure not getting shut out, you'll also forgo standing in immense ticket booth lines for admiring actual artwork.

Left Ceiling of the Sistine Chapel, Vatican City **Right** Palazzo degli Uffizi, Florence **Below** Piazza San Marco, Venice

↓ PHOTOGRAPHY

Besides standard no-flash rules, some Italian museums do not allow photography of any kind (Sistine Chapel), selfie sticks or tripods. Always check the photography rules in advance or be prepared to check your equipment in.

FREE SUNDAYS

From October to March, state-run museums and cultural sites offer free admission on Sundays, known as *domenica al museo* (Sundays at the museum). If your plans are flexible, a trove of cultural treasures can be viewed while saving euros for pasta!

Best Art Experiences

▶ **Skip the crowds on an off-the-beaten-path tour of Rome's lesser-known art and cultural treasures.** (p56)

▶ **Take a walk back in time eyeing Milan's Liberty architecture, Italy's answer to art nouveau.** (p112)

▶ **Follow Italy's unsung graphic arts history around Veneto, where 17th-century caricatures spawned modern-day cartoons.** (p134)

▶ **Scout alfresco street art in Rome's Tor Pignattara neighbourhood, an open-air mural museum.** (p52)

ITALY BEST EXPERIENCES

SEVEN ROMAN WONDERS

Pantheon
(Rome)

Herculaneum
(Ercolano)

Ostia Antica
(Rome)

Colosseum
(Rome)

Hadrian's Villa
(Tivoli)

Roman Forum
(Rome)

Pompeii

RUINS &
RELICS

If the ruins of Rome on Italian soil stopped at the Colosseum, Palatino and Forum, Italy's ancient architectural offerings would still be earth-shattering by anyone's call. But they carry on: centuries-old cities dug out from under volcanic ash, lava and mud; extraordinarily preserved Roman mosaics; lavish, 2000-year-old villas and therapeutic baths; majestic city gates and ornate bridges. Simply put, Italy's astounding relics are unrivalled.

ALEXANDRA BRUZZESE/LONELY PLANET ©

→ PIZZA BREAK

Pizzeria Gino Sorbillo (p211) near Napoli Sotterranea is as authentic a pizza experience as you'll get in Naples: queues, gruff but super-quick waiters and sensational pizza.

Left Colosseum, Rome **Right** Pizza at Gino Sorbillo, Naples **Below** Mosaic of Neptune and Amphitrite, Herculaneum

COLOSSEUM QUEUES

If you find yourself staring down an excessively long queue for Rome's Colosseum, grab tickets at Palatino (Via di San Gregorio 30; p68) instead.

ALYSTA/SHUTTERSTOCK ©

↑ HERCULANEUM

Herculaneum (p210) is a smaller city destroyed by the same 79 CE Vesuvius eruption as Pompeii, but with more impressively intact, less heavily touristed ruins.

Best Ancient Experiences

▶ Immerse yourself in Julius Caesar's Rome, the epicentre of a flourishing global empire on the brink. (p60)

▶ Discover extraordinary Renaissance Florence through the eyes of Dante Alighieri, Italy's supreme poet. (p166)

▶ Fall under the spell of seductive southeastern Sicily and its honey-hued southern baroque towns. (p214)

▶ Admire Greek, Byzantine, Norman and medieval architecture in a trio of ancient Calabrian villages. (p206)

FOODIE FACTS

Modern pizza was invented in Naples in the early 19th century.

Garlic bread, pepperoni and Caesar salad are not Italian.

Say *'Buon appetito!'* before digging into a meal.

EPICUREAN
DELIGHTS

Italy's epicurean endeavours are recreated, reinvented and copied on a daily basis all around the world, but they are never equalled. Pizza! Pasta! Gelato! Parmesan! No cuisine has permeated the palates of more people on earth than Italian, but forget all that. You haven't eaten Italian food until you've eaten it in Italy. So grab a knife and fork and clear your schedule – it's time to eat. *Buon appetito!*

RESERVATIONS

Italy is old school – few traditional establishments use restaurant reservation apps or websites. Pick up the phone (a week in advance is usually fine).

Left Gelato **Right** Pasta with wild hare
Below Pizza oven, Naples

FARE LA SCARPETTA

Bread is not for dipping in olive oil and balsamic vinegar – it's for sopping up leftover sauce. Known as *fare la scarpetta* (do the little shoe), it's named as such for the movement you do with the bread into the sauce, like dipping a little shoe into all that leftover liquid love.

↑ PIZZA NAPOLETANA STG

Associazione Verace Pizza Napoletana (AVPN) is the governing body of *pizza napoletana* (STG; Specialità Tradizionale Garantita or Traditional Guaranteed Speciality). For the real deal, look for one of its 255 member pizzerias.

Best Food Experiences

▶ **Embark on a farm-to-fork foodie tour through some of Tuscany's lesser-trampled culinary corners.** (p170)

▶ **Devour a cavalcade of iconic Emilian specialities in Bologna, Italy's pasta and pork paradise.** (p146)

▶ **Canvas the culinary corners of Naples on an epic street food expedition (eat pizza, too!).** (p192)

▶ **Taste your way around Slow Food's home in the Piedmontese countryside around Alba and Bra.** (p96)

COUNTLESS
VINEYARDS

It's one of Italy's most iconic images: impossibly pastoral vineyards draped across waves of rolling hills peppered with centuries-old villas and castles.

Rightfully so! Italy is one of the oldest and greatest Old World wine countries – in fact, the world's largest producer of *vino* – and every region is in on the action. *Salute!*

TOP: JANOKA82/GETTY IMAGES ©. BOTTOM: EKATERINA IATCENKO/SHUTTERSTOCK ©

★ HOUSE WINE

While you might shy away from house wine back home, pleasant surprises await in Italian restaurants. *Vino della casa* is usually good and good value.

Best Wine Experiences

▶ **Tackle Tuscany on the ultimate road trip through its fairy-tale vineyards and wonderful wines.** (p168)

▶ **Pop some bubbly in Conegliano and Valdobbiadene, home to Italy's Unesco-listed grapevines.** (p142)

▶ **Burrow in with bottles of Barolo and Barbera at Asti's boozy Douja D'Or festival.** (p82)

← TASTINGS

Wineries in Italy aren't as tasting-room-savvy as, say, in California. Always call ahead. **Movimento Turismo del Vino** (*movimento turismovino.it*) tracks Italian vineyards that welcome visitors.

Above left Vineyard, Tuscany **Left** Wine and food, Manarola, Cinque Terre **Above right** Riomaggiore, Cinque Terre

FAIRY-TALE
ROMANCE

████ Chocolates and flowers are nice and all, but few gestures pack the same sort of starry-eyed wallop as whisking that special someone off to Italy on a trip of a lifetime. When it comes to romance, Italy has few rivals. It's impossible not to get swept up in it all: intoxicating Roman piazzas, stunning honey-coloured historic centres, stupendous viewpoints – hell, everything! Italy is *amore*.

Best Romantic Experiences

▶ Wander hand in hand around the monumental ruins, pretty piazzas and fetching fountains of the Eternal City. (p46)

▶ Be seduced by the commanding allure of the Italian Riviera like myriad literary masterminds before you. (p92)

▶ Fall in love in Verona, one of Italy's most romantic cities. (p140)

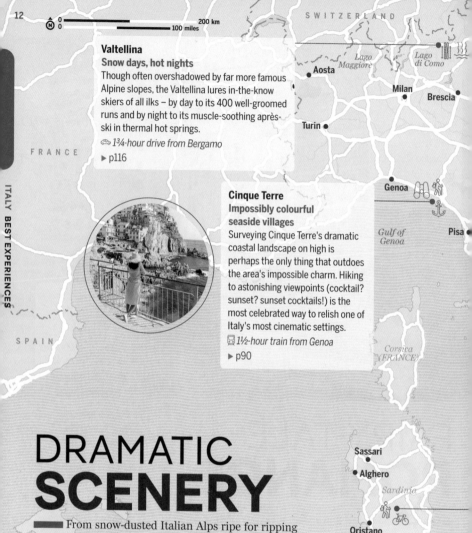

SWITZERLAND

0 ____ 200 km
0 ____ 100 miles

Lago Maggiore

Lago di Como

Aosta

Milan

Brescia

Turin

Genoa

Pisa

Gulf of Genoa

Corsica (FRANCE)

FRANCE

SPAIN

Valtellina
Snow days, hot nights
Though often overshadowed by far more famous Alpine slopes, the Valtellina lures in-the-know skiers of all ilks – by day to its 400 well-groomed runs and by night to its muscle-soothing après-ski in thermal hot springs.

🚗 1¾-hour drive from Bergamo

▶ p116

Cinque Terre
Impossibly colourful seaside villages
Surveying Cinque Terre's dramatic coastal landscape on high is perhaps the only thing that outdoes the area's impossible charm. Hiking to astonishing viewpoints (cocktail? sunset? sunset cocktails!) is the most celebrated way to relish one of Italy's most cinematic settings.

🚆 1½-hour train from Genoa

▶ p90

DRAMATIC
SCENERY

From snow-dusted Italian Alps ripe for ripping to sun-drenched road- and mountain-biking routes in Sardinia, Italy is an Eden of outdoor recreation. Skiing, cycling, hiking and sailing lead the way to unforgettable sunsets in Cinque Terre, foraging for porcini mushrooms in Calabria and colourful villages along the waterways around Milan.

Sassari

Alghero

Sardinia

Oristano

Cagliari

Mediterranean Sea

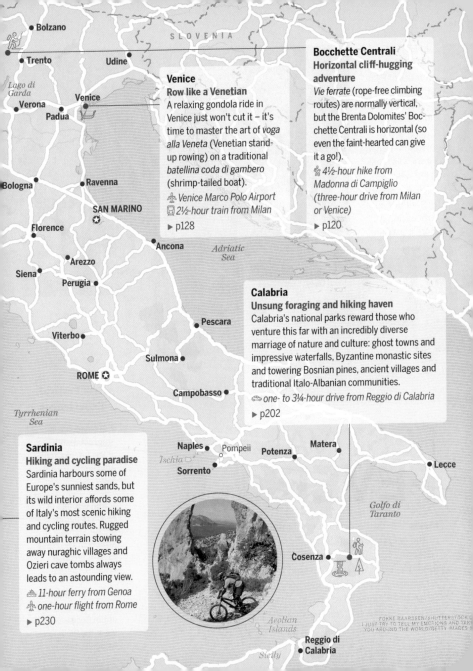

Bolzano
Trento   **Udine**
Lago di Garda
Verona   **Venice**
Padua

S L O V E N I A

Venice
Row like a Venetian
A relaxing gondola ride in Venice just won't cut it – it's time to master the art of *voga alla Veneta* (Venetian stand-up rowing) on a traditional *batellina coda di gambero* (shrimp-tailed boat).

🛫 *Venice Marco Polo Airport*
🚆 *2½-hour train from Milan*

▶ p128

Bocchette Centrali
Horizontal cliff-hugging adventure
Vie ferrate (rope-free climbing routes) are normally vertical, but the Brenta Dolomites' Bocchette Centrali is horizontal (so even the faint-hearted can give it a go!).

🥾 *4½-hour hike from Madonna di Campiglio (three-hour drive from Milan or Venice)*

▶ p120

Bologna   **Ravenna**

SAN MARINO ✪

Florence

Arezzo
Siena
Perugia

Adriatic Sea

Ancona

Pescara

Viterbo

Sulmona

ROME ✪

Campobasso

Tyrrhenian Sea

Calabria
Unsung foraging and hiking haven
Calabria's national parks reward those who venture this far with an incredibly diverse marriage of nature and culture: ghost towns and impressive waterfalls, Byzantine monastic sites and towering Bosnian pines, ancient villages and traditional Italo-Albanian communities.

🚗 *one- to 3¼-hour drive from Reggio di Calabria*

▶ p202

Sardinia
Hiking and cycling paradise
Sardinia harbours some of Europe's sunniest sands, but its wild interior affords some of Italy's most scenic hiking and cycling routes. Rugged mountain terrain stowing away nuraghic villages and Ozieri cave tombs always leads to an astounding view.

⛴ *11-hour ferry from Genoa*
🛫 *one-hour flight from Rome*

▶ p230

Naples **Pompeii** **Potenza**   **Matera**
Ischia
Sorrento   **Lecce**

Golfo di Taranto

Cosenza

Reggio di Calabria

Aeolian Islands

Sicily

FESTIVAL FEVER

Celebration is part of the Italian ethos. Festivals in the *bel paese* (beautiful country) often revolve around recurring refrains: religion, rivalry, history, music and food. Be it the arrival of coveted truffles in Piedmont, a hair-raising, cross-neighbourhood battle of equine skill in Siena or the inevitable arrival of Lent nationwide, Italians take to the streets in enthusiastic revelry. Spy a poster promoting a *festa* or *sagra*? That's where it's at.

Best Festival Experiences

▶ Overindulge in 'fragrant diamonds' at the International Alba White Truffle Fair. (p82)

▶ Join throngs of revellers parading through the streets at the Festa di Sant'Efisio in Cagliari. (p228)

▶ Get your groove on while sipping Barolo at the Collisioni Festival in the Piedmontese hills. (p82)

UNSPOILED
TERRAIN

Cloud-kissing jagged mountaintops; rolling hills of wavy, impossibly picturesque vineyards; cerulean seas headbutting craggy coastlines and floury sands; and three of the world's most active volcanoes together form an astonishing arsenal of natural landscapes. From museum to mountain, Italy entices from a united front.

Best Outdoor Adventures

▶ Summit one of Italy's most active volcanoes: the fiery 3326m Mount Etna near Catania. (p214)

▶ Cycle the interior of Sardinia's Golfo di Orosei, a two-wheel paradise for mountain-bike enthusiasts. (p230)

▶ Seek out unseen sands and idyllic islands along southern Italy's dramatic Amalfi Coast. (p196)

← CAI
Club Alpino Italiano
(cai.it) constructed and maintains nearly 800 huts and shelters and manages 7000km of hiking trails connecting all 25 Italian national parks.

TOP: STUART WILSON/SHUTTERSTOCK ©; BOTTOM: MY EMOTIONS AND TAKE YOU AROUND THE WORLD/GETTY IMAGES ©

★ TRAIL DIFFICULTY SCALE
Hiking trails are rated as follows: T (Tourist/Turistico), E (Hiking/Escursionistico), EE (Expert Hikers/Escursionisti Esperti) and EEA (Equipped Expert Hikers/Escursionisti Esperti con Attrezzatura).

Far left Festa di Sant'Efisio, Cagliari **Above left** Walking Mt Etna, Sicily **Left** Cycling, Sardinia

ENCHANTING ISLANDS & SANDS

Italy clocks up 7600km of coastline and 450 islands. Dramatic mountainous coastlines spilling onto postcard-perfect beaches and impossibly charming seaside villages are mainland highlights. Islands like Sardinia and Sicily, among others, have extremely rich cultural identities too, home to ancient civilisations and distinct cuisines.

SWITZERLAND

Lago Maggiore

Lago di Com

● Aosta

Milan

● Turin

● Genoa

FRANCE

Gulf of Genoa

SPAIN

Elba
Protected national marine park
Seven islands and islets off the Tuscan coast make up Parco Nazionale Arcipelago Toscano, Europe's largest marine national park. Here beach-peppered coves yield to perfect cerulean waters – a far cry from Chianti, but pure magic just the same.

⛴ one-hour ferry from Piombino

▶ p172

● Sassari

Alghero ●

Sardinia

Oristano ●

Sardinia
Pristine island paradise
The second-biggest island in the Mediterranean packs a sun-kissed wallop – many of Italy's most coveted shores are here. Lazing about Sardinia's unspoilt cream-sand beaches is a European rite, but don't discount the fantastic hiking, biking and seafood in paradise, either.

⛴ 11-hour ferry from Genoa

✈ one-hour flight from Rome

▶ p222

● Cagliari

Mediterranean Sea

ALGERIA

TUNISIA

Borromean Islands
Baroque wonderland, lake islands
Isola Bella and Isola Madre make up Lago Maggiore's Borromean Islands, two *palazzo*-harbouring havens once home to the aristocratic House of Borromeo. Impeccably manicured botanical and terrace gardens and a bevy of baroque await.

🚆 1¾-hour train from Milan
▶ p114

Amalfi Coast
Off-the-radar beaches and islands
The dramatic Amalfi Coast is a melange of craggy cliffs perched over tucked-away beaches, some of which aren't reachable by land and are appropriately dreamy as a result. In the gulf, a trio of islands beckons sunseekers, nature enthusiasts and cultural connoisseurs.

🚗 1½-hour drive from Naples
🚆 70-minute train from Naples
▶ p196

Procida
Authentic fishing village
Big tourism hasn't affected this small Phlegraean island's authentic way of life. Locals live in colourful villas, fish for sustenance and generally go about their down-to-earth business amid a wealth of natural splendour.

⛴ one-hour ferry from Naples or 25 minutes from Ischia
▶ p196

Sicily
Raging volcanoes, ancient temples
Summit scarily active Mt Etna (Europe's tallest active volcano), explore ancient Greek treasures and cook local delicacies with a duchess on this fascinating isle.

🚆 nine-hour train from Naples
⛴ 20-minute ferry from Villa San Giovanni
▶ p214

AUSTRIA

Bolzano

Trento

Lago di Garda

Brescia Verona Venice

HUNGARY

0   200 km
0   100 miles

Bologna Ravenna

CROATIA

BOSNIA & HERZEGOVINA

SERBIA

SAN MARINO

Florence

Pisa Arezzo

Siena Perugia Ancona

MONTENEGRO

Piombino

Viterbo Pescara

Sulmona

ROME

Adriatic Sea

ALBANIA

Naples

Ischia Sorrento Amalfi

Matera

Potenza

Lecce

Golfo di Taranto

Tyrrhenian Sea

Cosenza

Aeolian Islands

Villa San Giovanni

Palermo

Reggio di Calabria

Trapani Mt Etna

Sicily

Catania

Agrigento

Ionian Sea

Syracuse

Ragusa

August marks the high season for Italian holiday-making – touristy spots are packed while everywhere else all but shuts down.

← Spoleto Festival

A world-renowned arts event, serving up 17 days of international theatre, opera, dance, music and art in June/July.

- 📍 Spoleto
- ▶ festivaldispoleto.it

↘ Paradise Beaches

Italians summer at the beach and few rival those in Sardinia. Explore the island's best patches of paradise from La Pelosa (Stintino) to the Golfo di Orosei.

- 📍 Sardinia
- ▶ p222

← Estate Romana

Rome summer calendar of music, dance, literature and film events turns the city into an outdoor stage.

- 📍 Rome
- ▶ estateromana. comune.roma.it

JUNE

Average daytime max: 22°C
Days of rainfall: 4 (Rome)

JULY

Italy in
SUMMER

⬊ Il Palio di Siena

Daredevils in tights thrill the crowds with this chaotic bareback horse race around Siena's world-famous medieval piazza on 2 July and 16 August.

⬤ Siena

↑ Rome's Outlying Treasures

Rome's sights are expectedly crowded in summer – make your escape to the Eternal City's lesser known arts and culture gems.

⬤ Rome

▶ p56

Ferragosto

One of Italy's biggest holidays, the Feast of the Assumption, is marked on 15 August. Naples goes nuts!

Average daytime max: 25°C
Days of rainfall: 2 (Rome)

AUGUST

Average daytime max: 22°C
Days of rainfall: 3 (Rome)

Demand for accommodation peaks during summer. Book tours and overnight adventures in advance at lonelyplanet.com/italy/activities.

🧳 Packing Notes

Hat, sunglasses, sunscreen and insect repellent are a solid investment for the Italian summer.

Check out a full calendar of events

→ Culinary Call

Festival-frenzied Piedmont celebrates throughout the year, but foodies won't want to miss Asti's Festival delle Sagre in September.

◆ Asti

▶ p82

Eurochocolate

Over a million chocoholics pour into Perugia in October for the city's 10-day celebration of the cocoa bean.

◆ Perugia

▶ eurochocolate.com

→ Regata Storica

In early September, gondoliers in period dress work those biceps in Venice's Historic Regatta along the Grand Canal.

◆ Venice

▶ regatastoricavenezia.it

← Love in the Time of Verona

Idyllic September weather is perfect for a romantic jaunt through the amorous alleyways of Verona.

◆ Verona

▶ p140

SEPTEMBER

Average daytime max: 21.5°C
Days of rainfall: 6 (Rome)

OCTOBER

Italy in
AUTUMN

Strike a Pose...Voga!

The *voga alla Veneta* rowing style defines Venice's historic gondoliers. October marks last call each year for learning this unique art.

📍 Venice

▶ p128

↖ Towers of Tortellini

Bologna's annual Tour-tlen tortellini festival in October is the perfect time to overindulge in one of Italy's irrefutable gastronomic capitals.

📍 Bologna

▶ p146

↑ Truffle Season

From the Piedmontese towns of Alba and Asti to Tuscany's San Miniato and Le Marche's Acqualagna, November is perfect for sniffing about for truffles.

Average daytime max: 17°C
Days of rainfall: 8 (Rome)

NOVEMBER

Average daytime max: 12°C
Days of rainfall: 10 (Rome)

← A Tipple in Tuscany

A dip in crowds coupled with a magic autumnal glow makes autumn an ideal time for a vineyard jaunt through Tuscany.

 Packing Notes

Cobblestone-friendly shoes, a light sweater or waterproof jacket and – once again – insect repellent.

Christmas Day, 26 December (St Stephen's Day), New Year's Day and 6 January (Epiphany) are public holidays. Cities go quiet for family time.

↖ Hit the Slopes

Let it snow! Top ski resorts pepper the northern Alps and the Dolomites, but offer pristine powder, too.

↘ Natale

Religious events nationwide lead up to the Christmas holiday, including remarkable nativity scenes (*presepi*), especially in Naples.

Weather aside, Italy in winter means less crowded archaeological sites, less busy museums, Christmas markets, winter comfort food and lower prices. Not too shabby.

DECEMBER

Average daytime max: 8.5°C
Days of rainfall: 9 (Rome)

JANUARY

Italy in
WINTER

↓ Carnevale

Leading up to Ash Wednesday, many Italian towns stage pre-Lenten carnivals, with whimsical costumes, confetti and festive treats.

↑ Opera Season

Four world-renowned opera houses – La Scala (Milan), La Fenice (Venice), Teatro San Carlo (Naples) and Teatro Massimo (Palermo) – fire up mid-October through March.

Dining with da Vinci

January is Milan's coldest month. What better time to tuck away indoors admiring *The Last Supper*?

♥ Milan

▶ p108

FEBRUARY

Average daytime max: 7.5°C
Days of rainfall: 7 (Rome)

Average daytime max: 8°C
Days of rainfall: 8 (Rome)

→ A Walk on the Roman Side

It's a tad chilly but Rome's fascinating street art remains an open-air museum to explore in the Eternal City.

♥ Rome

▶ p52

📦 Packing Notes

Winter jacket, scarf, hat and gloves. An umbrella, too – it can be wet.

Liberation Day (25 April) and Labor Day (1 May) often create a holiday *ponte* (bridge). Accommodation prices can inflate the entire week.

Buon Compleanno, Lucio!

Casa di Lucio Dalla organises events, concerts and street celebrations to celebrate the 4 March birthday of Bologna's beloved musical son.

📍 Bologna

▶ p152

↓ Settimana Santa

Pope-led candlelit procession and Easter blessings from St Peter's Square in Rome; processions take place in cities nationwide.

→ Cin cin!

The Primavera di Prosecco festival (March to June) kicks off Italian bubbly season. Head north of Venice/Treviso to Valdobbiadene and raise a glass.

📍 Valdobbiadene

▶ p142

MARCH

Average daytime max: 10°C
Days of rainfall: 7 (Rome)

APRIL

Italy in
SPRING

Head for the Hills

Here comes the sun! Join the Romans piling up to the Castelli hills for their rustic, no-frills *osterie* (casual taverns) known as *fraschette*.

📍 Rome

▶ p66

↖ La Biennale di Venezia

Europe's premier arts show-case, alternating between art (odd-numbered years) and architecture (even-numbered years) despite its name.

📍 Venice

▶ p132

↖ Salone Internazionale del Mobile

April sees Milan celebrate the world's most prestigious furniture fair with design exhibits, events and parties.

📍 Milan

▶ salonemilano.it

ITALY PLAN BY SEASON

Average daytime max: 13°C
Days of rainfall: 9 (Rome)

MAY

Average daytime max: 17.5°C
Days of rainfall: 6 (Rome)

← Cycle Milan's Canals

Spring affords the most amicable weather for exploring the waterways of Milan by bike, including the Naviglio Grande and Naviglio di Bereguardo.

📍 Milan

▶ p110

 Packing Notes

A light sweater or waterproof jacket, and comfy shoes. Mosquitoes emerge in March (bring repellent!).

ITALIAN ALPS
Trip Builder

TAKE YOUR PICK OF MUST-SEES AND HIDDEN GEMS

Italy's extraordinary Alpine landscape blankets the country's northernmost regions, offering an unparalleled trio of culinary wow, snow-capped mountains, including the Unesco-recognised Dolomites, and Germanic-influenced pockets of Tyrolean fairyland.

🗺️ Trip Notes

Hub towns Turin, Trento, Bolzano

How long Allow 12 days

Getting around Car hire recommended – public transport tapers off beyond major transit hubs.

Tips *Rifugi* (mountain huts) fill up fast, especially in summer – book at least a week or two in advance. Forget about pizza, lasagna and *ragù* and indulge in local Alpine-influenced specialities such as *pizzocheri* (buckwheat pasta), *canederli* (dumplings) and speck (dry-cured, smoked ham).

Mt Pirchiriano
Hike to the cloud-kissing Sacra di San Michele atop 888m Mt Pirchiriano, a majestic mountain sanctuary in the Susa Valley that inspired Umberto Eco novels.
🕐 *half-day*

Mont Blanc (Monte Bianco)

Aosta

VALLE D'AOSTA

Turin

FRANCE

Cuneo

SWITZERLAND

Turin
Tour grandiose Unesco World Heritage–listed House of Savoy palaces before making a break for higher elevations.
🕐 *2 days*

Valtellina
Conquer powder-dusted Alpine peaks by ski or snowboard; soak inevitably weary muscles in this picturesque valley's therapeutic hot springs.
🕐 3 days

Alagna Valsesia
Discover fascinating religious sanctuaries, *rifugi* and Walser communities tucked away in Italy's 'land of mountains'.
🕐 2 days

Bocchette Centrali
Get sideways on the most famous *via ferrata* in the Brenta Dolomites, the horizontal Bocchette Centrali, in Trentino.
🕐 3 days

Vercelli
Gaze upon one of only four existing Old English poetic codices, staunchly preserved Romanesque monuments and pretty piazzas in one of Italy's oldest cities.
🕐 1 day

AUSTRIA

TRENTINO ALTO ADIGE

Merano

Bolzano

Cortina d'Ampezzo

FRIULI-VENEZIA GIULIA

Dolomites

Lago Maggiore

Lugano

Sondrio

Trento

Rovereto

Varese

Lago di Como

Lecco

Como

Bergamo

Brescia

Lago di Garda

Verona

VENETO

Ivrea

Novara

Milan

LOMBARDY

Cremona

Mantua

Po

Piacenza

Alessandria

PIEDMONT

Parma

Modena

Alba

Bologna

Genoa

EMILIA-ROMAGNA

Ravenna

Savona

Gulf of Genoa

LIGURIA

Rimini

an emo

Florence

Urbino

Arezzo

Siena

Perugia

NORTH OF ITALY
Trip Builder

TAKE YOUR PICK OF MUST-SEES AND HIDDEN GEMS

■■■ Italy's indelible workhorse, the north harnesses industry, fashion and design fuelled by incredible culinary traditions, enthralling history, incomparable architecture and stunning coastline.

🗺 Trip Notes

Hub towns Milan, Genoa, Bologna

How long Allow 16 days

Getting around The north is well connected by fast, efficient train service; buses too, but with trains this good, why bother? Excellent roads make car hire logical as well.

Tips Northern Italy is not tropical – dress appropriately and bring repellent (mosquitoes can be vicious). Skip *aperitivo* (apart from in Milan where it's considered art) – incredible regional dishes are served at dinner.

Lago Maggiore
Visit lavish lake palaces on Isola Bella and Isola Madre, two opulent Borromean islands on Lago Maggiore.
🕐 *1 day*

SWITZERLAND

Lago Maggiore

Como

Langhe
Embark on a Slow Food culinary crawl around the Piedmontese countryside near Alba and Bra. Don't miss truffle fairs and other festivals if the timing is right.
🕐 *2 days*

● Turin

PIEDMONT

● Alessandria

Bra
● ● Alba

LIGURIA

● Cuneo

Genoa ●
● Savona

Gulf of Genoa

San Remo ●

Milan
Admire the Lombardian capital's baroque-influenced Liberty-style architecture (Italy's own version of art nouveau) and dance the night away in Ortica.
🕒 *2 days*

Venice
Learn the unique rowing art of *voga alla Veneta* and explore Venice's undiscovered (read: uncrowded!) corners and graphic arts scene.
🕒 *3 days*

Verona
Steer your partner away from Shakespeare clichés and dig deeper into the romantic fairytale that is Verona.
🕒 *1 day*

Motor Valley
Fulfil your need for speed in the museums and factories of iconic supercars Ferrari, Lamborghini, Pagani and more; while you're at it, get behind the wheel, too!
🕒 *2 days*

Cinque Terre
Hike to a cavalcade of spectacular viewpoints and sunset cocktail perches peppering the Italian Riviera's signature showpiece: the colourful, Unesco-listed fishing villages of Cinque Terre.
🕒 *3 days*

Bologna
Loosen your belt for the lasagna and tortellini onslaught in one of Italy's most vibrant medieval cities. Save time for late musician Lucio Dalla's wild abode.
🕒 *2 days*

Bolzano

Trento

Treviso

VENETO

Vicenza

Padua

Venice

Lago di Como

Bergamo

Lago d'Iseo

Lago di Garda

LOMBARDY

Brescia

Verona

Milan

Mantua

Ferrara

EMILIA-ROMAGNA

Modena

Maranello

Bologna

Adriatic Sea

La Spezia

Pistoia

Lucca

Pisa

SAN MARINO

TUSCANY

Livorno

N 0   50 km
  0   25 miles

CENTRAL ITALY
Trip Builder

TAKE YOUR PICK OF MUST-SEES AND HIDDEN GEMS

▬▬▬ Central Italy is a tale of two alluring cities. The Italian capital, Rome, whose remnants of its ancient versions make for some of the continent's most spellbinding sights; and Florence, a Renaissance juggernaut surrounded by the vineyard-rich Tuscan countryside.

🗺 Trip Notes

Hub towns Florence, Pisa, Rome

How long Allow three weeks

Getting around Trains are efficient in Tuscany, Lazio and Marche (Umbria is more rail-challenged), but tracks taper as you head south. Consider a car, especially for the countryside.

Tips Lazio and Tuscany are two of Italy's most popular regions – always pre-book tickets to museums and sights (especially in Rome and Florence); avoid crowds by arriving early or late.

Montaione
Sniff out white truffles, coddle Chianina calves and mingle with a Florentine count at utterly idyllic organic *agriturismo* (farm-stay accommodation) Bar-bialla Nuova in the rural Tuscan countryside.
🕐 *2 days*

Parma
Modena
EMILIA-ROMAGNA
Pistoia
Lucca
Empoli
Pisa
Livorno
Gorgona
Ligurian Sea
Capraia
Elba
Bastia
Pianosa
CORSICA (FRANCE)
Montecristo
Giglio

Parco Nazionale Arcipel-ago Toscano
Escape to the *other* Tuscany, on the idyllic island of Elba, home to Parco Nazionale Arcipelago Toscano, Europe's largest marine national park.
🕐 *3 days*

SARDINIA

Florence
Revel in Renaissance Florence through the compelling story of the city's powerful Medici dynasty. Follow Dante's footsteps around Tuscany's crown jewel, too.
🕐 4 days

Chianti
Sip your way around the impossibly scenic, world-class vineyards of Tuscany, where Chianti and Sangiovese are born, bred and bottled for your drinking pleasure.
🕐 3 days

Val d'Orcia
Hop between Renaissance towns, magnificent abbeys and postcard-perfect plains in this rich, Unesco-recognised agricultural valley in central Tuscany.
🕐 2 days

Rome
Explore incredible ruins, vibrant street art and off-the-beaten-path attractions in the Italian capital. Save room for famed beef and chicory-stuffed sandwiches at Mercato Testaccio.
🕐 4 days

Castelli Romani
Escape to the foodie-friendly hills outside Rome, where rustic taverns know as *fraschette* serve hyper-local food and wine to throngs of ravished Romans.
🕐 1 day

Parco Regionale della Maremma
Ramble across a maze of walking trails connecting pine forests, marshy plains and pristine coastline in this picturesque regional park in Tuscany.
🕐 2 days

Adriatic Sea

0 — 100 km
0 — 50 miles

N

Rimini
Pesaro
Urbino
Ancona
rato
Florence
San Gimignano
Arezzo
Gubbio
Macerata
Siena
TUSCANY
Perugia
Lago di Trasimeno
Assisi
LE MARCHE
Orvieto
Spoleto
Ascoli Piceno
UMBRIA
Grosseto
Lago di Bolsena
Terni
Rieti
L'Aquila
Pescara
Viterbo
Tiber
LAZIO
Lago di Bracciano
Avezzano
Civitavecchia
Tivoli
ROME
Frascati
ABRUZZO
Albano Laziale
Frosinone
Tyrrhenian Sea
Ischia
Capri

SOUTH OF ITALY
Trip Builder

TAKE YOUR PICK OF MUST-SEES AND HIDDEN GEMS

Southern Italy has more in common with Turkey than Trieste. Stereotypes hail from here (brasher people, crazier drivers), but its rich cultural identity, rugged landscapes, regional cuisines and much better weather make the south marvellous.

🗺 Trip Notes

Hub towns Naples, Reggio di Calabria, Taranto

How long Allow 17 days

Getting around Large towns are connected by public transport, but less so than the north. You're probably going to want your own wheels here.

Tips Southern Italy moves at a slower pace (so should you). Summer tourist season (especially August) gets spectacularly crowded – consider visiting in shoulder seasons, when the sun still shines but on fewer people.

Naples
Dig into fantastic *napoletano* street food staples like *frittatina di pasta* (fried macaroni croquettes). Explore ancient labyrinthine tunnels hiding Greek-era grottoes, palaeo-Christian burial chambers and spooky catacombs.
🕐 3 days

M O L I S E

Campobasso

C A M P A N I A

Naples
Procida
Pompeii
Ischia
Salerno
Vietri su Mare
Sorrento
Capri

Golfo di Salerno

Procida
Savour a small, authentic slice of Italian island life in the fascinating and colourful fishing village of Procida, where life carries on defiantly unaltered by tourism.
🕐 2 days

Amalfi Coast
Dawdle around one of Europe's most dramatic coastlines, where cliff-hugging towns, hidden beaches and lush islands form a cinematic backdrop – the stuff Italian dreams are made of.
🕐 3 days

Tyrrhenian Sea

Aeolian Islands

Parco Nazionale dell'Aspromonte
Explore hauntingly beautiful ghost towns lost to the extremes of weather and geography such as Pentedàttilo and Roghudi Vecchio inside this national park once used as a refuge by Calabrian kidnappers.
🕐 2 days

Salento
Grab a partner and dance the *pizzica* at the wildly popular festival La Notte della Taranta in Melpignano – or any time, anywhere in Salento!
🕐 *2 days*

Vietri sul Mare
Survey the kaleidoscope of colours in Vietri sul Mare, the birthplace of the vibrant ceramic tiles that adorn the Amalfi Coast.
🕐 *1 day*

Parco Nazionale del Pollino
Hike to 16th-century churches and prehistoric art inside Parco Nazionale del Pollino, immersing yourself in the culture of the Italo-Albanian Arbëreshë people along the way.
🕐 *2 days*

Parco Nazionale della Sila
Crane your neck admiring the tremendously tall larch pines – the Fallistro Giants – that kiss the sky across Parco Nazionale della Sila in Calabria.
🕐 *2 days*

Foggia

Adriatic Sea

Matera

PUGLIA

Brindisi

Potenza

BASILICATA

Taranto

Lecce

Agropoli

Parco Nazionale del Cilento, Valle di Diano e Alburni

Golfo di Taranto

Otranto

Melpignano

Gallipoli

Golfo di Policastro

Cosenza

Crotone

CALABRIA

Catanzaro

Golfo di Gioia

Ionian Sea

Messina

Reggio di Calabria

SICILY

0   50 km
0   25 miles

SICILY & SARDINIA
Trip Builder

TAKE YOUR PICK OF MUST-SEES AND HIDDEN GEMS

Italy's isles cast a wide net, from Tuscany's Gorgona off the central coast to southerly Lampedusa, which nearly kisses the African continent. Sicily and Sardinia hog most of the headlines; together, they're roughly the size of Slovakia.

🗺️ Trip Notes

Hub towns Cagliari, Catania, Olbia

How long Allow 11 days

Getting around Planes and ferries are obviously essential (Sicily is reachable by train). On land, car hire is ideal for reaching far-flung beaches and sights, though bus services exist.

Tips Sicily and Sardinia are the Mediterranean's two largest islands – don't underestimate distances and travel times. If food is your focus, choose Sicily; for some of Europe's most dazzling beaches, head to Sardinia.

Stintino
Bathe in remarkably translucent Gulf of Asinara waters at La Pelosa beach in Sardinia's extreme northwest – under the watchful eye of the ancient Saracen Torre del Falcone (Falcon Tower).
🕐 2 days

Cabras
Spoil yourself on pasta dusted with treasured *bottarga* (cured and air-dried grey mullet roe) – the best in the world is plucked right from the coastal pools surrounding Cabras.
🕐 1 day

Cagliari
Join throngs of pious revellers in Italy's longest religious procession, the 65km-long Festa di Sant'Efisio, feverishly celebrated on 1 May. Indulge in sweet *seadas* (fried pecorino and honey pastries), too!
🕐 2 days

CORSICA
(FRANCE)
Ajaccio
Bonifacio
Santa Teresa di Gallura
Sassari
Alghero
Nuoro
SARDINIA
Oristano
Cagliari
Carbonia
Pula

MEDITERRANEAN SEA

ALGERIA

0 200 km
N 0 100 miles

Ogliastra
Seek out delicacies such as ravioli-like *culurgionis d'Ogliastra* (dough filled with boiled potatoes, olive oil, pecorino cheese, garlic, mint, nutmeg and more), which go down especially nicely around Dorgali.
🕐 *1 day*

Golfo di Orosei
Set your spirits soaring as you hike magnificent clifftop trails on the Golfo di Orosei and cycle tough mountain roads in its thrilling hinterland.
🕐 *2 days*

Mt Etna
Hike among ancient lava flows, whisk up to the summit of Europe's tallest active volcano and drink volcanically enhanced *vino* in Sicily.
🕐 *1 day*

Baunei
Stake out a patch of paradise on the wild Cala Goloritzé beach, a national-monument-designated pearl of white-pebbled heaven formed by a 1960s landslide.
🕐 *1 day*

Piazza Armerina
Be awed by one of the finest Roman floor mosaics in the world, including a 64m-long hunting scene, at the monumental Unesco-listed Villa Romana del Casale.
🕐 *1 day*

Adriatic Sea

Pescara

L'Aquila

LAZIO

ABRUZZO

Termoli

ROME ✪

MOLISE

Foggia

Campobasso

PUGLIA

Olbia

Potenza

BASILICATA

Orosei

Dorgali

Tyrrhenian Sea

CALABRIA

Cosenza

Stromboli

Ustica

Salina

Aeolian

Lipari

Islands

Vulcano

Messina

Palermo

Cefalù

Reggio

Trapani

Mt Etna

Calabria

Taormina

Marsala

SICILY

Enna

Caltanissetta

Catania

Agrigento

Syracuse

Pantelleria

Gela

Ragusa

MALTA

TUNISIA

7 Things to Know About
ITALY

INSIDER TIPS TO HIT THE GROUND RUNNING

1 Don't Order Cappuccino after Breakfast

Italians take their gastronomic culture extremely seriously. There are rules. Cappuccino after 11am? Never! Order an espresso or macchiato. Parmesan on seafood pasta? No. Looking for spaghetti *bolognese*? It doesn't exist (it's *tagliatelle* with *ragù*). Share a pizza? Not on their watch! Of course, it's a free country, but behind-your-back snickers often follow culinary crimes.

2 Tailor Your Trip

Italy, along with China, boasts the most Unesco World Heritage Sites of any country – resist the temptation of trying to see them all in one trip! Honing in on particular regions (Italian Alps, the south) or interests (gastronomy, art, architecture) will result in a far more rewarding, less hurried experience. Take your cues from locals, whose slower pace of life is quintessentially Italian – they invented Slow Food, after all.

Arrivederci

3 Service Charge

At bars and cafes, it's cheaper to stand at the counter. A service fee is charged if you sit. It's not a scam or because you're a foreigner – it's because you took a load off.

▶ See more about money on p241

4 Ciao!

'Ciao!' is an informal greeting/farewell between friends and family. Saying *'ciao!'* to strangers, authority figures or elders *could* cause unintentional offence; use *'salve'* (hello) and *'arrivederci'* (goodbye) instead.

Ciao

5 Validate Your Ticket

Electronic train tickets are the norm these days; however, paper tickets for regional trains purchased from in-station ticket machines must be validated in the green-and-white machines (usually found in station lobbies and/or at platform entrances) before boarding. Don't forget – you'll be fined! Don't board earlier trains, but catching later regional trains (up to four hours) is generally permitted.

▶ See more about getting around on p238

7 Beware the Colpo d'Aria

The dreaded *colpo d'aria* (literally 'blast of air') is a much-feared, uniquely Italian meteorological phenomenon that terrorises the country's population as the weather cools in autumn. Italians deeply believe a cold gust or cool draught will level you with illness. Do not challenge them on this.

▶ See more about weather on p18

6 Four Countries in One

Italians often joke that Italy is four countries in one: the mountainous, German-speaking autonomous region of Trentino-Alto Adige-South Tyrol; the modern, industrious north (Piedmont, Lombardy, Liguria, Veneto, Emilia-Romagna etc); the heart of central Italy (Tuscany, Lazio, Umbria etc); and the more rustic, considerably warmer south and islands (Abruzzo, Campania, Calabria, Sicily, Sardinia and so on).

As the Italian Republic was forged from numerous, often culturally diverse city-states and maritime republics, there's some truth to the joke and visitors will notice staunch differences as they travel the length of the country. An owner of a Gasthof (guesthouse) in Alto Adige has very little in common with a Sardinian sheep farmer, for example. Language, gastronomy, culture, history, architecture, driving habits, physical appearances – even personality quirks! – can change faster than a Ferrari as you cross regions.

With the Vatican and San Marino, it's actually six – but who's counting?

Read, Listen, Watch & Follow

 READ

La divina commedia (Dante Alighieri; c 1307–21) Italian literature's singular work; a hereafter chronicle of love and loss.

I promessi sposi (Alessandro Manzoni; 1827) Star-crossed epic defining the modern Italian language.

Il nome della rosa (Umberto Eco; 1980) Monastic murder mystery from renowned Italian semiotician.

L'amica geniale (Elena Ferrante; 2011) First in a wildly popular Neapolitan contemporary coming of age series.

 LISTEN

Tintarella di luna (Mina; 1960) Italy's most famous voice, a feminist style icon with a three-octave vocal range.

Una donna per amico (Lucio Battisti; 1978) Singer-songwriter Battisti's seminal album, a sonic breeze of infectious jazz-blues.

Come è profondo il mare (Lucio Dalla; 1977) Dalla's genre-bending introduction as both songwriter and composer, recorded in solitude in Isole Tremiti.

E=MC² (Giorgio Moroder; 1977) The world's first digitally recorded album; from the 'father of disco'.

THOMAS QUACK/SHUTTERSTOCK ©

XFM (Sangue Misto; 1994) Bologna's Sangue Misto's lone album, a brooding US West Coast–inspired revolution in underground Italian hip-hop.

WATCH

Roma città aperta (1945) Neorealist war drama set in Nazi-occupied Rome.

Ladri di biciclette (1948) Resilient post-WWII saga of a man's hunt for his stolen bicycle.

La dolce vita (1960; top right) Federico Fellini's hedonistic, post-war Roman adventure.

Il postino (1994) Fictional account of exiled Chilean poet Pablo Neruda's bond with his Italian postman.

La vita è bella (1997; bottom right) Academy Award–winning film about a father shielding his son from holocaust horrors.

 FOLLOW

@chiaraferragni
Fashionista about town – Italy's top influencer.

italia.it
Official Italian-government tourism website.

THE LOCAL
thelocal.it
English-language culture/travel news.

italymagazine.com
Travel, dining, accommodation and culture.

ilpost.it
Italian-language daily news.

Sate your Italy dreaming with a virtual vacation

ROME

ART | HISTORY | FOOD

**Experience
Rome online**

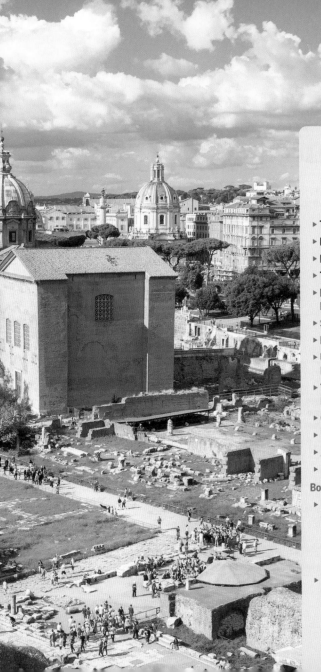

Bonus Online Experiences

- **Lost World of the Etruscans**

- **Get Away on the Appian Way**

Enjoy the delicious confections and charming ambience of **Confetteria Moriondo & Gariglio** (p71)
⏱ ½ hour

TRIONFALE

PRATI

VATICAN CITY
(CITTÀ DEL
VATICANO)

BORGO

AURELIO

CENTRO STORICO

Take in the Eternal City from **Piazza Garibaldi** on the Janiculum hill (p47)
⏱ 1 hour

Gianicolo (Janiculum)

TRASTEVERE

Villa Doria Pamphilj

AVENTINO

Devour local flavours at one of Rome's best street-food innovations, **Trapizzino** (p70)
⏱ 1 hour

MONTEVERDE

TESTACCIO

GIANCOLENSE

PORTUENSE

ROME
Trip Builder

Behold the futurist architecture of Rome's city-within-a-city, **EUR** (p64)
⏱ ½ day

▬▬▬▬ Fabulous food and outdoor escapes, hidden romance and out-of-the-way art, Rome has it all. But remember, Rome wasn't built in a day, so be sure to take your time to enjoy the moment, whether that's voraciously exploring everything the city offers or just relaxing in a picturesque piazza.

Tiber

Explore bookable experiences in Rome online

Discover Italy's modern art heritage at **La Galleria Nazionale** (p69)
🕒 ½ day

Soak up the serenity of **Villa Borghese** on bicycle, boat or foot (p69)
🕒 ½ day

Get to the heart of Roman history with a visit to **Palazzo Massimo** (p69)
🕒 ½ day

Bring on the baroque at **Palazzo Barberini** (p69)
🕒 ½ day

Explore neighbourhood **Tor Pignattara** for some of Rome's most epic works of *en plein air* art (p52)
🕒 ½ day

Feast on *porchetta* and *coppiette* from the **Castelli Romani** (p66)
🕒 1 day

Villa Borghese

NOMENTANO

SALARIO

RI-
ENTE

SALLUSTIANO

CASTRO
PRETORIO

TREVI

MONTI

TIBURTINO

SAN
LORENZO

Parco del
Colle
Oppio

ESQUILINO

Parco
del
Celio

CELIO

TUSCOLANO

APPIO-
LATINO

GARBATELLA

OSTIENSE

APPIO
PIGNATELLI

Castelli
Romana

ELENA ODAREEVA/SHUTTERSTOCK ©. ANNA PAKUTINA/
SHUTTERSTOCK ©.MARCOVARRO/SHUTTERSTOCK ©

0   0
         1 miles   2 km

Practicalities

MARCO RAMERINI/SHUTTERSTOCK ©

ARRIVING

⚓ **Leonardo da Vinci (Fiumicino) Airport**
Direct trains run to Stazione Termini, €14; slower
trains stop at Trastevere, Ostiense and Tiburtina,
€8. Buses to Termini are cheaper but slower,
from €7. Set taxi fare to city centre is €48.

⚓ **Ciampino Airport** Buses run to Stazione
Termini. Tickets, available in the arrivals hall,
start at €6. Taxis cost €30.

🚉 **Stazione Termini** Rome's main train station.
Continue from here by bus, metro or taxi.

WHEN TO GO

DEC–FEB
Cold, short days and
low-season rates.

MAR–MAY
Lovely weather, Easter, crowds
and peak prices.

JUN–AUG
Very hot with plenty of
outdoor events.

SEP–NOV
Sunny days make this a popular
time until rain in November.

HOW MUCH FOR A

Slice of pizza
€3

Aperitivo
€8–12

Colosseum ticket
€16

GETTING AROUND

Metro and buses The metro
is the quickest way of getting
around Rome, but the network
is limited. Two main lines (A and
B) serve the centre, crossing at
Stazione Termini. Trains run from
5.30am to 11.30pm (1.30am on
Fridays and Saturdays). Buses
serve most areas, running from
5.30am until midnight, with
limited night services.

Walking The best way of moving
around the historic centre is on
foot. Distances are not great and
you'll see far more.

Tickets and passes Public transport tickets are valid on buses,
trams and metro lines. A standard
100-minute ticket costs €1.50.
You can also get 24-/48-/72-hour
passes for €7/12.50/18. Children
under 10 travel free.

EATING & DRINKING

Roman pastas Iconic Roman pasta dishes include carbonara (with guanciale pork and a sauce of egg and pecorino romano cheese), *alla gricia* (with guanciale and pecorino romano), *amatriciana* (with a chilli-spiked tomato and guanciale sauce; pictured) and *cacio e pepe* (with pecorino romano and black pepper).

Street food Rome's favourite fast food is *pizza al taglio* (sliced pizza) but you can also snack on *supplì* (fried rice balls with fillings) and crispy *fritti* (fried foods). Round your meal off with a delicious gelato.

Best coffee Sciascia Caffè (p71)

Must-try pizza Bonci Pizzarium (p70)

CONNECT & FIND YOUR WAY

Wi-fi Available free in hostels, hotels, bars and cafes, though signal quality varies. If you have an Italian mobile number you can register and use hotspots run by WiFimetropolitano (*cittametropol itanaroma.it/wifimetropolitano*).

Navigation Fairly straightforward – Google maps and other phone apps work fine or you can pick up paper maps at tourist information points dotted around the city.

DISCOUNT CARDS

The **Roma pass** (€28/38.50 for 48/72 hours) offers free and discounted admission to museums, sites and events, plus unlimited city transport. Details at romapass.it.

WHERE TO STAY

Rome is busy and expensive, so it pays to book ahead. Accommodation options range from five-star hotels to hostels, B&Bs and *pensioni,* as well as boutique suite and apartment hotels.

Neighbourhood	Pro/Con
Centro Storico	Atmospheric, beautiful area in the heart of the action. Expensive. Few budget options.
Tridente, Trevi & the Quirinale	Good for sightseeing and shopping. Quiet after dark. Mostly midrange and top-end hotels.
Vatican City, Borgo & Prati	Ideal for the Vatican's big sights. Accommodation for all budgets plus shops and restaurants.
Monti, Esquilino & San Lorenzo	Budget options around Stazione Termini. Buzzing nightlife. Some dodgy streets near Termini.
Trastevere & Gianicolo	Gorgeous, picturesque area with sights, restaurants and nightlife. Can be noisy.

MONEY

Carry some cash for smaller shops and trattorias. When eating out, if service isn't included, a tip of a euro or two is fine in pizzerias and trattorias, no more than 5% to 10% in smarter restaurants.

01 Romantic ROME

ART | ARCHITECTURE | ROMANCE

Rome, by its very name, is a romantic city. Turn the word Roma around and you have *amor* (love). And then turn around any corner and you'll find love on every street and piazza in beautiful architecture, gorgeous colours and rich hued skies.

FJJPHOTO/SHUTTERSTOCK ©

🗺 How to

Getting around Put your best foot forward, pick up a bus pass or grab a taxi.

When to go More important than the time of year is the time of day. Walking the city in the early morning or late evening is when the romance of Rome reveals itself. Just pay attention to the weather, dress accordingly and wear comfortable shoes.

Seasonal snack Pick up a *grattachecca*, a syrup-infused shaved ice at the neighbourhood kiosks along the Tiber.

ALEXANDER DEMYANENKO/SHUTTERSTOCK ©

Set the Scene

Morning romance An early morning wander around a very quiet Rome brings out a special kind of *amore*. **Villa Borghese's Pincio**, a wide platform terrace, offers a romantic morning view across **Piazza del Popolo** to **St Peter's Dome**, and is best followed by a walk into the park to **La Casina dell'Orologio**, a tiny bar nestled amid magnolia trees.

Afternoon delight Private, pretty and serving prosecco, **Terrazza Borromini** (terrazzaborromini.com) rooftop terrace peeks onto Rome's prettiest piazza, Piazza Navona, with its beautiful Bernini-designed Four Rivers Fountain, while **Piazza Garibaldi** on the Janiculum has a beautiful outlook over the entire city. Or else, paddle around Villa Borghese's famous *laghetto*, a tiny lake with an ersatz Roman temple as backdrop.

Sunset strip A walk down the **Lungotevere**, the sycamore-lined promenade alongside the Tiber, from **Ponte Garibaldi** to **Ponte Cavour** at dusk is spectacular. As you stroll from one historic bridge to the next, Rome's technicolour skies make a stunning backdrop to the dramatic architecture.

Late-night lovers In the late evening, Rome quiets and umber-coloured palaces seem to catch fire. Meander the side streets from the **Pantheon** to **Piazza Navona** and through the Navona neighbourhood to the **Ponte degli Angeli**, Rome's beautiful Angel bridge that sets the scene for the nearly two-thousand-year-old **Castel Sant'Angelo** (castelsantangelo. com), originally Emperor Hadrian's tomb turned papal stronghold and scene for the denouement of the opera *Tosca*.

Far left Piazza Navona
Bottom Villa Borghese **Near left** Castel Sant'Angelo

📷 Rome with a View

Romance is all about the scene, or better yet, the view. **Terrazze delle Quadrighe**, atop the **Altare della Patria** (vittoriano.beniculturali. it) in the very epicentre of Rome, boasts a bird's-eye view of the city, from its ancient past to its contemporary present.

Or else take in the full splendour of the Colosseum from the rooftop of **Palazzo Manfredi** (palazzomanfredi.com), a luxury hotel with an unobstructed front-row view of the world's best arena.

Trattoria 2.0

**THE TRADITIONAL
ROMAN EATERY
EVOLVES**

Forget about checked
tablecloths and
brusque waiters,
Rome has a new
generation of
trattorias and *osterie*
where the quality
of ingredients and
recipes complements
a curated focus on
contemporary design
and gastronomic
experience.

Left and middle Dishes at Bistrot 64
Right A dish at Barred

Think of a Roman trattoria and you most likely conjure up
images of rustic boltholes with red-and-white checked
tablecloths, brown-paper placemats and Chianti bottles
doubling as candelabras. Rome is filled with yesteryear-
styled *osterie* and trattorias, some with decor from
decades ago and others ersatz design for the postcard
experience. But look again. The Rome restaurant scene
has evolved from Alberto Sordi's *Un'Americano a Roma*
to the next generation of trattoria that upends these
stereotypes.

Food is still the hero of this new generation of trattorias,
but it's not just what ends up on your plate that holds
importance. Equal focus is placed on where the ingredients are sourced and how the dishes are put together, as
well as affordability. It's more than a design choice, it's a
sustainability-leading ethos embracing ethical sourcing,
waste and recycling, as well as heritage preservation – and
of course, great food.

Giuseppe Lo Iudice and Alessandro Miocchi had all this
in mind when they opened **Retrobottega** (retro-bottega.
com). Forging together their Michelin backgrounds, Lo
Iudice and Miocchi created a trattoria/*laboratorio*, where
they experiment with traditional recipes and techniques
as a starting point – whether in foraging, sourcing from local producers or developing recipes or design. Retrobottega's sleek dark tones, woods, and open-kitchen stations
are exactly the opposite of the trattoria cliché. And its
location in the heart of the *centro storico* (historic centre)
near the **Pantheon**, an area some would say suffers from
overtourism, is key. 'We wanted to create something for
the residents of this neighbourhood that was contem-

porary, in line with today's restaurants in Paris, London, New York, without sacrificing our heritage,' Lo Iudice explains.

Across the city near the Maxxi Museum, chef Kotaro Noda had a similar idea when he created **Bistrot 64** (bistrot64. it). Noda plays on the bistro model where affordability and a simplified decor are as much a part of the menu as Noda's unique dishes, which mix his Japanese heritage, technique and flavours with Roman tradition. Awarded a Michelin star, Noda eschews the stellar prices that often accompany the culinary acknowledgement by curating a range of affordably priced tasting menus specifically geared to keep the vibe casual and friendly.

> Retrobottega's sleek dark tones, woods, and open-kitchen stations are exactly the opposite of the trattoria cliché.

In San Giovanni, the Palucci brothers keep things contemporary with **Barred** (barred.it), where minimal, Nordic-inspired aesthetics match a tapas-style menu featuring creative twists on traditional recipes, with a focus on seasonal and often foraged vegetables, herbs and fruit. Paying homage to their Roman origins, the chefs adopt a waste-not mentality, where everything is used – offal is on the menu and leftovers are reimagined into new dishes. Lining the walls are niche biodynamic and natural wines, primarily from Lazio. The Palucci brothers' no-frills approach is distinctly Roman and entirely contemporary, and like Retrobottega and Bistrot 64, is helping to redefine a new generation of Rome's much-loved trattorias.

Carbonara King

Luciano Monosilio is Italy's reigning King of Carbonara – his take on the traditional Roman dish vaulted the chef to the Michelin constellation. Monosilio stepped down from the stars to open his eponymous **Luciano** (lucianocucinaitaliana.com), a pioneer of Rome's new-wave trattorias, where the award-winning chef features the humble Roman dish as well as more epicurious creations inspired by traditional recipes and waste-not ingredients.

02 Rome's Vibrant
MARKETS

FOOD | VINTAGE | SHOPPING

Cornerstone of the local communities, Rome's neighbourhood markets are the best place to experience a slice of village life in the heart of the city. Often located near or on top of archaeological sites, each market is different in spirit, but you're always bound to find bargain clothes, shoes, homewares, seasonal produce and all manner of delectable food products.

PEDRO RUFO/SHUTTERSTOCK ©

How to

Getting here Metro B for Campagna Amica Farmers Market (Circo Massimo), Mercato Testaccio (Piramide). Metro A for Borghetto Flaminio (Flaminio) and Via Sannio (San Giovanni). Porta Portese is near Trastevere train station.

Cost Entry is €1.60 for Borghetto Flaminio. Sundays, Vintage Market entry is by donation from 2pm.

Hidden gem Visit the archaeological site of ancient Rome's 'Emporium' port for goods storage underneath Mercato Testaccio (mercato ditestaccio.it/area -archeologica).

KRAFT74/SHUTTERSTOCK ©

Top left Mercato Campo de' Fiori
Bottom left Porta Portese

Find Your Shopping Style

Food Campagna Amica Farmers Market near the Circus Maximus offers a great chance to meet local producers and sample the flavours of the Lazio region. Held on weekends, it is here that discerning Romans come to buy guanciale (cured pork), truffle sauces, goat milk *stracchino* (creamy fresh cheese) and bread made with ancient grains. Daily **Mercato Testaccio** is the place for exquisitely fresh groceries and ready meals such as lasagna, fresh pasta and pizza, perfect for a quick dinner after a long day of sightseeing. Try the hearty sandwiches filled with Roman classics from Mordi e Vai.

Flea markets To find anything from vintage Sophia Loren–worthy sunglasses to '70s Italian rock vinyl, head to one of the city's flea markets such as **Porta Portese** Sunday market, Rome's largest, and daily **Mercato di Via Sannio** in San Giovanni. Though the stalls of Via Sannio are fewer than in its heyday in the '60s to '80s, you can still find unconventional costumes, hats or bags – and its popular leather jackets – for a good bargain.

Vintage Every Sunday, at locals' favourite **Borghetto Flaminio**, secondhand dealers display vintage homewares, clothes and antiques on their makeshift stalls. Head to the larger **Vintage Market** to find emerging fashion designers and artisans selling unusual handmade gifts, organic foods and craft beers. Currently in Piazza Ragusa; for future locations, check its Facebook page (facebook.com/vintagemarketroma).

Best of the Rest

Mercato Campo de' Fiori

Central and popular among tourists, the booths of Campo de' Fiori daily market display anything from seasonal veg to clothes, flowers, homewares and souvenir-worthy goods.

Mercato Trionfale

Near the Vatican museums, Mercato Trionfale is one of Rome's most iconic and largest food markets, famous for its seasonal produce, meat, freshly baked bread, herbs and spices.

Nuovo Mercato Esquilino

A stone's throw from Santa Maria Maggiore Basilica and Termini train station, this loud and colourful covered market offers a true international bazaar experience. Here you'll find foods from around the world, from all types of spices to the ingredients for a perfect South American meal.

03 Street Art **STROLL**

STREET ART | WALKING | MORNING TRIP

▬▬▬ Tor Pignattara's street art scene shows off some of the most incredible murals in the city as part of Rome's latest art renaissance. An open-air museum, the neighbourhood is also a canvas for off-the-radar stencils and smaller works of art by acclaimed artists from around the world.

ALBERTO PIZZOLI/AFP/GETTY IMAGES © ARTWORK BY DAVID DIAVÙ VECCHIATO

📍 Trip Notes

Getting here From Termini Station, take Metro C (atac.roma.it) or a taxi for a 30-minute ride to **Malatesta** (Piazza Roberto Malatesta) in Tor Pignattara. Be sure to head out after the morning traffic rush.

When to go All year round, but spring is the loveliest.

Top tip Head to **Piazza Perestello** with your drone (and permission) or find a bird's-eye view for an overhead glimpse of the massive curled up woman nestled in the square; she's one of the mind-blowing anamorphic murals by French artists **Ella & Pitr** (instagram.com/ellapitr).

🖼 Mural Magic

Tor Pignattara was the favourite neighbourhood of director and intellectual **Pier Paolo Pasolini**; he's honoured by Italian artist Nicola Verlato in *Hostia*, a 10m-high mural building facade on **Via Galeazzo Alessi**, considered the Sistine Chapel of Tor Pignatttara. Adjacent **Pigneto** also boasts murals by world-recognised artists Mr Klevra, and more.

PIGNETO

Malatesta

01 Unmissable at 32m high, **Coffee Break** (Via Ludovico Pavoni 171) by Etam Cru is the tallest mural in Rome and emblematic of **#IloveTorPigna**.

Piazza Perestello

02 Walk up and down **Via della Marranella** and its side streets to discover some hidden masterpieces by legendary artist Jef Aerosol.

Via della Marranella

Via di Acqua Bullicante

03 Around the corner on **Via dell'Acqua Bullicante 24**, artist Diavù brings back Italian silver-screen icons Pier Paolo Pasolini (pictured left), Anna Magnani, Mario Monicelli (below) and more to now-closed Cinema Impero.

TOR PIGNATTARA

Hostia

Via Casilina

04 A walk along **Via di Tor Pignattara** is an artistic treasure hunt for works of art by acclaimed artists including C215, Carlos Atoche, Diavù, Agostino Iacurci and MP5.

Via di Tor Pignattara

05 Behold **It's a New Day** (Via Ludovico Antino), a trippy wave of larger-than-life children's faces that grin back at you, by **AliCè** (alicepasquini.com) in her signature psychedelic palette.

ALBERTO PIZZOLI/AFP/GETTY IMAGES ©
ARTWORK © DAVID DIAVÙ VECCHIATO

N

0
0
500 m
0.25 miles

MURALES
Romane

01 Popstairs

The larger-than-life portrait series by Italian artist Diavù spotlights actress Elena Sofia Ricci on a Trastevere staircase.

02 Piccolo Hulk

Ron English's iconic *Baby Hulk* is the centrepiece of the Quadraro street-art project and open-air museum.

03 Frida Kahlo

A dreamy vision of the Mexican icon by Italian artist UMAN, in collaboration with the association Pittori Anonimi Trullo, in the Trullo neighbourhood.

04 Big City Life

Bambino Redentore by French artist Seth is one of 22 larger-than-life murals scaling the facades of the Tor Marancia housing complex.

05 Hunting Pollution

Created by Italian artist Iena Cruz, this 1000-sq-metre of regenerative street art covers seven stories and uses smog-cleansing paints.

06 Il Nuotatore

Italian artist Agostino Iacurci's technicolour swimmer adorns the facade of a former fish market in the Ostiense neighbourhood.

07 Outside In

Dutch artist JDL created a 250-sq-metre split image of LGBTIQ+ icon Karl du Pigné, made with paints that purify air. Neighbourhood: San Paolo.

04 UNCOVER
Secret Rome

CULTURE | ARCHAEOLOGY | ART

With its iconic history and countless masterpieces, Rome is a city where it can be hard to find a quiet moment – but not impossible. While far from the city centre it's easier to spot under-the-radar gems, some intriguing and less-known wonders stand right next to the iconic sights that attract large crowds every day. Leave the rush of the Spanish Steps and start hunting for hidden treasures.

MONADORI PORTFOLIO/GETTY IMAGES ©

🗺 How to

Getting here Metro B for Sant'Agnese Fuori Le Mura (St Agnese/Annibaliano) and Centrale Montemartini (Garbatella). Tram 8 for Santa Cecilia Basilica (Mastai stop). Roma Giardinetti tram (Berardi stop) for Saints Marcellino and Pietro Catacombs.

Cost Santa Cecilia Basilica undergrounds €3. Catacombs of Saints Marcellino and Pietro €8. Sant'Agnese Complex €10. Centrale Montemartini €10.

Gelato stop Try the daring flavours of Otaleg all-natural gelato in Trastevere (Via San Cosimato 14A).

SIBIL PHOTOS/SHUTTERSTOCK ©

Top left Statue of Santa Cecilia, Santa Cecilia Basilica **Bottom left** Centrale Montemartini

Hidden Cultural Riches

Inside the walls Tourist-trodden Trastevere hides some of Rome's best-kept secrets. Many flock to Santa Maria, but few cross the road to **Santa Cecilia Basilica**. The street-level 5th-century church hosts baroque sculptor Stefano Maderno's intimate marble statue of the martyr in the recumbent position she was found in. Underground is her crypt, decorated with a forest of arches and pillars, along with 2nd- to 4th-century buildings, thermal baths, a mosaic floor and ancient jars.

Outside the walls Venture outside the walls to explore less-known relics of ancient Rome, including the rich complex of **Sant'Agnese Fuori Le Mura** (santagnese.org) off Via Nomentana. Alongside stunning mosaics of the saint, the complex includes a 7th-century basilica, catacombs and the ruins of a 4th-century covered cemetery and worship place, known as *basilica costantiniana,* built by Emperor Constantine's daughter near the martyr's tomb. Also worth a visit are the little-known, beautifully frescoed catacombs of **Saints Marcellino and Pietro Ad Duas Lauros** (santimarcellinoepietro.it) in Tor Pignattara, which were dug around the 3rd century and became the last resting place for wealthy Christians.

Contemporary For more contemporary history and architecture, discover relics of Rome's industrial archaeology in the Ostiense area, including the old Gasometer and **Centrale Montemartini** (centralemontemartini.org), the city's former power plant turned into a fascinating museum where classic Roman and Greek art stands beside giant boilers and turbines.

Mithra Temples

Immerse yourself in ancient Rome's worship of the deity Mithras with a visit to the cult's atmospheric underground temples. Book ahead.

Circus Maximus

Discover the large sanctuary near the cages of the Circus Maximus from where the chariots set off for the races.

San Clemente Basilica

Descend below the surface of this basilica to a 3rd-century all-round carving depicting Mithras killing the bull.

Baths of Caracalla

Step into the underground labyrinth of the Baths of Caracalla to find one of the largest sanctuaries in Rome devoted to the cult of Mithra.

Palazzo Barberini

Explore the undergrounds of Palazzo Barberini to see a rare example of a frescoed Mithra temple.

Tales of Rome's Master-pieces

IN THE FOOTSTEPS OF ROME'S GREATEST ARTISTS

With majestic buildings, romantic sculptures and marble fountains, the enduring beauty of Rome's cultural riches conveys a palpable sense of *la dolce vita*. Yet behind the making of the city's eternal masterpieces hides extraordinary stories of rivalry, love affairs and animosity between noble families.

From left Wall of the Sistine Chapel; Facade of St Peter's Basilica; Four Rivers Fountain

Sculptor, painter and unequalled artistic genius, Michelangelo Buonarroti is known as a leading figure of the Italian Renaissance – and for his bad temper. Among those who bore the brunt of it was Biagio Martinelli, the papal master of ceremonies, who declared the painted nudities of *The Last Judgement* as more suitable to public baths or local taverns rather than the Sistine Chapel. In return, Michelangelo represented Martinelli as Minos, donkey-eared judge of the underworld. To Martinelli's complaint, the pope patiently replied that since hell was out of his jurisdiction, the painting had to remain the way the artist had envisioned it.

Those who lived and worked within the mighty Vatican walls also witnessed the legendary competition between two of the greatest baroque artists, Gian Lorenzo Bernini and Francesco Borromini. 'Eclectic and polyhedric, Bernini was often in charge of important projects thanks to his more accommodating and diplomatic character, whereas Borromini's temperamental personality made him less fit to be welcomed into elite circles,' explains Michele Di Monte, renowned art historian at Palazzo Barberini.

The troublesome relationship between the two peers began with the construction of Palazzo Barberini, but reached notorious heights in the building of the ill-fated bell towers of St Peter's Basilica facade, commissioned to Bernini by Pope Urban VIII and demolished even before their inauguration. Even though the debacle was mainly due to unstable ground rather than Bernini's miscalculation, the fact that an intervention by Borromini was crucial to their demise contributed to his fierce rival's fall from grace. This fall was further worsened by the death

of Urban VIII, a member of the Barberini clan and a long-time supporter of Bernini's genius, and the ascension to the papal throne of Innocent X, member of the rival Pamphilj family and patron of Borromini.

The pair's perpetual game of one-upmanship led to many more legends, including the famous tale that one of the statues of Bernini's Four Rivers Fountain covers its eyes to avoid seeing the facing church of Sant'Agnese in Agone, designed by Borromini. 'Bernini's fountain was erected before the facade of the church where Borromini worked only for a few years, so it's safe to say that this is only unfounded hearsay,' explains Di Monte.

> Michelangelo represented Martinelli as Minos, donkey-eared judge of the underworld.

Even though Borromini was the leading artist under the supremacy of the Pamphilj family, Bernini won the commission to build the Four Rivers Fountain in Piazza Navona thanks to his savoir-faire and a clever ruse. He gave Olimpia Maidalchini, the pope's sister-in-law, a model of his fountain's design to be placed in Palazzo Pamphilj where Innocent X was sure to be seen. One look was enough to make the decision and the shrewd artist scored a gig that contributed to bringing him back in the spotlight.

'Myths like the one linked to Piazza Navona's Four Rivers Fountain are to be found in the well-known rivalry that saw Bernini and Borromini competing on several occasions,' adds Di Monte. A rivalry that remains alive many centuries later.

Raphael's La Fornarina

Renaissance artist Raphael was a true Casanova and the subject of his *La Fornarina* painting is a portrait of his lover. When working for the Chigi family on the frescoes of Villa Farnesina in Via della Lungara in Trastevere, apparently Raphael fell head over heels for Margherita Luti, the daughter of a local baker, after seeing her taking a bath in the river. Raphael's frequent outings prompted Agostino Chigi to allow Margherita into his house so that the artist could work at a faster pace.

Michele Di Monte, *art historian and curator, Gallerie Nazionali Barberini Corsini – Palazzo Barberini, where La Fornarina is on display*

05 Caesar's ROME

ARCHAEOLOGY | HISTORY | WALKING

Julius Caesar left an indelible mark on Rome as one of history's most epic military leaders and dictators, but not much remains of Rome's Republic, and even less of Julius Caesar. Here's where to trace the legacy of the Roman general and self-declared leader of the ancient city.

How to

Getting around Literally a walk in the park, an archaeological park and surrounding streets. With the Capitoline Hill as base camp, dedicate at least a few hours for exploration.

When to go Any time of year, but check the weather for extreme heat or rain. Plan for mornings and book museum and site entrances well in advance. Try to avoid weekends and public holidays.

Terre e Domus Our pick for a taste of traditional Roman dishes, like carbonara or *ovuli*, the emperors' preferred mushrooms. (palazzovalentini.it/terre-domus)

From Humble Origins

Born in 100 BCE, **Gaius Julius Caesar** was raised in the rough-and-tumble neighbourhood known as **Subura**, away from the rich enclaves of the elite like the Palatine. Today, Subura is part of the **Monti** district. Wander the neighbourhood sheltered by a massive 35m-high, 300m-long fire wall that shielded the 1st-century **Forum of Augustus** from the ancient slum.

Caesar's rise from slum dog to top dog was meteoric. By 63 BCE, he was elected *pontifex maximus*, following a successful military career, and was obligated to live in the epicentre of the city in the Roman Forum's *domus publica*, next to **Temple of Vesta**. Traces of the *domus'* pavement are visible as you wander through the House of the Vestal Virgins.

Via dei Fori Imperiali

The 850m straight shot Via dei Fori Imperiali connecting Piazza Venezia to the Colosseum is punctuated with reproductions of statues of ancient Rome's most important emperors. A bronze statue of Julius Caesar guards the Forum Julium, and each year on the Ides of March, wreaths are placed at its base.

Top left House of the Vestal Virgins.
Bottom left Forum of Augustus. **Above** Statue of Julius Caesar, Roman Forum.

On the Rise

General Pompey the Great, Caesar's most dynamic rival, eventually formed an unstoppable alliance with Caesar and Marcus Licinius Crassus. Together, the triumvirate dominated the Senate and Pompey left his own mark on history with the **Teatro di Pompeo**, Rome's largest theatre. Today you can walk its curves in the side streets of **Campo de' Fiori** and even explore its remains in the subterranean levels of **Constanza Hostaria** (hostariacostanza.it) and **Trattoria der Pallaro** (trattoriaderpallaro.it).

Caesar's military victories vaulted him to cult status and he celebrated by carving out the **Forum of Caesar** (Forum Julium) as the very first extension of the Roman Forum. His new forum, with ancestral **Temple of Venus Genetrix**, was the social scene and included the famous Cleopatra and equestrian statue of himself, of course.

🚶 Walk Like Caesar

Trace Julius Caesar's last footsteps starting out from the **Capitoline Hill** (Campidoglio), the smallest and most important of Rome's famous seven hills, for a great outlook over the Roman Forum.

Head down via Monte Tarpeo to the **Forum Holitorium**, Rome's ancient marketplace and exchange. Go underground **San Nicola in Carcere** to explore the Republican-era temples.

Make your way past the **Portico di Ottavia** in the Ghetto neighbourhood to Largo di Torre Argentina, Temple B, where Caesar was assassinated.

Local insight by Darius Arya, *a Rome-based archaeologist,* ancientromelive.org, @dariusaryadigs

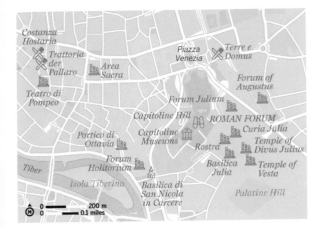

Left Roman Forum **Below** Temple in Area Sacra, Largo di Torre Argentina

From Man to God

On 15 March 44 BCE, Caesar was assassinated by Senate members leading the Republic into an Empire. The murder took place at the Curia, behind **Temple B of Largo di Torre Argentina**. Set in the heart of a busy neighbourhood, the open-air archaeological site is also known as the **Area Sacra** and hosts four beautiful Republican-age temples.

Some 14 months after his death, Caesar was declared a god and the **Temple of Divus Iulius** was built in the centre of the Roman Forum on the site of Caesar's cremation. Across the piazza is the **Rostra**, where Mark Antony's famous oration stirred up the crowd to action.

An Enduring Legacy

Caesar set out to leave a mark in all he did, including architecture, urban planning and entertainment. The **Theatre of Marcellus** was completed near the **Forum Holitorium** by nephew Augustus, who also was key in the completion of the **Basilica Julia** and the **Curia Julia**, in the Roman Forum.

The **Capitoline Museums** (museicapitolini.org), the world's oldest public museums, will catch you up on Rome's history from Iron Age origins to Empire magnificence. Look for Caesar's name on the Consular and Triumphal Capitoline Fasti lapidary, listing leaders from Romulus to the Augustan age.

Futurist Rome

**BACK TO THE FUTURE
WITH CONTEMPORARY
ARCHITECTURE**

Rome is a palimpsest of architecture and ornament that chronicles the city's millennia of culture. Ancient temples, resplendent Renaissance *palazzi* (mansions) and beautiful baroque churches make up the incredible landscape, but it's the follies of modern architecture that cultivate the city's enduring appeal.

From left Palazzo della Civiltà Italiana; Palazzo dei Congressi; Stadio dei Marmi

Drive 15 minutes south of Rome and you're in the future. Or at least, a future conceptualised by dictator Benito Mussolini for the 1942 World's Fair. E42, or Esposizione Universale Roma – now known as **EUR** – was designed to celebrate the 20th-century empire and promote the fascist agenda through rationalist architecture, a style inspired by the scale, structure and symmetry of ancient Roman architecture. WWII halted the project and the fair never happened, but in the 1950s construction of the ultra-modern palaces and buildings by architects such as Marcello Piacentini, Aldaberto Libera and Luigi Moretti was completed.

The city-within-a-city was inspired by imperial town planning. Axially planned streets and bombastic boulevards are lined with austere and monumental buildings referencing Roman classical and Renaissance styles, made with high-quality and precious materials like travertine, limestone, tuff and marble, all associated with Roman Empire architecture.

Looming over the neighbourhood is the landmark **Palazzo della Civiltà Italiana**, now fashion house Fendi's headquarters. Nearly 60m in height, the travertine **Colosseo Quadrato**, as it is fondly called, is a square copy of the ancient Colosseum, with six levels of symmetrical open arches. Across the boulevard is **Palazzo dei Congressi**, a temple-like congress hall considered one of the best examples of 1930s Italian architecture, combining modernism and classical styles. Grandiose colonnades at the **Palazzo dell'Ina** and **Palazzo dell'Inps** were modelled after Trajan's markets. The 45m-tall **Marconi obelisk** made of Carrara marble forms the focal point for the entire neighbourhood. With such a dramatic departure from Rome's traditional

architecture, it's no wonder EUR has featured as a backdrop for futuristic films such as *Titus* and *The Machinist*.

Fascist iconography also features strongly in the **Foro Italico**, a stadium complex built as a stage for the 1940 Olympics, north of the city in the residential neighbourhood of Flaminio. At the entrance is an unmissable, 17.5m-high white marble obelisk carved with the names Mussolini DUX (Latin for Il Duce), while the pavement is decorated with modern mosaics with athletes and fascist text. The nearby outdoor **Stadio dei Marmi** is one of the most beautiful running tracks perimetered by 4.5m-tall statues depicting muscular Italian athletes in classical style and low-rise marble stadium seating. Inside the sporting complex is the indoor Olympic-sized swimming pool with floor-to-ceiling mosaic walls decorated with divers, swimmers, athletes and mythological animals, while on a floor above is Mussolini's private lap pool, where the Duce waded around astrological symbols in the mosaics.

> Axially planned streets and bombastic boulevards are lined with austere and monumental buildings referencing Roman classical and Renaissance styles.

Traces of rationalist architecture appear in central Rome as well. Trastevere's **Casa del GIL** (wegil.it), the former Fascist Youth House, is a rationalist jewel designed by Luigi Moretti with an austere travertine tower, marble pavements, long lines, elliptical stairwell and a relief celebrating Italy's 1936 conquests in Africa. Across town is the whimsical **Posta di Piazza Bologna**, an undulating wave of travertine.

Step into the 21st Century

Although new architecture in Rome is rare, especially in the historic centre, there are some 21st-century monuments to the Eternal City's landscape including Richard Meier's minimalist travertine box **Museo dell'Ara Pacis** (arapacis.it), Zaha Hadid's **MAXXI Museum** (maxxi.art) and Renzo Piano's **Auditorium Parco della Musica** (auditorium.com).

Connecting the city are two modern arch bridges, **Ponte Settimia Spizzichino** and pedestrian **Ponte della Musica**, while just outside of the city centre are Meier's beautiful **Jubilee Church** and hometown architect Massimiliano Fuksas' **Nuvola**, a futurist glass-enclosed cloud.

06 A Country **FEAST**

FOOD | WINE | DAY TRIP

Forget Michelin-starred fine dining. For a Roman banquet to travel for, do as the locals do and head to the Castelli Romani. Just south of town, this scenic wine-producing area of verdant slopes and volcanic lakes has long been a favourite with day-trippers who flock here to feast on country food at rustic trattorias known as *fraschette*.

🗺 **How to**

Getting here Regular trains run from Rome's Stazione Termini to Frascati, Castel Gandolfo and Albano Laziale, from where it's an easy walk to Ariccia.

When to go The area is best in spring (April to mid-June) and autumn (September and October).

Cost Most *fraschette* offer fixed-price menus, typically costing from €15 to €25.

Walk off your meal Explore Frascati's historic centre, hilltop Castel Gandolfo or nearby Lago Albano.

Tradition *Fraschette* have been part of Castelli life for centuries. Initially they were little more than pop-up wine shops. 'When the local peasants made their wine, if they had enough to sell they would put a *frasca* (branch) outside their house as a sign,' explains tour guide Silvia Prosperi 'And it's from this *frasca* that we get the word *fraschetta*.'

Fraschette Today, almost all *fraschette* serve food, even if many are still housed in *cantine* (cellars) and are no-frills affairs with wonky tables and wooden benches. You'll find them all over the Castelli but for the full-on *fraschetta*

Top right Platter of food with red wine **Bottom right** *Porchetta di Ariccia*

🍇 Castelli Wines

With its own microclimate and fertile volcanic soil, the Castelli Romani is ideal wine country. Its most famous wine is Frascati but other important DOC wines include Velletri, Montecompatri-Colonna, Colli Lanuvini, Castelli Romani and Colli Albani. Most Castelli wines are white but you'll also find reds and rosés, as well as Frascati's sweet Cannellino wine.

By Silvia Prosperi,
tour guide,
afriendinrome.it

experience, head to Ariccia, a small town renowned for its *porchetta* (boneless, seasoned roast pork).

The menu A typical *fraschetta* meal consists of a lavish antipasto followed by a classic Roman pasta dish and/or a simple cut of grilled meat. All, of course, accompanied by carafes of local wine. Helpings are generous so don't be shy of calling a halt after the pasta dish – most people do.

Headline dish The star of the show is almost always the antipasto spread. Featuring platters of *porchetta*, *coppiette* (jerk-like strips of pork spiked with chilli), prosciutto, vegetables marinated in olive oil, bulbs of creamy mozzarella, olives and crusty farmhouse bread, it's the stuff of foodie fantasies.

Listings

BEST OF THE REST

Roman Relics

Colosseum

Rome's iconic amphitheatre encapsulates all the blood and thunder of the ancient city. Climb the stands and imagine the roar of the crowd as the gladiators slugged it out below.

Pantheon

A 2000-year-old temple turned church, this is Rome's best preserved ancient monument and, with its soaring dome and marble-clad interior, one of the most influential buildings in the Western world.

Palatino

The haunting remains of the imperial palace adorn the Palatine Hill, the oldest and most exclusive part of the ancient city, where Romulus supposedly founded Rome in 753 BCE.

Roman Forum

These sprawling ruins are what's left of ancient Rome's showcase centre, a teeming district of temples, law courts and vibrant public spaces. For great Forum views head up to Piazza del Campidoglio.

Ostia Antica

A mini-Pompeii, the remnants of ancient Rome's sea port make for one of Italy's most compelling archaeological sites.

Appia Antica

In Rome's southern suburbs, the ancient Appian Way is steeped in drama. This is where Spartacus and his slave army were crucified and the early Christians buried their dead in catacombs.

Villa Adriana

One of two Unesco World Heritage Sites in Tivoli, Hadrian's colossal villa is quite magnificent. By Cotral bus, it's an easy day trip.

Heavenly Art

Vatican Museums

Home to the Sistine Chapel and one of the world's greatest art collections, this vast museum complex boasts a stunning array of classical sculpture alongside masterpieces by Michelangelo, Raphael et al.

Museo e Galleria Borghese

The best Roman museum you've never heard of. Its collection provides a great introduction to Renaissance and baroque art, culminating in a series of astounding sculptures by Gian Lorenzo Bernini.

St Peter's Basilica

The Vatican's showpiece basilica is an astonishing sight with its landmark dome, monumental facade and colossal, art-clad interior. Chief among its priceless treasures is Michelangelo's *Pietà* sculpture.

Michelangelo's *Pietà*, St Peter's Basilica

Capitoline Museums

On the Capitoline Hill, the world's oldest public museums showcase one of Rome's finest collections of classical sculpture as well as paintings by major-league European artists.

Chiesa di San Luigi dei Francesi

This beautiful church in central Rome boasts a trio of Caravaggio paintings.

Gallerie Nazionali: Palazzo Barberini

One of Rome's finest baroque palaces, Palazzo Barberini was designed by three of the most important 17th-century architects and now houses an eclectic and wonderful collection of art.

Galleria Doria Pamphilj

This lavish private gallery displays works by big-name artists, including Raphael, Titian, Caravaggio, Bernini, Velázquez and Pieter Bruegel the Elder.

Piazzas, Parks & Street Life

Piazza Navona

With its trio of flamboyant fountains, baroque *palazzi* and colourful cast of street artists, hawkers and tourists, Piazza Navona is Rome's elegant showpiece square.

Villa Borghese

Rome's Central Park boasts wooded glades, a lake, a Shakespearean theatre and a string of magnificent museums.

Trevi Fountain

Throw a coin into Rome's most celebrated fountain and legend says you'll return to the city.

Spanish Steps

A magnet for foreigners for centuries, this statement staircase provides the picture-perfect backdrop to Piazza di Spagna.

MURATART/SHUTTERSTOCK ©

Trevi Fountain

Piazza di Santa Maria in Trastevere

The focal piazza of the attractive Trastevere district where students, tourists, locals, diners, drinkers and street hawkers cheerfully mingle.

Parco Savello

With its heavenly views of St Peter's dome, this hilltop Aventino garden, known to Romans as the Giardino degli Aranci (Orange Garden), is romance central.

◎ Under-the-Radar Gems

Museo Nazionale Romano: Palazzo Massimo alle Terme

Often overlooked by visitors, this terrific museum near Termini train station will blow you away with its stunning frescoes, mosaics and breathtaking ancient sculpture.

La Galleria Nazionale

Housed in a vast belle-époque palace in Villa Borghese park, this fantastic modern art gallery boasts works by many of the most important artists of the 19th and 20th centuries.

Museo Nazionale Etrusco di Villa Giulia

Pope Julius III's 16th-century palace in Villa Borghese provides the setting for Italy's finest collection of Etruscan treasures.

Cimitero Acattolico per Gli Stranieri

An air of Grand Tour romance hangs over Rome's 'non-Catholic' cemetery in Testaccio. Poets Keats and Shelley are buried here as well as Italian political thinker Antonio Gramsci.

Basilica di Santa Maria in Trastevere

Reckoned to be the oldest church in Rome dedicated to the Virgin Mary, this discreet Trastevere basilica hides a superb display of 12th-century apse mosaics.

Roman Cuisine

Flavio al Velavevodetto €€

Rome's Testaccio neighbourhood is the spiritual home of *cucina romana* and this is one of its finest trattorias.

Trattoria Da Cesare al Casaletto €€

Heavy on taste and light on attitude, this is one of Rome's top trattorias. It's in the Monteverde district but well worth the hike.

La Tavernaccia €€

Cheery helpful staff, a convivial atmosphere and excellent Roman cooking combine to make this Trastevere trattoria a super-hot dining ticket.

L'Arcangelo €€€

A long-standing favourite in the upmarket Prati district, L'Arcangelo keeps diners happy with its updated takes on traditional Roman dishes.

Salumeria Roscioli €€€

The Roscioli name is a guarantee of good things to come as you'll discover at this, its flagship deli-restaurant. Traditional dishes are prepared with premium ingredients and peerless skill.

🚚 Street Food

Bonci Pizzarium €

Sliced pizza by Gabriele Bonci, Rome's most acclaimed pizza chef, draws the crowds to Pizzarium near the Vatican Museums. Squares of spongy base are topped by combos of prime seasonal ingredients.

Forno Roscioli €

One of Rome's best bakeries, Forno Roscioli is much-loved by lunching locals who stop by this city-centre spot for luscious sliced pizza and hunger-sating *supplì* (fried risotto balls).

Trapizzino €

The Testaccio home of the *trapizzino*, a cone of doughy bread stuffed with fillers such as *polpette al sugo* (meatballs in tomato sauce). They're messy to eat but quite delicious.

Fatamorgana €

Natural, artisanal gelato comes in myriad flavours at several city centre branches. Anyone for citrus and ricotta?

🍴 Fraschette

Osteria da Angelo €

One of many popular *fraschette* (rustic trattorias) in Ariccia serving a slap-up menu of *porchetta* and prize Castelli Romani specialities.

Pizza from Bonci Pizzarium

La Selvotta   €

An outdoor *fraschetta* in a woody glade in Ariccia. Great food, wooden benches and plenty of space for the kids to run around in.

Cantina Simonetti   €

For an authentic Castelli feast of *porchetta*, cold cuts, cheese and local white wine, search out this atmospheric *cantina* in Frascati.

Cafes, Bars & Speakeasies

Sciascia Caffè

Head to this polished, old-school cafe in the Prati district for some of Rome's finest coffee.

Sant'Eustachio Il Caffè

Almost always full, this workaday *centro storico* cafe is reckoned by many to serve the capital's best coffee. The secret to its creamy deliciousness is a jealously guarded secret.

Rimessa Roscioli

Part of the Roscioli culinary empire, this central Rome wine bar is for true aficionados with labels from all over Italy and a menu of exquisite wine-tasting dinners.

Open Baladin

Open Baladin has long been a leading light in Rome's craft beer scene. A laid-back pub, it offers up to 40 beers on tap and an encyclopedic selection of bottled brews.

Jerry Thomas Project

A trend-setting speakeasy requiring a password to get in, this Prohibition-styled hideaway specialises in craft cocktails prepared by master mixologists.

Sant'Eustachio Il Caffè

Boutiques & Artisanal Style

Marta Ray

Women's ballerina flats and everyday bags in rainbow colours and super-soft leather feature at this smart city centre boutique.

Confetteria Moriondo & Gariglio

Set up by the Torinese confectioners to the royal house of Savoy, this historic shop sells handmade chocolates and confections, many prepared from 19th-century recipes.

Tina Sondergaard

Sublimely cut and whimsically retro-esque, Tina Sondergaard's creations for women are a hit with Rome's fashion cognoscenti.

Fausto Santini

Nothing screams Roman style more than a pair of shoes from the city's best-known shoe designer, known for his beguilingly simple architectural designs.

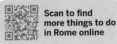

Scan to find more things to do in Rome online

Experience
Turin,
Piedmont
& Cinque
Terre online

TURIN, PIEDMONT & CINQUE TERRE

OUTDOORS | VILLAGES | WINE

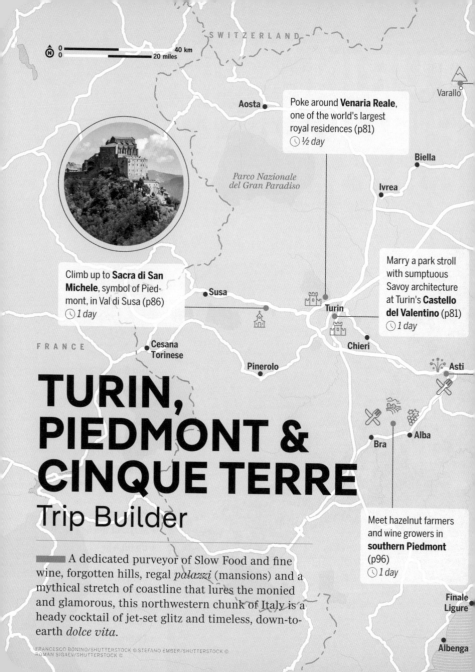

SWITZERLAND

0 ——————— 40 km
0 ——————— 20 miles

Varallo

Aosta

Poke around **Venaria Reale**, one of the world's largest royal residences (p81)
🕐 ½ day

Biella

Parco Nazionale del Gran Paradiso

Ivrea

Climb up to **Sacra di San Michele**, symbol of Piedmont, in Val di Susa (p86)
🕐 *1 day*

Susa

Turin

Marry a park stroll with sumptuous Savoy architecture at Turin's **Castello del Valentino** (p81)
🕐 *1 day*

FRANCE

Cesana Torinese

Chieri

Pinerolo

Asti

TURIN, PIEDMONT & CINQUE TERRE
Trip Builder

Bra   Alba

Meet hazelnut farmers and wine growers in **southern Piedmont** (p96)
🕐 *1 day*

▰▰ A dedicated purveyor of Slow Food and fine wine, forgotten hills, regal *palazzi* (mansions) and a mythical stretch of coastline that lures the monied and glamorous, this northwestern chunk of Italy is a heady cocktail of jet-set glitz and timeless, down-to-earth *dolce vita*.

Finale Ligure

Albenga

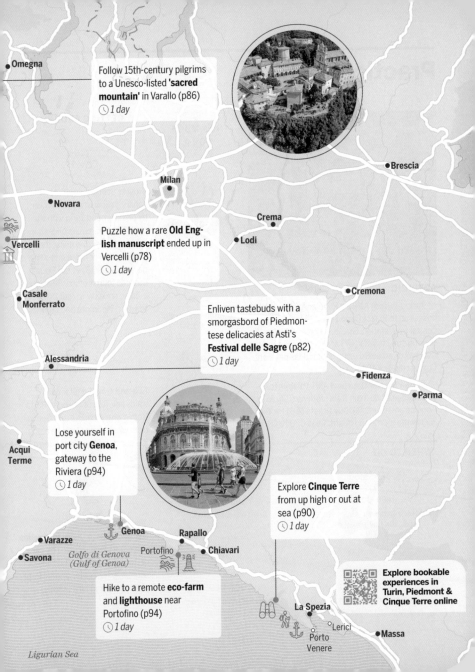

Follow 15th-century pilgrims to a Unesco-listed **'sacred mountain'** in Varallo (p86)
🕒 *1 day*

Omegna

Brescia

Milan

Novara

Crema

Vercelli

Lodi

Puzzle how a rare **Old English manuscript** ended up in Vercelli (p78)
🕒 *1 day*

Casale Monferrato

Cremona

Enliven tastebuds with a smorgasbord of Piedmontese delicacies at Asti's **Festival delle Sagre** (p82)
🕒 *1 day*

Alessandria

Fidenza

Parma

Acqui Terme

Lose yourself in port city **Genoa**, gateway to the Riviera (p94)
🕒 *1 day*

Explore **Cinque Terre** from up high or out at sea (p90)
🕒 *1 day*

Varazze

Genoa

Rapallo

Savona

Golfo di Genova (Gulf of Genoa)

Portofino

Chiavari

Hike to a remote **eco-farm** and **lighthouse** near Portofino (p94)
🕒 *1 day*

Explore bookable experiences in Turin, Piedmont & Cinque Terre online

La Spezia

Lerici

Porto Venere

Massa

Ligurian Sea

Practicalities

TTPHOTO/SHUTTERSTOCK ©

ARRIVING

 Turin (Torino) Airport Regular Arriva shuttle buses run to Piazza Carlo Felice 39 by Turin's central train station, Stazione Porta Nuova, in 30 minutes; buy tickets (€7) at machines in the arrival hall or on board using contactless payment. Costs roughly €40 by taxi.

 Genoa (Genova) Airport AMT Volabus to/from Genoa's two main train stations (Piazza Principe and Brignole); buy tickets (€6) for the 30-minute journey on board. Taxis €20 to €30.

WHEN TO GO

APR–JUN
Fewer crowds, warm days on the coast, ideal hiking conditions.

JUL–AUG
Beach season on the busy Italian Riviera.

SEP
The grape harvest begins; food festivals in Turin and the Langhe.

OCT–DEC
White truffles are hunted with dogs around Alba.

HOW MUCH FOR A

Glass of Barolo
€5–20

Cinque Terre train
€4

Truffle hunt
€70

GETTING AROUND

Bicycle Scoop up a set of canary-yellow wheels to power by pedal around Turin with the city's [To]Bike public bike-sharing scheme; subscribe using the [To]Bike app or buy a one-/two-day card (€8/13) at the Piazza Castello tourist office. Bikes and e-bikes are easy to rent in most towns in Piedmont and Liguria.

Bus and train Regular daily trains link Turin's Stazione Porta Nuova with Alba, Bra and Genoa, from where trains trundle along the coast, via the Cinque Terre villages, to La Spezia.

Car and scooter Away from cities and main towns, touring by car or Audrey Hepburn–style Vespa scooter is the better option. Rent at airports or in city centres.

EATING & DRINKING

Apericena Turin's answer to the *aperitivo* is a bar-buffet feast equivalent to dinner. Find fabulous spreads in student-loving San Salvario and the Quadrilatero quarter: bars **Beerba** and **Pastis** are favourites.

Riviera street food On the coast, build picnics from *focaccia alla genovese* covered with salt and rosemary, *farinata* (thin, chickpea-flour 'pizza'; pictured top right) and paper cones of tiny fried fish, calamari or octopus. In San Remo, go for *sardenara* (pizza-like focaccia topped with tomatoes, onions, capers and sardines; pictured bottom right).

Must-try pasta Osteria del Boccondivino (p97)

Best sunset spritz Al Faro di Portofino (p98)

CONNECT & FIND YOUR WAY

Wi-fi Freely available on arrival at airports and at post offices, tourist offices and motorway service stations region-wide. To track down free wi-fi hotspots in Genoa and the surrounding Liguria region, check regioneliguriawifi.it.

Navigation Getting lost in Genoa's *caruggi* (old-town alleys) is unavoidable. Download offline maps or buy a paper map before hiking in rural Piedmont and Liguria.

DISCOUNT CARDS

The **Torino+Piemonte Card** (one/two/three days €28/36/43) covers admission to 190 monuments and museums in Piedmont. Genoa's **Card Musei** (24/48hr €12/16) assures free admission to 20-plus city museums.

WHERE TO STAY

Turin, the Cinque Terre villages and seaside resorts on the Italian Riviera are expensive. Coastal accommodation fills up quickly April to September; advance reservations are essential.

Place	Pro/Con
Turin	Hotels for every budget and numerous character-filled B&Bs.
Genoa	Beautiful boutique hotels and B&Bs in the historic centre; elsewhere, mediocre but highly affordable hotels.
Alba	Attractive B&Bs in town; chic villas, traditional B&Bs and on-trend farm stays in the surrounding Langhe countryside.
Golfo dei Poeti	Main town La Spezia is an affordable spot to stay en route to Cinque Terre; upmarket Lerici and Porto Venere have B&Bs and apartment rentals.
Cinque Terre	For the most choice, hit Monterosso for hotel accommodation, Manarola for outstanding apartment stays, and Corniglia for decent B&Bs.

MONEY

In Cinque Terre, walkers need cash at trailheads to buy a **Cinque Terre card** (€7.50/14.50 for unlimited one-/two-day use of paths and electric buses). Otherwise, contactless payment is increasingly the norm.

07 Hidden
VERCELLI

CULTURE | DAY TRIP | FOOD

Right in the middle of the rice fields of the Po Valley, Vercelli is the perfect city for a day trip. With a rich heritage that dates back to the Middle Ages, a quiet centre beckoning for a stroll and some unmissable culinary gems, here's why Vercelli deserves to be discovered.

DI LUCA PONTI/SHUTTERSTOCK ©

📖 How to

Getting here The easiest way from either Turin or Milan is with the Torino-Milano regional train, which leaves from both cities every hour.

When to go Year-round, but autumn, spring and early summer are especially lovely.

Top tip On your way from the train station to the city centre you can stop at the **ATL Vercelli** (atlvalsesiavercelli.it) for some detailed information about the city.

GERVASIO S. - EUREKA_89/SHUTTERSTOCK ©

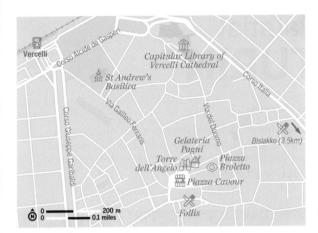

Top left Interior, St Andrew's Basilica
Bottom left A piazza in Vercelli

Unique sights Vercelli might be relatively small, but it packs a good punch. Its **St Andrew's Basilica** is one of the oldest and best-preserved Romanesque monuments in Italy, and walking around it you can already see the influences of soon-to-be popular Gothic architecture. Most importantly, the **Capitular Library of Vercelli Cathedral** (tesorodelduomovc.it) houses the **Vercelli Book** – one of the only four surviving Old English codices in the whole world and still shrouded in mystery, since it's not yet clear how it arrived in Vercelli during the Middle Ages.

Squares There are many picturesque sights to enjoy while ambling through Vercelli's city centre. The medieval **Torre dell'Angelo** overlooks the city's main square, **Piazza Cavour**, where the local farmers market takes place every Tuesday and Friday; not too far away, the tiny **Piazza Broletto** (also known as Fish Square) feels like stepping back in time to the 14th century.

Piano and voice Vercelli is home to the **Viotti International Music Competition** (concorsoviotti.it), which has been taking place here since the 1950s. The competition switches from voice to piano each year and attracts thousands of accomplished and internationally famous musicians. It's held from late October to early November over several weekends.

✂️ Must-Have Munchies

You can't leave Vercelli without trying its typical risotto dish, *panissa*, featuring locally produced rice, beans and salami as well as red wine and lard. One of the best places to indulge in it is midrange restaurant **Bislakko** (bislakko.com). If you have a sweet tooth, you'll want to try local spice-rich *bicciolani* biscuits and liquor-laced *tartufata* cake, which you can pick up at the **Follis pastry shop** (follis.it). You might also want to sample the award-winning *fondente* (dark chocolate) gelato flavour of **Gelateria Pagni** (Via Gioberti 9, closed Mondays), or its beloved coffee with cream.

Recommended by Marta Mattea, *Vercelli-based tour guide*

08 Palatial TURIN

ARCHITECTURE | CITY WALK | HISTORY

Turin is a city with royal blood, and its history as a seat of dukes and kings is clear to see in its elegant porticoes, paved squares and splendid palaces – all of them Unesco World Heritage Sites. Here's a guide to the royal residences of Turin to help you on your kingly tour.

TARA VAN DER LINDEN PHOTO/SHUTTERSTOCK ©

🗺 How to

Getting here Residences within the urban area of Turin are easily reachable on foot or with public transport; there are trains and dedicated buses for those in suburban areas.

When to go Year-round, but the warmest season is the best option (even though it might be when it's most crowded).

Cost Tickets average €10, with a vast range of possible reductions; there's also the **Royal Card**, which gives you full access for seven days.

LORENZOBOV/SHUTTERSTOCK ©

Heart of the city The most central and best-known residence is the **Royal Museums complex** (museireali.beniculturali.it), which centres on the city's central Piazza Castello. The complex includes the lavish **Palazzo Reale**, chief of the Savoy residences in Piedmont and centre of Piedmontese politics for at least three centuries, as well as other unique sights like the invaluable collections of the **Biblioteca Reale** and the **Cappella della Sindone**, where the Shroud of Turin is housed (on display only for select periods).

Inside Turin There are many other residences in Turin's historic city centre, most within walking distance of the Palazzo Reale. At the top of **Palazzo Madama** you can enjoy amazing views over Turin's centre; a visit to the **Castello del Valentino** might include a stroll through the extensive Valentino Park and its open-air museum **Borgo Medievale** for a glimpse of Turin in the Middle Ages; and **Palazzo Carignano**, with its museum, is the perfect place to learn about the history of Italy's unification in the 19th century.

Outside Turin Among the residences and hunting lodges just outside Turin's urban area, the most famous is by far **La Venaria Reale**, the Royal Palace of Venaria, with its breathtaking Galleria Grande and sprawling gardens.

Far left Palazzo Reale **Bottom left** Valentino Park **Near left** Palazzo Carignano

 Turin's Table

For a top-end stop between throne rooms and royal bedchambers, look no further than **Ristorante Del Cambio** (delcambio.it), right in front of Palazzo Carignano. Since the 18th century, history has been made at its tables, with politicians (including Count Camillo Cavour, who helped unify Italy during the 19th century), musicians, actors and poets like Frederich Nietzsche, Giuseppe Verdi and Audrey Hepburn passing through its halls.

Recommended by Gloria Faccio, *Tourism Office of Turin*

09 Festivals by the
BARREL

FOOD | DRINK | MUSIC

▬▬▬ Food is a pillar of Italian culture, and it's no exception for Piedmont. All throughout its mountains, hills and plains, the region is dotted with festivals and events dedicated to its most typical and delicious culinary and alcoholic specialities – the perfect recipe for great times and memorable feasting!

🗺 **How to**

Getting here Bigger cities like Asti and Turin can be reached via train; for smaller towns and villages, renting a car is the best way to go.

When to go Festivals happen year-round, but the best time to enjoy outdoor drinking and eating is definitely the warmer months (May–early October).

Essential gear Some festivals (especially those focused on drinking) offer you the chance to buy a pouch you can hang around your neck to carry your glass – free hands and easy access all in one!

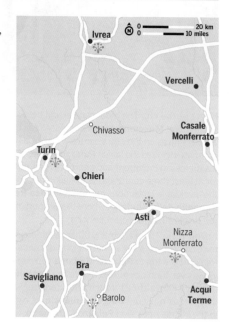

Eating You can find festivals dedicated to Piedmontese delicacies like *bagna càuda* (a hot garlic-and-anchovy dip), *toma* cheese, truffle or agnolotti all throughout the region. If you want to sample more dishes at once, though, then the **Festival delle Sagre di Asti**, held each September, is your best bet – all the villages and towns surrounding Asti come together, each offering their own speciality. And for something sweeter you might enjoy **Cioccolatò** (cioccola-to.eu), usually held in November, where the main squares of Turin become a chocolate-filled heaven.

Top right Battle of the Oranges, Ivrea **Bottom right** Cioccolatò, Turin

⚜ Festival Tips

Dress comfy City streets in Italy can be tricky, so pick shoes for all kinds of terrain.

Arrive early Lots of people (and cars) will show up and it's first come, first served.

Take it easy Chaos and queuing are festival staples. So enjoy it as part of the experience!

Advised by the team at Nizza Monferrato's tourist office

Drinking Together with the Festival delle Sagre, Asti also hosts the **Douja D'Or**, one of Piedmont's most important wine festivals, where you can stock up on Barolo, Barbera and the other wines the region has to offer. There are also several festivals dedicated to beer, especially artisanal beer; find them using websites like **Itinerari Nel Gusto** (itinerarinelgusto.it).

Partying For unique experiences that aren't (directly) related to drinking and eating, check out Nizza Monferrato's annual **barrel race** (corsadellebottinizza.com), where runners spin huge wine barrels down the town's streets; or Barolo's **Collisioni Festival**, where you can catch performances from international music artists; or Ivrea's Carnevale, with its famous **Battle of the Oranges** (storicocarnevaleivrea.it).

A BOUNTY OF COLOUR
Liguria's Cinque Terre

01 Manarola
Small but charming Manarola perches improbably high on the sea cliffs and marks the start of the famous Via dell'Amore.

02 Neptune
Neptune, Roman god of the sea, still juts out from a rock spur in Monterosso al Mare even after WWII bombings.

03 Ligurian Pesto
The emerald green of basil leaves and of their favoured destiny, pesto, is a familiar sight in Cinque Terre.

04 Lemons
Each year, Monterosso al Mare is painted yellow by the lemons filling the streets during the festival dedicated to them.

05 Riomaggiore
The colourful stone buildings of Riomaggiore cluster around a picturesque tiny harbour – best enjoyed at sunset.

06 Vernazza
Breathtaking Vernazza, with its coloured houses gathered around the harbour, is Cinque Terre at its finest.

07 Nativity Scene

Since the '60s, Manarola lights up at Christmas time with the world's largest nativity scene, colourfully stretching across an entire hillside.

08 Maritime Pine

Everywhere you go in Cinque Terre, you're surrounded by the Mediterranean scrub and its most recognisable trees, maritime pines.

09 Local Wine

Cinque Terre has its own wine, the Schiacchetrà, produced in the typical terraced vineyards you can see around the villages.

10 Torre Aurora

The Torre Aurora served as a lookout to protect Monterosso al Mare, but especially Genoa, from the incursions of pirates.

11 Corniglia

Corniglia is the only one of the Cinque Terre villages not directly on the seashore, but its height does make for a rather magnificent observation point.

10 Piedmont
PEAKS

NATURE | CULTURE | HIKING

Mountains are an integral part of Piedmont's landscape and heritage – it's even there in the name, which means 'at the foot of the mountain'. From the highest peaks to the gentler slopes of the Prealps, here are some of the treasures you can find as you start climbing up.

🗺 How to

When to go The best months are the mildest ones, where you can enjoy walking and hiking without extreme weather. Weekends and holidays are likely to be more packed than regular weekdays.

Cost Entrance at the Sacra is about €8; for cabins, half-board prices vary from €40 to €150 a night.

Mountain expertise There are many options for all skill levels – from easy hikes everyone can tackle to glacier treks that require experience and a dedicated guide.

SWITZERLAND
Matterhorn Monte Rosa
Capanna Margherita Rifugio Pastore Sacred Mountain of Varallo
Alagna Valsesia Varallo
St-Vincent
Aosta
Parco Nazionale del Gran Paradiso
Biella
Ivrea
Sacra di San Michele
Chivasso
Turin
0   20 km
0   10 miles

Snow and saints Among the many mountain religious sanctuaries in Piedmont, you can't miss the **Sacra di San Michele**, the official symbol of the region and said to have inspired the abbey in Umberto Eco's *The Name of the Rose*. Picturesquely perched on a mountaintop in the Susa Valley, it can be reached with a calm walk of around 800m, a 600m fixed rope climb, or even a three-hour mountain-bike ride. Another peculiar sight is the **Sacred Mountain of Varallo** (sacromontedivarallo.org) in Valsesia, a Unesco World Heritage devotional complex

Top right Sacra di San Michele
Bottom right Hiker, Monte Rosa

⛰ Mountain Cultures

The **Walser** reside between Valle d'Aosta and the northernmost parts of Piedmont. According to the team of the **Walser Museum** in Alagna Valsesia, a great way to see Walser traditions come alive is during the celebrations of Alagna's patron saint, John the Baptist, in late June.

To the west is the Italian part of **Occitania**, a cultural area that also spans France and Spain. To enjoy traditional Occitan music dating back to the 10th century, follow the suggestion of Espaci Occitan Association and check out the **Occit'Amo Music Festival**.

with chapels dotted along the mountain representing stories from the life of Christ. You can reach it with a cableway (tickets €5) from Varallo.

High cabins If you fancy a climb and some alpine wilderness, there are numerous *rifugi* (mountain cabins) you can trek to. For something not too taxing, head to **Rifugio Pastore**, some 50 minutes out of Alagna Valsesia; or with more fortitude, you might try for the *rifugi* of Monte Rosa, the second-tallest mountain in the Alps. Expert mountaineers can aim for the **Capanna Margherita** (4554m), the highest mountain cabin in Europe and one of the highest scientific observatories in the world.

11 Music by
THE SEA

MUSIC | CULTURE | FESTIVALS

Liguria is a place of mountains diving straight into the sea and of breathtaking sights that go far beyond the rightly famous Cinque Terre. It's also a region of music, having being the home of some of the greatest singer-songwriters in Italy's history. Here's a guide to where you can live some of that music.

ANDREA RAFFIN/SHUTTERSTOCK ©

🎤 How to

Getting here Most of the Riviera is connected by Trenitalia trains, which might run late but solve the tricky issue of finding parking spots.

When to go Sanremo Music Festival and the Premio Tenco are usually held around February, but the warmer months are also lovely.

Evergreen snack It doesn't matter if it's breakfast or lunch time, a piece of focaccia is always a good idea.

LUCIANO VITI/GETTY IMAGES ©

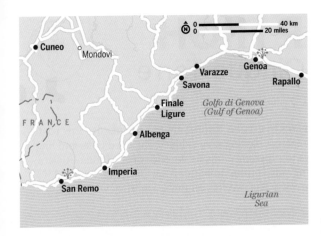

Top left Pinguini Tattici Nucleari perform at the Sanremo Music Festival, 2020 Bottom left Fabrizio De André

Waves & Notes

The Genoa School Genoa is one of the hearts of the long Italian tradition of singing-songwriting. During the '60s, the so-called 'Genoa School' included artists that have left their forever mark on Italian culture – chief among them being **Fabrizio De André**, quoted as a veritable poet on high-school literature books. The life and works of De André (or Faber, as he's also known) are told at the small **Via Del Campo 29 Rosso museum** (viadelcampo29rosso.com), located in Genoa's historic city centre in a street that lends its name to one of Faber's most famous songs.

At the Ariston The words 'music' and 'Liguria' together conjure up one thing and one thing only in every Italian's mind – the **Sanremo Music Festival**. The most famous song contest in the country *and* one of the inspirations for Eurovision, it usually happens in February, lasts five nights and airs on national television. While tickets are on the pricier side and get snatched up fast, if you want to see what an Italian variety show looks like (the good and the bad) then the festival is the event to attend. Around the same time, San Remo also hosts the **Premio Tenco**, organised by the club of the same name (clubtenco.it), a renowned singer-songwriter competition dedicated to another great name of the Genoa School, Luigi Tenco.

🏛 Rolli Days

If you're in Genoa either in spring (around April) or autumn (around October), then you can't miss the **Rolli Days** (visitgenoa.it/rolli). 'Rolli' is the collective name for the more than a hundred old noble palaces of the city, which were declared a Unesco World Heritage Site in 2006 and have been periodically opened to the public since 2009.

During the Rolli Days everyone can visit the gorgeous halls that shaped the destiny of Genoa when it was one of the maritime republics during the Renaissance, and the city organises several events that go along with the opening of the Rolli doors.

12 UP HIGH
in Cinque Terre

HIKING | DAY TRIP | VIEWS

Nothing quite compares to Cinque Terre's sublime setting: five tiny pastel-hued gem-villages nestled against soaring green slopes, chiselled cliffs and blue sea. There are myriad ways to experience this iconic slice of the Italian Riviera, but a particularly rewarding way is from up high, rising above the crowded beaches, footpaths and narrow village streets on the seashore down below.

ELLOBO1/GETTY IMAGES ©

How to

Getting here Trains travel the coast between Genoa and La Spezia, stopping at each Cinque Terre village (roughly two hours from either town).

When to go April to June and October mean cooler weather and fewer crowds; July and August are sizzling hot and packed.

Get organised Local, eco-conscious tour operator **ArbaSPàa** (arbaspaa.com) arranges village accommodation, tours, boats, water sports and activities galore (including sunset e-biking on mountain trails, paragliding and rock climbing).

GIORGIO PARAVAGNA/SHUTTERSTOCK ©

Far left Hiker near Manarola **Bottom left** Grape harvest, Manarola **Near left** Torre Aurora, Monterosso

Choose Your Viewpoint

On the trail Cinque Terre hiking translates as constant killer views of the big blue Med interspersed with cinematic snapshots of one of the five ingeniously constructed fishing villages, hacked, chiselled and shaped on terraced cliffs tumbling down to the water. Skip the over-run coastal **Sentiero Azzurro** (12km Blue Trail; marked SVA on maps) for the lesser-known, sublimely vertiginous **Alta Via delle Cinque Terre** (38km; AV5T on maps), a flat high route linking Porto Venere and Levanto. Or consider a **Sanctuary Walk** above a village: in Riomaggiore many trek the waterfront trailhead (trail 593V) to 18th-century chapel **Santuario della Madonna di Montenero**; for a more peaceful route, follow the trail signposted on Via Colombo at the top of the village instead.

Meet the makers Exploring the Cinque Terre's steeply terraced vineyards provides an alternative perspective on the celebrity villages and a precious opportunity to meet passionate winegrowers whose fearless tenacity and nothing-short-of-heroic efforts to cultivate the gravity-defying land is the bedrock of Cinque Terre. Dizzying views of the coast and 70 hand-tended terraces plunging down to the sea are highlights of tours and vertical Sciacchetrà tastings with Bartolomeo Lercari and Lise Bertram at Vernazza's **CheO** (cheo.it) winery. Winegrower Andrea Pecunia at Riomaggiore's **Terre Sospese** (terresospese.it) cellar explains how he ages his boutique wines in traditional terracotta amphorae during his bespoke vineyard tours.

🍸 Drinks with a View

Torre Aurora
'Sea, cuisine and cocktails' is the vibe of this hip little drinking 'n' dining spot, atop a sturdy 13th-century tower in Monterosso. Expect a soul-soaring panorama from its sea-facing terrace. (torreaurora cinqueterre.com)

A Piè de Campu
Savour a guided tasting with sommelier and sensational bird's-eye sea view at this mythical wine bar, hidden in the heights of Manarola. (facebook. com/apiedecampu. experience)

La Scuna
Be it a cocktail or mint beer, brewed at Birrificio La Taverna del Vara using mint grown in the gardens of Corniglia's Il Magàn-Cinque Terre B&B, La Scuna doesn't disappoint. Sea and sunset views stun. (facebook.com/laScunaBarCorniglia)

13 Love on the
RIVIERA

HISTORY | BEACH | GLAMOUR

Italy's crescent of Mediterranean coast has been immortalised in art and literature since the 18th century when Grand Tour romantics flocked to the Riviera to 'fall damnably in love' with its cinematic scenery and glamour. The seduction remains timeless.

🗺 How to

Getting here/around Genoa is well-connected to the rest of Italy by (slow) train. Motoring around is spectacular but not for the faint of heart.

When to go Spring or September to October, when the days are warm and the crowds less overwhelming.

Best gelato A scoop of *panera* (a Genovese coffee-and-cream blend), creamy Sorrento lemon or bitter orange in a cone from Genoa's enchantingly old-fashioned and elegant Gelateria Profumo (facebook.com/profumogenova).

Seductive Sands

It's hard not to fall in love with the golden-sand beaches of **Fiascherino**, cradled in a captivating twinset of sheltered bays. English writer DH Lawrence certainly did when living in a villa-with-sea-view here in 1913–14. To discover the curvaceous coastline from his perspective, rent a kayak. Paddle 1km south to **Tellaro**, a port village of faded pink and orange houses where Lawrence collected his mail each week and sipped *spritz* at sundown. Hit the terrace at port-side **Bar La Marina** and do the same.

Romantic Vistas

In **Porto Venere**, on the western promontory of the so-called **Golfo dei Poeti** (Gulf of Poets), watch gulls helicopter above the craggy cove and let your heart soar with the

☼ Sunset Romance

After a beautiful day spent exploring the Riviera, there is no more romantic setting for an aperitif with a view over the entire Gulf of Genoa than **Bar Dai Muagetti**, a 1960s bar outside tiny San Rocco. Tables are few, reservations mandatory.

By Lorenzo Marsano, *Genoese bon vivant, @L_Marsano*

Top left Fiascherino. **Bottom left** Tellaro. **Above** Grotta Arpaia (Grotta di Byron), Porto Venere.

sensational Cinque Terre panorama that unfolds from the suitably dishevelled and affecting rocky terraces of **Grotta Arpaia** (affectionately nickamed Grotta di Byron), a vista much admired by 19th-century English Romantics, English poet Lord Byron included.

Serene Eco-Hikes

A world away from Portofino's jet-set glitz, **Parco Naturale Regional di Portofino** safeguards 60km of hiking trails. At eco-farm

La Portofinese (laportofinese.it) abandoned vineyards, olive groves and oil mills are once again worked using traditional techniques.

Coastal Strolls

Magnolia, yew and cedar trees adorn the 1930s public gardens at **Lerici**, a seductive fishing hamlet turned exclusive seaside resort of terraced villas clinging to cliffs. From its wild cliff-backed shoreline, a scenic 3km coastal path tangoes northwest to **San Terenzo**, a

🚶 Favourite Passeggiate

Genoa A *passeggiata* through the city I love, from the Renaissance church of Santa Maria Assunta di Carignano, through the School of Architecture where I studied on Collina di Castello, to medieval San Donato, Palazzo Ducale, the cathedral and the sea.

Portofino to San Fruttuoso, built in a tiny bay to prevent Saracen attacks. The 1½-hour walk is easy and surprising: a pathway through meadows, pines, junipers, myrtles and olive trees, above the sea.

Riserva Naturale Statale Agoraie di Sopra e Moggetto This is a protected park with perennial glacial lakes – a mountain wilderness with an alpine climate not far from Genoa.

By Filippo **Casaccia**, *Genoese novelist and screenwriter,* @DzigaCacace

Left San Fruttuoso
Below Dolceacqua

discrete village with sandy beach, Genoese castle and evocative vertiginous tumble of pastel houses. Writers Percy Bysshe and Mary Shelley lived in the waterfront **Villa Magni** in the 1820s; the villa is closed, but catching a summertime movie beneath stars in the villa's park is a fabulous second-best.

Desert Islands

Not quite deserted, but refreshingly devoid of crowds, pinprick **Palmaria** is home to 50-odd people. A walk along its wild coastline, famously featured in the background of Sandro Botticelli's iconic Renaissance masterpiece, *The Birth of Venus* (1484–86), takes in picturesque cliffs, coves and rocky beaches.

Cinematic Back Alleys

Many an illicit kiss has been stolen and romantic love affair born, in the twisting maze of *caruggi* – dark, narrow old-town streets – in medieval Genoa and elsewhere. Bursting with backstreet charm and lines of clean washing hung out to dry, *caruggi* promising on-the-spot seduction include Via Orefici and Vico all Chiesa delle Vigne, home to the stunning Primo Piano art gallery, in **Genoa**; the labyrinthine cobblestone paths of **La Pigna**, the overlooked old town of **San Remo**; and almost every steeply inclined lane in the medieval heart of **Dolceaqua**.

14 A Slow Food **JOURNEY**

FOOD | SUSTAINABLE TRAVEL | ROAD TRIP

The rolling green hills, verdant valleys and tiny tradition-steeped towns of southern Piedmont are northern Italy's redolent pantry. Endowed with sweet hazelnuts, rare white truffles, arborio rice, delicate veal and Nebbiolo grapes that become revered Barolo and Barbaresco wines, this naturally gourmet region is where the Slow Food movement took root in 1986 and continues to flourish.

ROSTISLAV GLINSKY/SHUTTERSTOCK ©

🗺 How to

Getting here Frequent trains link the Langhe region's vibrant, pretty capital of Alba with Bra, Turin and other Italian towns.

When to go The grape harvest (August to October) is an exhilarating time to visit, with mellow temperatures and beautiful light; spring promises the perfect touring climate.

Touring tip For complete *dolce vita* immersion, slow down on the back of a Vespa or e-bike; **Langhe Experience** (langhe -experience.it) in Alba arranges rental.

TENNIS/SHUTTERSTOCK ©

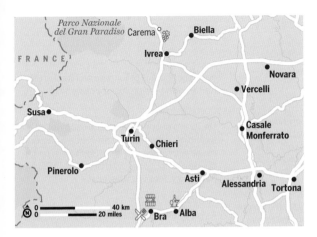

Top left Cheeses on a market stall, Bra **Bottom left** Nebbiolo vineyards, Carema

Best Slow Food Dining

A place to best breathe in Slow Food philosophy is **Osteria del Boccondivino** in Bra. It is in the courtyard of our headquarters, Carlo Petrini himself founded it before dedicating himself to Slow Food, and there are always many Slow Food Presidia (artisanal food products, many at risk of extinction) on the menu. Two iconic dishes are always available: *tajarin*, a fresh pasta with a unique craftsmanship, made by hand every day. It is like tagliatelle but very very thin and is made with 40 eggs for every kilo of flour). Boccondivino's panna cotta is a dessert that no one has ever returned claiming they have found a better one.

By Roberto Burdese, *executive committee member of Slow Food International and former president of Slow Food Italy, @SlowFood*

Earth markets Small town **Bra** – headquarters to Slow Food – showcases the movement's work in building a global network of farmers markets promoting 'good, clean and fair food'. Shop and mingle with farmers at **Mercato della Terra di Bra** (Bra Earth Market). Alfresco stalls beneath golden arches overflow with cured meats, honey, hazelnuts, raw-milk sheep and cow cheeses, *saras* (local ricotta) and other regional produce. Watch for sheep-milking, cheese-making and baking workshops.

Cooks' alliance Slow Food's commitment to uniting chefs with local, small-scale producers extends beyond the kitchen. In **Alba** at stylish **Soda** masterfully prepared cocktails are paired with innovative vegan dishes, invariably using regional produce. Sassy craft-gin cocktails blend lemongrass, celery and pepper perhaps; and a 'slow', deconstructed Bloody Mary mixes smoked vodka with cherry tomatoes, rosemary and rock salt. As per 'Slow Food' tradition, ice cubes are chiselled by hand.

At risk of extinction Forget Piedmontese heavyweights Barolo and Barbaresco. Curious wine lovers: head north to **Carema** where pergola-trained vines once laced every house facade and garden in the rural village. Covering 12 hectares of gravity-defying steep terraces today, the vines twist around pergolas supported by stone pillars that heat by day in the sun to create a nighttime microclimate for the Nebbiolo grapes. Visiting Carema and sampling its dry red AOC wine provides precious insight into Slow Food's work with independent wine-growers and producers to protect endangered food productions and sustainable agricultural practices.

Listings

BEST OF THE REST

Aperitivi

Al Faro di Portofino   €€

Stunningly set by Portofino's lighthouse, this iconic terrace lounge-bar enjoys mesmerising sea views from its clifftop perch. Sink in a deckchair, sip a first-rate *spritz* and spot dolphins waltzing in the waves below.

Bar Cavour   €€€

Named for its most famous barfly, the ubiquitous Count Cavour, this beautiful historical room in Turin combines a magical, mirrored setting with sharp contemporary art and artfully prepared cocktails accompanied by quality snacks.

Farmacia Del Cambo   €€

At home in an 1830s pharmacy, this glamorous all-day space in Turin's bar- and restaurant-peppered 'Cambio Corner' 'hood is a coffee and *aperitivo* hotspot. Kick back beneath dark shelves, by the theatrically open kitchen, or outside on the piazza.

Bardotto   €

Hobnob with Turin's cool crowd over well-mixed cocktails, *spritz* or craft beer and *aperitivo* snacks (€2) at this fashionable bookshop and literary cafe-bar.

Boia Fauss Pensavo Peggio   €

Lap up local vibe in Alba over excellent microbrews, interesting Langhe wines and a legendary *aperitivo* buffet at this brewery restaurant.

Art & Architecture

Museo Casa Mollino

For 20th-century art and architecture lovers, a guided tour of this little-known house-museum in Turin – a testament to the deliriously lush aesthetic and skill of Turinese architect-artist Carlo Mollino – is profoundly rewarding.

Castello di Rivoli

On Turin's outskirts discover Piedmont's wealth of contemporary art inside a baroque castle with amazing views. Don't miss neighbouring Villa Cerruti, with works by Modigliani, Kandinsky, Picasso, Klee et al.

Podere Case Lovara

A visit to this clifftop farm, only accessible on foot from Levanto by a 1¾-hour coastal hike, delivers extraordinary insight into traditional architecture and sustainable agriculture in the Cinque Terre.

Rice, White Truffles & Hazelnuts

Osteria More e Morcine   €

Be it a swirl of *tajarin* pasta or *risotto alla piemontese* (risotto with butter and cheese), this village eatery is La Morra's star turn for regional cuisine.

La Mandragola   €€

Nestled beneath the crumbling walls of San Gimignano's 14th-century fortress, the

Al Faro di Portofino

Mandrake serves outstanding handmade pasta – the *tortelli* stuffed with truffles and artichokes is divine – in a beautiful courtyard.

Fiera del Tartufo   €€€

October's precious white-truffle crop is celebrated at this Alba festival (aka the International Alba White Truffle Fair) every weekend from mid-October to mid-November. Watch princely sums exchanged and sample autumn's gloriously pungent, tasty bounty.

Gaudenzio   €€

There's no finer spot in Turin to sample Piedmontese hazelnuts than this on-trend space, celebrated for its innovative but sublimely local dishes featuring some fantastic and unexpected food- and natural wine-pairings.

Perino Vesco   €

In Turin, cult Slow Food baker Andrea Perino crafts fragrant *torta langarola* (hazelnut cake), naturally yeasted panettone and focaccia that draws sighs from homesick Ligurians. Join the queues for takeaway pizza and focaccia slices.

 ## Wine Tasting

Rocche Dei Barbari

In wine town Barbaresco, tasting rare wines made from exceptionally ripe grapes at this historic winery is a treat. Invariably it's the winemaker who leads the complimentary tastings in his boutique cellar, and the stories he weaves are enchanting.

Agrilab Wine Tasting Tour

Tucked behind the village castle, this modern tasting room brings a dash of verve to Barolo. Swirl, sniff, sip and spit some 36 different wines, including Barolo, Barbaresco and Barbera, and obscure varietals like Nascetta, Ruche and Pelaverga.

Enoteca Sciacchetrà

When in the colourful dolls-house village of Vernazza, overlooked by steeply terraced

Procession during Fiera del Tartufo, Alba

vineyards, tasting Cinque Terre's celebrated Sciacchetrà – an amber-yellow dessert wine sold in 375mL bottles – is a rite of passage.

The Great Outdoors

Parco Naturale Alpi Marittime

Hiking through wild-flower-peppered meadows to spectacular topaz lakes, shimmering glaciers and craggy peaks – some soaring over 3000m – is a highlight of this protected alpine playground in Piedmont.

Monte Rosa

A trio of wild backcountry valleys – Ayas, Gressoney and Valsesia in northern Piedmont – promise white-knuckle adventure in buckets. Think white-water rafting, hardcore hiking, canyoning and some of Europe's finest off-piste and heli-skiing.

Whale Watch Liguria

Spotting a whale on a half-day boat tour, run from Genoa's Porto Antico in consultation with the WWF, is magic. Once at sea, an onboard biologist provides fascinating background on the world's largest mammal.

 Scan to find more things to do in Turin, Piedmont & Cinque Terre online

MILAN &
THE LAKES

ART | HISTORY | OUTDOORS

Experience
Milan & the
Lakes online

MILAN & THE LAKES
Trip Builder

Move beyond the fashion boutiques to discover Milan's millenary history and vibrant contemporary culture, between offbeat neighbourhoods and local hang-outs, or use the city as a base to explore the sparkling Italian Lakes, all just a day trip away.

Admire da Vinci's forgotten frescoes at **Castello Sforzesco** (p118)
🕐 *3 hours*

Attend an opera or ballet performance at Milan's **La Scala** theatre (p119)
🕐 *3 hours*

Make a reservation for da Vinci's **The Last Supper** masterpiece (p108)
🕐 *2 hours*

Visit Milan's **Duomo** and head to the rooftop for unbeatable views (p118)
🕐 *2 hours*

Piazza Carbonar

ISOLA

Via Melchiorre Gioia

Parco Biblioteca degli Alberi

Piazza della Repubblica

Giardini Pubblici Indr Montanelli

Parco Sempione

Parco Pallavicino

Via Lodovico Ariosto

BRERA

Via Manzoni

QUADRILATERO D'ORO

Corso Vercelli

Corso Magenta

Via Dante

Parco Don Giussani

Parco delle Basiliche

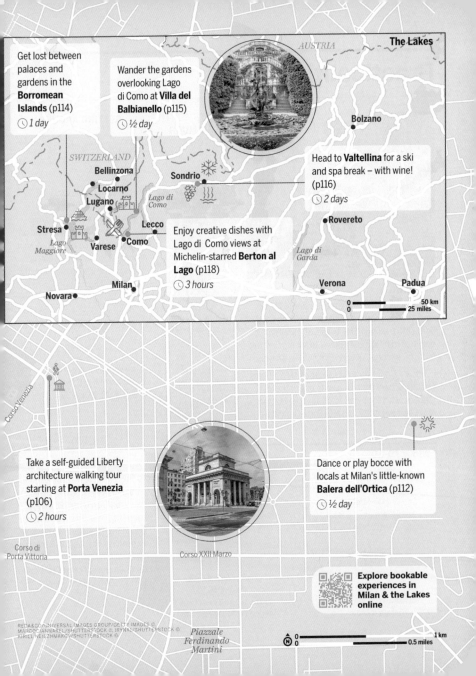

The Lakes

AUSTRIA

Get lost between palaces and gardens in the **Borromean Islands** (p114)
🕐 1 day

Wander the gardens overlooking Lago di Como at **Villa del Balbianello** (p115)
🕐 ½ day

Bolzano

Head to **Valtellina** for a ski and spa break – with wine! (p116)
🕐 2 days

SWITZERLAND

Bellinzona

Locarno

Sondrio

Lugano

Lago di Como

Stresa

Lago Maggiore

Varese

Lecco

Como

Rovereto

Enjoy creative dishes with Lago di Como views at Michelin-starred **Berton al Lago** (p118)
🕐 3 hours

Lago di Garda

Milan

Verona

Padua

Novara

0 —— 50 km
0 —— 25 miles

Corso Venezia

Take a self-guided Liberty architecture walking tour starting at **Porta Venezia** (p106)
🕐 2 hours

Dance or play bocce with locals at Milan's little-known **Balera dell'Ortica** (p112)
🕐 ½ day

Corso di Porta Vittoria

Corso XXII Marzo

Piazzale Ferdinando Martini

Explore bookable experiences in Milan & the Lakes online

0 —— 1 km
0 —— 0.5 miles

Practicalities

RESUL MUSLU/SHUTTERSTOCK ©

ARRIVING

 Malpensa Airport Frequent trains (€13 one way) to Milano Centrale (55 minutes) and Cadorna (40 minutes). Buy tickets at the airport, or online at trenitalia.com. Buses to Milano Centrale (€10, 60 minutes) depart right outside Arrivals.

 Milano Centrale/Porta Garibaldi Most trains (including from the lakes) go to one of these stations, where you can connect to the M2 and M3 (Centrale) or M2 and M5 (Porta Garibaldi).

HOW MUCH FOR A

Aperol spritz €6

Cotoletta alla milanese €20

Como–Bellagio ferry €10.40

GETTING AROUND

Metro Milan has an excellent metro system, with four lines. Trains run from 5.30am to midnight; single tickets (also valid on buses and trams) are €2 (24-hour tickets €7). Contactless bank cards can be used to pay directly at ticket gates.

Tram Vintage trams from the 1920s are still used regularly on lines 1, 5, 10, 19 and 33.

To the lakes Lago di Como: take a train to Como Lago (from Milan Cadorna) then ferry to Bellagio. Lago Maggiore: take a Stresa-bound train then ferry to the Borromean Islands. Lago di Garda: take a Verona-bound train from Centrale and get off at Desenzano to reach Sirmione.

WHEN TO GO

JAN–MAR
Quietest time to visit; cold but rarely snows.

APR–JUN
Mild and sunny weather with some rainstorms. Busiest time.

JUL–SEP
Hot and sunny. Milan is virtually empty in August.

OCT–DEC
October is a great time to visit, then it gets cold, rainy and foggy.

EATING & DRINKING

Milanese cuisine Traditional Milanese food is hearty and meat-heavy, with dishes like *ossobuco con risotto alla milanese* (veal osso buco with saffron risotto) and *cotoletta alla milanese* (veal schnitzel; pictured top right). Trattorias are good places to try Milanese specialities.

Lakeside dining Restaurant menus around the lakes often feature fresh, locally caught lake fish like *persico* (perch), *lavarello* (whitefish) and trout, served with pasta or risotto or as a *secondo* (main dish). It's worth splurging on a Michelin-starred restaurant if your budget allows.

Best trattoria La Balera dell'Ortica (p112)

Must-try lake fish Lido 84 (p118)

MILAN & THE LAKES FIND YOUR FEET

CONNECT & FIND YOUR WAY

Wi-fi Phone signals are generally very good everywhere in Milan and around the lakes. There are free wi-fi hotspots in all of Milan's public libraries, museums and at several locations marked as 'Open Wi-Fi Milano'. Como also has free outdoor hotspots.

Navigation Navigation apps work well in Milan and the lakes.

CAR RENTAL

To move around lake towns and villages, it's best to rent a car. Hire companies have Milan and Malpensa Airport offices (credit card required).

WHERE TO STAY

Both Milan and the lakes are fairly expensive, but it's possible to find good hotel deals when visiting outside peak season. Other options: hostels and apartment rentals.

Neighbourhood/Town	Pro/Con
Milano Centrale	Many options for all budgets, close to Milan's biggest transport hub. Bit sketchy at night.
City Centre	Best area for shopping and sightseeing, but most expensive part of Milan.
Navigli	Very quaint and great for Milan nightlife; can get noisy and crowded.
Stresa	Scenic Lago Maggiore town, convenient for the Borromean Islands.
Sirmione	Best location for a Lago di Garda break, with a spa and lake beaches.

DISCOUNT CARDS

MilanoCard offers free public transport, discounts on airport transfers, museums and attractions, plus a welcome coffee. Available for one/two/three days (€11/17/19.50). Buy it online and collect it in Milan.

15 LIBERTY
Architecture Stroll

WALK | ARCHITECTURE | HISTORY

Liberty style was Italy's version of art nouveau, popular in the late 19th and early 20th centuries and characterised by flowing lines and nature-based decoration. Some of the best examples of Liberty architecture in Italy can be found in the quiet streets near Milan's Porta Venezia metro station, perfect to explore on a walking tour.

MASSIMO SERZIO/CIMITERO MONUMENTALE DI MILANO ©

🏛 Cimitero Monumentale

Several graves and mausoleums at Milan's Cimitero Monumentale date back to when Liberty style was at its peak. You'll find examples all over the cemetery, including Edicola Reyna, Monumento Elisi (pictured) and Edicola Origgi. Find their location at monumentale. comune.milano.it/ itinerari/liberty.

🗺 Trip Notes

Getting here All stops are located a maximum 15 minutes' walk from Porta Venezia M1 station. Allow about an hour to see them.

When to go Mornings are generally quieter. Please respect residents' privacy.

Coffee break Stop at **Casa Capitano** for a Neapolitan coffee and Valrhona pralines.

Guided tours Liberty-focused tours are on offer at **Walk Alternative Art Milan** (waamtours.com).

01 Start with the lavish facade of **Casa Galimberti**, two minutes' walk from Porta Venezia station, with elegant wrought-iron balconies and colourful, decorative tiles.

02 Just down Via Malpighi you'll find **Casa Guazzoni**, with *putti* (cherubs) and female heads intertwined with leaves and branches. Look out for the 2nd-floor wrought-iron balconies.

03 Around the corner between Via Melzo and Via Frisi you'll see the elegant Liberty facade of the former **Cinema Dumont**, Milan's first, now a public library.

05 Walk back towards Porta Venezia station to the last stop, **Casa Berri Meregalli**. Its style is quite eclectic, with mosaics and neo-Gothic gargoyles alongside decorative Liberty elements.

04 Fifteen minutes away, **Casa Campanini's** caryatids and elegant door are iconic Liberty-style examples, but the real marvels are the entrance's frescoes and stucco decorations.

Repubblica

Piazza della Repubblica

Turati

Bastioni di Porta Venezia

Porta Venezia

Porta Venezia

Giardini Pubblici Indro Montanelli

Corso Venezia

Via Malpighi

Via Melzo

Via Nino Bixio

Casa Capitano

Palestro

Via Cappuccini

Viale Luigi Majno

Via Poerio

Via Gustavo Modena

Via Castel Morrone

Via Vivaio

Via Carlo Goldoni

Piazza del Tricolore

Piazza Risorgimento

Corso Indipendenza

Corso Monforte

Viale Bianca Maria

San Babila

Dateo

Via Pasquale Sottocorno

Largo Marinai d'Italia

N

0 ——— 400 m
0 ——— 0.2 miles

In Awe of The Last Supper

REALISM, TECHNIQUE AND SURVIVAL

Other depictions exist but none are more celebrated than Leonardo da Vinci's. Capturing the dramatic moment Jesus foretells his betrayal, *The Last Supper* is charged with emotion. Its fragility, caused by Leonardo himself, and miraculous survival only add to the appeal.

From left *The Last Supper*; Basilica di Santa Maria delle Grazie, where the painting is kept; *Crucifixion*

The subject of countless reproductions, creative works and conspiracy theories, this iconic painting has long enthralled the world. And for good reason. Unesco World Heritage listed since 1980, *The Last Supper* is credited for heralding in the High Renaissance and praised for its subtleties of tone, complexity of details, ground-breaking technique and portrayal of human psychology. Standing before the immense 40-sq-metre mural, still luminous despite everything, it's not hard to imagine it was unlike anything that had come before.

Revolutionary Realism

According to Silvia Regonelli, art historian, art lecturer at IES (Institute for the International Education of Students) and a certified tour guide, it was Leonardo's ability to push the 'rules, traditions and impositions of a religious painting, and make something so real' that makes the work a masterpiece. The gestures of each apostle perfectly capture their range of emotions from disbelief, to confusion and anger. This may seem commonplace today but according to Regonelli, 'in the 1490s some of those gestures entered a painting for the first time'.

Even Judas is shown in a more human light. Instead of being separated from the other apostles as in previous depictions, he is naturally integrated into the scene. As Regonelli states: 'For the first time we are invited to relate to Judas.' He has spilled the salt upon hearing the news and we see the nervousness of his actions.

The painting also feels like a photograph. Leonardo achieved this by using both a central vanishing point and a mix of optical illusions to ensure that even if you were

viewing the painting from various points the distortion would be minimal. Compare the painting with the *Crucifixion* by Giovanni Donato da Montorfano on the opposite side of the room, which was started the same year, and you can see how Leonardo was light years ahead of his time.

Survival Against the Odds

Yet, in many ways the painting was a failed experiment. Dissatisfied with traditional fresco painting, Leonardo had experimented with a dry technique that let him work more slowly and make changes over time. Because of this the pigment failed to adhere to the wall and soon after completion the painting began to flake.

Adding insult to injury, in 1652 monastery residents chopped off Jesus' feet to install a door. Sadly, the painting's misfortune didn't end there. In the 18th century Napoleon Bonaparte's soldiers turned the refectory into a stable and reputedly flung bricks at the apostles' heads. During WWII the monastery was bombed, leaving the mural unharmed but exposed to the elements. Crude restorations made short work of what was left. Finally in 1999, after over 20 years of restoration, the painting was said to be Leonardo's again. Although a ghostly memory of the original, not only does it offer us an enthralling glimpse of the artist's greatness, it reminds us of the immense efforts of the many who sought to preserve it.

> The gestures of each apostle perfectly capture their range of emotions from disbelief, to confusion and anger.

Leonardo's Footsteps

After Leonardo was done painting for the day he would retire to nearby **Casa degli Atellani** (casadegliatellani. it), where he also happened to own a **vineyard** (vignadi leonardo.com) gifted to him by his patron, the Duke Ludovico Sforza. Now you, too, can do the same. Not only can you bunk down in the same 15th-century *palazzo* (mansion) as Leonardo did (comfortably fitted out with contemporary decor), you can also stroll his vineyard, meticulously recreated with the exact same variety of grapes.

16 **WATERWAYS**
Around Milan

CYCLING | NATURE | SPRING

Escape the bustle of Milan walking or cycling along one of the canals surrounding the city, between pretty villages and traces of Lombardy's agricultural past. Take your pick of four canals, or get away from it all with a day trip kayaking along the river Ticino, part of a protected nature reserve stretching all the way to Lago Maggiore.

CLAUDIO GIOVANNI COLOMBO/SHUTTERSTOCK ©

🗺 **How to**

Getting here Naviglio Grande: starts in the centre of Milan. Naviglio Martesana: starts near M2 Gioia. Naviglio di Bereguardo: train to Abbiategrasso (20 minutes). Canale Muzza: train to Cassano d'Adda (50 minutes). Bike supplement: €3 on trains.

When to go Spring and autumn; avoid weekends.

Bike rentals Smile and Bike rents bikes in four locations, including on Naviglio Grande and Martesana. Regular/e-bikes €20/45 daily.

AGF/GETTY IMAGES ©

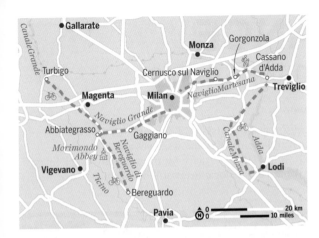

Top left Naviglio di Bereguardo
Bottom left Canale Muzza

Choose Your Canal

Closest to the city Start from the Darsena (dock) and ride along **Naviglio Grande** out of Milan through colourful Gaggiano. Keep following the canal as it turns north in Abbiategrasso, past genteel villas and medieval bridges. The cycleway ends 50km later at the striking Turbigo power station, with the snowy peaks of Monte Rosa in the background. Hop on a 45-minute train back to Milan from Turbigo station.

The secret one **Naviglio di Bereguardo** connects Abbiategrasso to the city of the same name, 18.5km to the south, passing ancient *cascine* (farmhouses), and corn and rice fields. It's rarely visited, especially during the week, making it perfect for a nature walk or bike ride. Don't miss the Romanesque **Morimondo Abbey**, about 1km from the canal.

Best for a walk Do you prefer walking to cycling? Head to **Naviglio Martesana**, flowing 42km from Milan to the river Adda. The M2 metro runs along the canal, offering chances to break up your walk into manageable stages. The 6km section between Cernusco sul Naviglio and Gorgonzola is especially picturesque.

Between fields and farmhouses Get deep into the agricultural heart of southern Lombardy with a relaxing bike ride along **Canale Muzza**, one of the oldest artificial canals in Europe, dating back to the 13th century. The 36km ride from Cassano d'Adda to Lodi on the unpaved path along the canal is the perfect escape from the city – especially in spring, when trees are in bloom.

Ticino Escape

The Lombard stretch of the Ticino is one of the cleanest rivers in northern Italy, blissfully free from overdevelopment. Most of the river has no banks, and shifts its course each year as it meanders through reeds, brambles and broadleaf forests. Spend a day on its waters kayaking or slow rafting and learning about biodiversity, before a sunset picnic with local products. Alternatively, opt for the ultimate Ticino adventure – a four-day descent from Lago Maggiore to Pavia, kayaking by day, and camping on the riverbank at night.

By Alberto Vincenzi,
owner/founder, Aqqua Canoa & Rafting, Vigevano, @aqqua_canoa_rafting

DANCE
with the Locals

DANCING | BOCCE | TRATTORIA

Tucked away in the city's eastern outskirts, La Balera dell'Ortica is the kind of place that every local and their nonno knows, loves and has a story about. A *balera* (dance hall) from 1925, it's a place far from the city's slick image of fashion and finance, where Milan's historic heart still beats and you can dance like in days gone by.

🗺 How to

Getting here From the city centre it's a half-hour ride on bus 54.

When to go Summer is the best time to visit, when it hosts concerts and open-air events with dancing and live music.

Check labaleradellortica. com for what's on.

Cost Meals €18 to €25; events free or from €7 to €30.

Other reasons to visit Its cosy trattoria and bocce field are open year-round.

LA PISTA DA BALLO
E' FATTA
PER BALLARE
E PER TROVARE
L' AMORE
NON PER FUMARE
E
BERCI UN DRINK

Far left and near left La Balera dell'Ortica **Bottom left** A sign at La Balera dell'Ortica, which translates as "The dance floor is made for dancing and finding love, not for smoking and drinking"

Back to life Originally the after-work haunt for railway workers in the area, La Balera dell'Ortica was a place for people to meet up, do the *liscio* (a dance originating in northern Italy), eat simple, hearty meals and play bocce. Sadly, after dance halls went out of fashion, replaced by discos then clubs, it spent 15 years languishing in disrepair. That is until 2012, when the Di Furia family stepped in. Marina Di Furia, manager of the venue recalls: 'My father, Antonio, dreamed about bringing La Balera back to life.' A regular there when he was young, Antonio saw the importance of saving this historic place and its unique mix of what Marina describes as 'authenticity, simplicity, live music and good Italian food'.

Dinner, dancing and bocce Now it's once again the place to swing a bocce ball and enjoy a meal amid the boisterous atmosphere of a *sagra* (local food festival). This time, however, the homey dishes of *polpette* (meatballs) and *arrosticini* (skewers of meat) are made by Marina's mother Rita. The decor has also been given a new kitsch slant that's somewhere between a '70s disco and your gran's living room.

The dancing, however, hasn't changed. Swing, lindy hop and *liscio* nights with live music are still a big part of the picture. The only difference is now you're likely to see fashionistas and hipsters rubbing elbows with the retirees on the dance floor.

Milan's Little-Known Village

A visit to La Balera dell'Ortica also gives you a chance to explore the charismatic **Ortica** district, famously immortalised in a song by local hero Enzo Jannacci in 1966. Originally considered to be outside of Milan, Ortica very much has its own identity as a former working-class village with industrial roots. Wander its small, intimate streets still lined with charming *case di ringhiera* (houses in northern Italy traditionally used by the poor), and appreciate the bold street art murals that proudly tell the district's history. And don't forget to stop by the humble **Church of SS Faustino and Giovita**; once the heart of this former village, it dates back to the 1200s.

18 Palace
ISLANDS

DAY TRIP | HISTORY | LAKES

Get deep into the sapphire heart of Lago Maggiore on a day trip to the Borromean Islands, with baroque palaces, lush gardens and wandering white peacocks. Start with fanciful Isola Bella, a dreamy palace surrounded by terraced Italian gardens, then hop across to its wilder sister, Isola Madre. Head back to Milan in time for dinner – or spend the night on an island!

LUCA LORENZELLI/SHUTTERSTOCK ©

🗺 **How to**

Getting here There are hourly trains between Milan Centrale and Stresa, where ferries depart. Seventy minutes travel time, €8.60 each way.

When to go The islands are open from March to October. May is a great month to see flowers in bloom. Avoid summer weekends.

Cost Access to Isola Bella is €18 per person; it's €15 for Isola Madre.

Spend the night Stay in luxury apartments in renovated fishermen's houses on Isola Bella (from €200).

EASY GOING/SHUTTERSTOCK ©

Top left Palazzo Borromeo, Isola Bella **Bottom left** Peacock, Botanical Gardens, Isola Madre

Explore the Islands

The showstopper Marvelling at the opulence of **Isola Bella**, it's hard to imagine it was once a nondescript rock on the lake, home to a few fishing families. In 1630, the Borromeo family began constructing a sumptuous *palazzo* surrounded by scenic Italian gardens, turning Isola Bella into the baroque wonderland it is today, looking like a ship sailing across the lake.

Start your visit at **Palazzo Borromeo**, place of legendary balls for Europe's rich and famous. Don't miss **Galleria Berthier**, with over 130 Old Master paintings, and the whimsical **Grottoes**, built to resemble the marine world. The main attraction in the Italian gardens is the **Teatro Massimo**, with 10 terraces topped by a unicorn statue, and rare plants and flowers.

The family home Learn about the Borromeo family's private side visiting **Isola Madre**, the largest Borromean island. In contrast with Isola Bella's opulence, the style in Isola Madre's **Palazzo** is elegant yet sober, with furniture and decorations from Borromeo palaces all over Lombardy. The Marionette Theatre and Venetian Lounge with its delicate *trompe l'œil* ceiling are two of the most interesting places to visit.

The rest of the island is occupied by the English-style **Botanical Gardens**, defined by Gustave Flaubert as 'the most voluptuous place I've seen in the world'. The mild lake climate is the ideal habitat for a host of exotic plants, from camellias to rhododendrons and South African proteas. White peacocks, pheasants and parrots wander freely across the grounds.

Other Lake Palaces

Vittoriale degli Italiani

Near Gardone Riviera on the western shore of Lago di Garda, the Vittoriale was the former estate of soldier-poet Gabriele d'Annunzio. Start your visit at the **Priory**, where the poet's eccentric spirit is reflected in the decoration, then move on to the unique gardens, housing an amphitheatre and a warship.

Villa del Balbianello

This stunning 18th-century villa on Lago di Como may look familiar – it was a filming location for *Star Wars: Attack of the Clones* and *Casino Royale*. The villa was home to explorer Guido Monzino and still preserves memories of his journeys. End your visit with a stroll around the gardens, with wisteria-covered porticoes overlooking the lake.

19

Slopes & Springs in
VALTELLINA

SPORT | RELAXATION | WINTER

While often overshadowed by its flashy sibling the Dolomites, this sinuous valley on the border between Italy and Switzerland more than holds its own. Not only does it have dramatic mountain landscapes, hard-earned wines and a buttery rich cuisine, it also offers up invigorating hot springs and peerless skiing all year round.

SLAWOMIR KRUZ/SHUTTERSTOCK ©

📷 How to

Getting here It's around two hours by train from Milan and almost three hours from Bergamo. Tickets are available from trenord.it.

When to go Various ski areas and hot springs are open year-round, but peak season is from December to March.

Cost A one-day adult ski pass is priced from €37 to €45. Entry to the Bormio Terme costs €15, while QC Terme costs between €42 and €64.

DIEGO BONACINA/SHUTTERSTOCK ©

Top left Snowboarder, Livigno
Bottom left QC Terme Bagni Nuovi, Bormio

Skiing, snowboarding and freeriding With over 400km of well-groomed runs, snow parks and epic freeride routes, the Valtellina satisfies newbies, experts and powder-chasers alike. It's also unique according to alpine guide and Valtellina native Giuliano Bordoni for its 'great variety of terrain' and because you can still find 'little-known ski resorts with few people where the sun always shines'.

One of the most popular towns is far-flung **Livigno**, famed for its tax-free shopping and skiing. It has wide slopes, some of the best snow parks in Europe and a long season from November to May. Historic **Bormio** has more challenging runs overall and lets you hurtle down the Stelvia slope like Men's World Cup competitors, who reach speeds over 100km/h. You can also ski during summer at the Stelvio Pass. Alternatively, **Madesimo** is your best option under two hours from Milan. It's home to the Canalone, a 3.5km corridor known for its exacting nature and rugged beauty.

Hot-spring immersion While Bormio has a number of hot springs to choose from, nothing quite compares to **QC Bagni Vecchi**, where you can steep your weary limbs in Roman baths dating back two thousand years. The **QC Terme Bagni Nuovi** is newer and the largest spa complex in the alps. In comparison, **Bormio Terme** is well located (near the centre of town) and better priced but more basic.

 Where Locals Soak for Free

Looking for something quite literally off a beaten track? Then hunt for the **Pozza di Leonardo** (Leonardo's Pool; it seems the artist couldn't resist a good soak). Here locals enjoy the hot springs without paying a cent. From Bormio drive in the direction of the Stelvio Pass and turn when you see the sign for Livigno. After a couple of kilometres you should see the parked cars and graffiti on your right. From there it's a short walk in the woods (be warned it gets slippery in the snow). You can't miss it. There's even a sign and some hooks where you can hang your clothes.

Listings

BEST OF THE REST

Mountain-Hut Dining

Rifugio Motta   €

This cabin on the Alpe Palù invites you in with its fairy-tale good looks. While it serves up hearty Valtellina cuisine, it's the plunging valley views that will leave you awestruck.

Rifugio Martina   €

Above Lago di Como, the views and bucolic setting are nothing to sneeze at – but it's the cuisine that steals the show. Creamy polenta and wild-meat dishes keep locals coming back.

Lakeside Restaurants

Berton al Lago   €€€

If you're looking for artistic dishes in sleek surrounds, you can't go past Berton al Lago. A 20-minute drive from Como, it also has soul-restoring views of the lake.

Lido 84   €€€

The view comes second only to the food at this Michelin-star restaurant five minutes' walk from Fasano. Run by two brothers, one being star chef Riccardo Camanini, it offers thoughtful Italian cuisine.

Cathedrals, Castles & Villas

Duomo di Milano

Milan's cathedral in the main square is an architectural marvel 600 years in the making. Topped with 135 spires and 3400 figures, its sheer extravagance makes it worthy of a visit.

Certosa di Pavia

Ten kilometres north of Pavia lies this lavish monastery commissioned by Gian Galeazzo Visconti, Duke of Milan. The church was intended to be his family's mausoleum, which accounts for its unabashed grandeur.

Castello Sforzesco

The mighty Sforzesco family once ruled from the lofty reach of this red-brick castle bordering Milan's main park. Frescoed by Leonardo da Vinci, it also houses several notable museums.

Palazzo Te

Next to Mantua's hippodrome, the pleasure palace of Federico II Gonzaga fulfils your wild imaginings. Mannerist-style architecture is matched with titillating artworks and mind-bending frescoes by Romano, pupil of Raphael.

Villa del Balbianello

This 18th-century villa on a woody headland in Lago di Como is dreamily cinematic. No wonder it was featured in *Star Wars* and *Casino Royale*. Accessible only by foot or boat from Lenno.

Art, Fashion & Opera

Fondazione Prada

Next to abandoned railway tracks lies Milan's gin distillery turned chic Prada gallery.

Certosa di Pavia

Cutting-edge exhibits go hand in hand with a gold-leaf-clad tower and a bar designed by Wes Anderson.

Pinacoteca Brera

Lovers of the Old Masters will want to dedicate time to this gallery upstairs from Milan's prestigious art school. It's home to Mantegna's emotionally charged *Lamentation of Christ* and Hayez' *The Kiss*.

Accademia Carrara

East of Bergamo's old city walls you'll find an excellent range of Italian masters originally collected by local art aficionado Count Giacomo Carrara. Highlights include works by Mantegna, Botticelli, Titian, Raphael and Canaletto.

Quadrilatero d'Oro

This exalted shopping district near Milan's centre is worth a stop, not only for its glossy flagship stores and flamboyant window dressings, but also for its equally flamboyant clientele.

La Scala

Where Verdi made his name and Maria Callas became an operatic legend. Behind Milan's Galleria, the exquisitely decked out La Scala is still *the* place to catch some world-class opera.

Wineries & Enoteche

Nino Negri

Winemaking is no easy affair in the Valtellina, but Nino Negri, in Chiuro's centre, rises expertly to the challenge. Discover its celebrated Sfursat 5 Stelle and other heady delights from its 33-hectare vineyard.

Cantine Isola

This cosy nook on the main thoroughfare in Milan's Chinatown has been a beloved drinking spot since 1896. The knowledgeable Sarais family, the owners, will steer your palate in the right direction.

Bergamo City Walls

Unesco Gems

Bergamo City Walls

Stroll along the 6km-long Venetian walls surrounding Bergamo's medieval Città Alta. They were built in 1561 to protect against enemy attacks that never came to pass – which accounts for their incredible condition.

Santa Giulia Museum

A stone's throw from Brescia's centre you'll find this massive former monastery founded in 753. Built over impressive Roman townhouses, the architecture is a fascinating mix from different epochs.

Rhaetian Railway

The Albula and Bernina lines of this historic railway connecting Italy to Switzerland are an engineering marvel and a charming way to experience the astonishing beauty of the Alps.

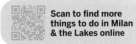

Scan to find more things to do in Milan & the Lakes online

20 Trip to a Mountain
VIA FERRATA

HIKING | MOUNTAINS | ADVENTURE

▬▬▬ You can hike, climb and scramble with 360-degree mountain views along the Bocchette Centrali *via ferrata*, a protected climbing route across the Brenta Dolomites. It progresses horizontally rather than vertically along natural ledges, making it ideal for those having a first *ferrata* experience. Here's how to plan your adventure!

HWO/GETTY IMAGES ©

🗺 How to

Getting here Drive to **Madonna di Campiglio**, about a three-hour drive from Milan and Venice. From there, you'll need two days (minimum) to hike Bocchette Centrali, spending one night at Rifugio Alimonta.

When to go Rifugio Alimonta is only open from 20 June to 20 September; July and August offer the best conditions.

Cost From €250 for a two-day package including guide, equipment rental and a night in a mountain hut (dorms only).

LUBOS CHLUBNY/SHUTTERSTOCK ©

Top left Bocchette Centrali
Bottom left Rifugio Alimonta

The approach From Madonna di Campiglio, it takes about 4½ hours to hike to **Rifugio Alimonta**, the closest mountain hut to Bocchette Centrali. Take a bus to Vallesinella waterfall, then start your ascent through a spruce forest. After about an hour, the mighty Brenta Dolomites will come into view.

Keep hiking up to reach **Rifugio Brentei**, ideal for a lunchtime stop surrounded by a rock amphitheatre, and then tackle the last uphill stretch to Rifugio Alimonta, your stop for the night. Don't miss the **enrosadira**, a natural phenomenon happening at sunset in the Dolomites, when the rocks take on a pink/orange hue – Alimonta is the ideal place to see it!

Hiking Bocchette Centrali It's best to tackle Bocchette Centrali first thing in the morning to maximise your chances of clear views. The start of the route is only half an hour from Alimonta via a rill, which may require the use of crampons. Five ladders will take you onto the panoramic ledges – the second is the most scenic one, a horseshoe-shaped path with views onto **Campanile Basso**, the most iconic peak in the Brenta Dolomites group. The route is as easy as *via ferrate* go, but there are some exposed sections with huge drops to the side. Fear not: your guide is there to help you at all times!

It takes between three and four hours to complete the *via ferrata*, plus a further hour to reach Rifugio Brentei, where you can rest and hike back to Madonna di Campiglio. It's advisable to go with an alpine guide. **Mountain Friends** (mountainfriends. it) offers tours between July and late September.

What is a Via Ferrata?

The term *via ferrata* is used throughout the Alps, and refers to a system of fixed ladders, cables and steps placed strategically to allow people to cross exposed mountain sections without ropes. Many *vie ferrate* in the Dolomites were created as supply routes during WWI, and later converted for tourist use. They are a great alternative to mountaineering for trekkers – but it's always recommended to go with a guide. In terms of equipment, you'll need a harness, helmet and a *via ferrata* lanyard (usually provided by your guide), plus a good head for heights!

VENICE &
THE VENETO

HISTORY | ART | WINE

Experience
Venice &
the Veneto
online

VENICE & THE VENETO
Trip Builder

It's a fact. Venice is like nowhere else on earth. But scan the Veneto horizon and you'll find so much more: honey-pot historic towns, smart modernist museums, Unesco-designated villas, cult wineries and rivers of prosecco with which to toast *la bea vita* (the good life).

Parco Nazionale Regionale della Lessinia

Bassano del Grappa

Schio

•Thiene

Admire the world's most harmonious architecture in **Vicenza** (p145)
🕐 *1 day*

Vicenza

Montecchio ∘ Maggiore

Verona

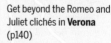
Get beyond the Romeo and Juliet clichés in **Verona** (p140)
🕐 *3 days*

Parco Regionale dei Colli Euganei

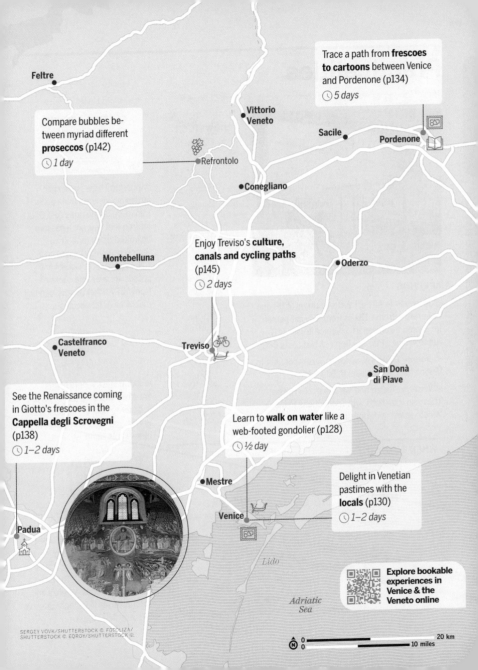

Trace a path from **frescoes to cartoons** between Venice and Pordenone (p134)
🕐 *5 days*

Compare bubbles between myriad different **proseccos** (p142)
🕐 *1 day*

Enjoy Treviso's **culture, canals and cycling paths** (p145)
🕐 *2 days*

See the Renaissance coming in Giotto's frescoes in the **Cappella degli Scrovegni** (p138)
🕐 *1–2 days*

Learn to **walk on water** like a web-footed gondolier (p128)
🕐 *½ day*

Delight in Venetian pastimes with the **locals** (p130)
🕐 *1–2 days*

Explore bookable experiences in Venice & the Veneto online

Feltre

Vittorio Veneto

Sacile

Pordenone

Refrontolo

Conegliano

Montebelluna

Oderzo

Castelfranco Veneto

Treviso

San Donà di Piave

Padua

Mestre

Venice

Lido

Adriatic Sea

0   20 km
0   10 miles

SERGEY VOVK/SHUTTERSTOCK ©, FOTOLIZA/
SHUTTERSTOCK ©, EQROY/SHUTTERSTOCK ©,

Practicalities

EQROY/SHUTTERSTOCK ©

ARRIVING

🛥 **Marco Polo Airport** Water shuttles (€15) and water taxis (from €110, or from €25 per person for shared taxis) depart to Venice. Buses (€8) run to Venice's Piazzale Roma. A taxi costs €40.

🛥 **Verona-Villafranca Airport** Buses connect to Verona (€6). A taxi costs €25 to €30.

🚆 **Venezia Mestre and Verona Porta Nuova** The main train hubs with connections to major Veneto towns and some international services.

HOW MUCH FOR A

Cicheto (bar snack) €1.50–5

Spritz €2.50–4

Risotto €8.50–12

GETTING AROUND

Vaporetto These passenger ferries are Venice's main public transport. Single rides cost €7.50; for frequent use, get a pass for unlimited travel (one-/two-/three-/seven-day passes cost €20/30/40/60). Tickets and passes are available dockside from ACTV ticket booths, vending machines or tobacconists.

Walking Most Veneto towns are easily walkable and often it is faster to walk in Venice, too. Bonus: you'll get to enjoy some remarkable sights en route.

Trains and buses The local train and bus network is frequent, inexpensive and reliable. Tickets can be purchased at ticketing machines in the station. Trains connects Venice with Treviso, Conegliano, Padua, Vicenza and Verona. Buses from Vicenza serve Bassano del Grappa.

WHEN TO GO

MAR–APR

Damp but lovely as ever indoors. Bargain rates.

MAY–AUG

Cycling season starts; major festivals draw crowds.

SEP–NOV

Crowds retreat but weather remains balmy; great for vineyards.

DEC–FEB

Chilly days; Christmas markets and Carnevale bring people out.

EATING & DRINKING

Lagoon larder Venetian cuisine revolves around the day's catch including *gò* (grass goby), *folpetti* (baby octopus), *peoci* (mussels), *seppie* (squid) and seasonal *moeche* (soft-shelled crabs). Fish are usually served whole, and the taste is not masked by sauces.

Risotto Rather than pasta, risotto is the Veneto's preferred staple. In Venice it is served with goby fish; in Treviso it is prepared with the famous *radicchio rosso* (pictured bottom right) in winter; and, in Bassano, it's served with the local, sweet, white asparagus.

Must-try risotto Toni del Spin (p144)

Best wine bar La Antica Bottega del Vino (p141)

CONNECT & FIND YOUR WAY

Wi-fi Available in hotels, B&Bs and rental apartments, and increasingly even in cafes. In Venice, you can also purchase a connection through Vènezia Unica.

Navigation Veneto towns are small and easily navigated on foot. The exception is the labyrinthine *calle* (alleys) of Venice. GPS works fairly well, but it does steer you down main thoroughfares with the crowds.

DISCOUNT CARDS

The **Vènezia Unica** (veneziaunica. it) card offers a range of discounts and services, including airport transfer, public transport cards, museum passes and wi-fi.

WHERE TO STAY

Venice and Verona are expensive particularly during Carnevale, opera season and school holidays. To secure the best bargains, book ahead. In Venice consider location carefully, and always look to stay near a *vaporetto* stop.

Place	Pro/Con
Dorsoduro	Venice's liveliest area, with design hotels near museums and seaside getaways along Zattere.
Castello & Cannaregio	Popular Venetian residential neighbourhoods full of good bars and reasonably priced restaurants.
Giudecca & Lido	Giudecca island is popular with artists and enjoys some of Venice's best views. Lido is Venice's leafy beach burb, best enjoyed from May to September.
Verona	Full of heritage hotels, B&Bs and apartments in the historic centre. Veronetta, east of the river, offers a less touristy experience.
Treviso	Has a small but attractive selection of characterful B&Bs and boutique hotels around the centre.
Vicenza	A great base in the heart of the region with lovely B&Bs, hotels and apartments in historic *palazzi*.

MONEY

There are multilingual ATMs throughout the region; €250 is the daily withdrawal limit. American Express and Diners Club aren't universally accepted.

21 Learn to
VOGA

CULTURE | ADVENTURE | VENETIAN ROWING

For thousands of years the *voga alla Veneta* – Venetian stand-up rowing – was the only way to navigate the shallow bowl of the lagoon and the city's intricate canals. Try mastering the art of the *gondolieri* for a unique perspective on the city. It's a peculiar experience finding yourself moving within a view – the canal – that you're used to glancing across. Like entering another dimension.

GIVAGA/SHUTTERSTOCK ©

🗺 How to

Getting here The marina is closest to the San Marcuola or Strada Nova *vaporetto* stops. Then follow Row Venice's directions to the meeting point on the Ponte de la Sacca bridge.

When to go You can row year-round, but the experience is best between April and September when the weather is warm.

Bar-hopping tip In summer, Row Venice runs a sunset row finishing with a drink at a local *bacarò* (bar).

FOOTTOO/SHUTTERSTOCK ©

CHRISDORNEY/SHUTTERSTOCK ©

Far left Gondolier, Venice **Bottom right** Gondola in a workshop **Near left** Gondola on the water, Venice

Learning the voga Find your footing on the lagoon with champion regatta rowers at **Row Venice** (rowvenice.org), who will show you how to propel a handcrafted *batellina coda di gambero* (shrimp-tailed boat) standing up. You'll start with some tuition in the sheltered Misericordia marina, where you'll be shown how to handle the 4m oar. Then you'll step up on the prow and head out into the quiet canal leaning forward into the *prèmer* (push) and pulling back for the *stalìr* (return stroke). It feels like weight lifting and surfing at the same time.

The art of the gondola Now you've tried your hand at *voga*, consider Luisella Romeo's behind-the-scenes tour of the boatyards and artist studios dedicated to building the mighty gondola – the prince of Venetian boats – through **SeeVenice** (seevenice.it). You'll meet the *squerariólo* (gondola makers) and *remèri* (oar makers), and even visit the foundry where must-have decorations are fashioned.

Lagoon views To explore the outer reaches of the lagoon, its abandoned islands and resident flamingos, you'll need more than arm power. **Classic Boats Venice** (classicboatsvenice. com) offer beautifully restored traditional wooden craft. Not only are these heritage boats great looking, but they are also powered by ecofriendly electric engines that won't disturb lagoon life. Before launch, you'll be given 30 minutes of training and equipped with a tracking device so you can't get lost.

⚜ Vogalonga

The annual **Vogalonga** (vogalonga.com), usually held in May, is Venice's most popular, non-competitive regatta and is open to the global rowing public. Established in 1975, it is the only day of the year when motorised traffic is banned from the Grand Canal. A cannon shot from Piazza San Marco launches over a thousand watercraft out into the lagoon in front of Palazzo Ducale. They then tackle a 30km circuit which loops past Burano and Murano before ending with cheers and prosecco at Punta della Dogana.

Unlike Carnevale, this is a real celebration of *vera Venezianità* (true Venetian-ness) when residents are more important than tourists and the deep connection between the lagoon and city is evident to see.

22

See Venice Like
A LOCAL

ART | HISTORY | CULTURE

Please take your seats. In this play, Venice assumes a dual role. There is Venice the city thousands of tourists visit and Venice the city where locals live. To navigate your way to the latter follow these tips for a glimpse behind the main stage.

⚲ How to

Getting around
Venice's reliable and regular public network of *vaporetti* (water buses) is run by **ACTV** (actv.avmspa.it). However, walking is more interesting and often quicker.

When to go In May when the blossom is out or early autumn for balmy days and fewer visitors.

Best sunset Grab a seat at the pint-sized kiosk **El Chioschetto** (Fondamente Zattere) and enjoy your *spritz* with an uninterrupted view across the Giudecca Canal.

Get Lost in the Labyrinth

Yellow signs may point the way to the landmarks of Basilica di San Marco and the Gallerie dell'Accademia, but the paradox of Venice is that in order to get to know it you need to lose yourself. In his book, *Venice is a Fish*, Tiziano Scarpa makes clear that Venice is first of all a physical experience that you must immerse yourself in. So, do as he suggests, learn to wander and take a ride down the palace-lined length of the **Grand Canal**. It's sound advice in a city that is itself a work of art.

Museums Locals Love

Don't be fooled by appearances, Venice's age-old traditions sit beside an electric contemporary art scene. Locals love the Klimts, Kandinskys and Grand Canal–side cafe at **Ca' Pesaro**, the cutting-edge exhibitions

⊙ I Am Not Making This Up

'This blog is intended to answer the question, "What is it like to live in Venice?" I'm never quite sure how to answer; it's like asking somebody what it's like to be a genius.' So says Erla Zwingle of her hilarious **blog** (iamnotmakingthisup.net) about Venice.

Top left and above Venice streets **Bottom left** Ca' Pesaro and Grand Canal

at one-time radical fashion house **Museo Fortuny**, the photography shows at **Casa dei Tre Oci**, the experimental video art at **Fondazione Prada** and the mega-installations at the **Punta della Dogana** (palazzograssi.it). Most recently, Russia's richest man opened the **V-A-C Foundation** (v-a-c.ru) bringing contemporary Russian art to the lagoon.

The Biennale

Despite *biennali* sprouting like weeds as far afield as Senegal and Korea, when connois-seurs talk about the Biennale, they still mean Venice. Nowhere is better suited to hosting an international art show than Venice. What's more, the epic event (labiennale.org), held between May and November, encompasses a huge fringe fair that is staged throughout the city's palaces and gardens, many of which are usually off-limits to the public. Plan ahead.

Superior Bar Bites

In Venice, it's natural for people to run into each other and stop to chat. More often than

Hidden Art Treasures

Oratory of the Crociferi (Campo dei Crociferi) The career climax of Palma II Giovane, pupil of Titian.

Elisabetta Mason (veniceoriginal.it/it/artigiani/37-elisabetta-mason) A modern Midas, Mason gilds gondolas with 24-karat gold leaf. Book for studio visits.

La Fonderia Artistica Valese (valese.it/fonderia-artistica-valese-venezia) Carlo Semenzato runs the Valese artistic foundry, where Venice's renowned brass door knockers and seahorses are cast.

Palazzo Cini (palazzocini.it) The house-museum of aristocrat Vittorio Cini located in the museum mile in Dorsoduro.

Recommended by Luisella Romeo, *Venetian tour guide* @luisella_romeo

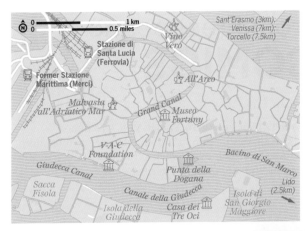

Left Ca' Macana **Below** Lido

not, they'll then invite each other for a quick drink. The world of *bacari* (bars), *ombre* (a small glass of wine) and *cicheti* (snacks) is the real Venice. The best bars to indulge are **All'Arco** (San Polo), **Cantina del vino già Schiavi** (Fondamenta Nani), **Malvasia dell'Adriatico Mar** (Dorsoduro) and **Vino Vero** (Fondamenta della Misericordia).

Authentic Experiences

To really get to know Venice, you have to see the city as the locals do. That means taking the leap beyond sightseeing and joining Venetians in their traditional pastimes. Learn to cook with Countess **Enrica Rocca** (enricarocca.com), make masks with a master at **Ca' Macana** (camacana.com), learn lampworking with **Davide Penso** (davidepenso.it) and practice the art of mosaic at **Artefact Mosaic Studio** (artefactmosaicworkshops.com).

Island Escapes

The lagoon that surrounds Venice is a watery garden where Venetians retreat to escape the 'city'. It offers idyllic retreats and outlandish escapes from reality. Push a boat out for the beaches of the **Lido**, the ancient Byzantine church and migratory birds of **Torcello**, the lagoon vineyard and restaurant **Venissa**, and the cycling trails and organic farms of **Sant'Erasmo**.

23

From Frescoes to
COMICS

GRAPHIC ART | CULTURE | ROAD TRIP

In summer 2019, Marvel's teen superhero, Spider-Man, was filmed holidaying in Venice. It was an apt destination for the comic book creation given the rich graphic design history of a region that launched the publishing industry. Spend a few days exploring this under-appreciated heritage.

TRAVELVIEW/SHUTTERSTOCK ©

🗺 Trip Notes

Getting around A car is most convenient. However, it's also easy to get everywhere on public transport.

When to go The countryside is most beautiful in late spring; Treviso's Comic Book Festival happens in September.

Top tip Make a pit stop in **Asolo**, a long-time haunt of literary types. **BellAsolo** (bellasolo.it) arranges visits to explorer Freya Stark's villa. Lunch at **Due Mori** (2mori.it) is also a must.

🚶 Bassano Basecamp

Bassano del Grappa (pictured) is a bucolic town that makes a great base for an extended trip. Stay at Julie's B&B, **Le 33** (le33bnb.com), and spend a few days cycling, hiking or white-water rafting. In the evening, toast happy hour at **Nardini** (nardini.it), Italy's oldest distillery.

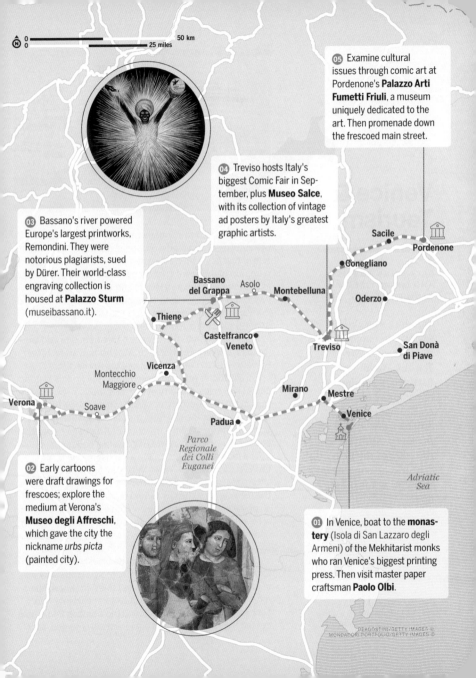

05 Examine cultural issues through comic art at Pordenone's **Palazzo Arti Fumetti Friuli**, a museum uniquely dedicated to the art. Then promenade down the frescoed main street.

04 Treviso hosts Italy's biggest Comic Fair in September, plus **Museo Salce**, with its collection of vintage ad posters by Italy's greatest graphic artists.

03 Bassano's river powered Europe's largest printworks, Remondini. They were notorious plagiarists, sued by Dürer. Their world-class engraving collection is housed at **Palazzo Sturm** (museibassano.it).

02 Early cartoons were draft drawings for frescoes; explore the medium at Verona's **Museo degli Affreschi**, which gave the city the nickname *urbs picta* (painted city).

01 In Venice, boat to the **monastery** (Isola di San Lazzaro degli Armeni) of the Mekhitarist monks who ran Venice's biggest printing press. Then visit master paper craftsman **Paolo Olbi**.

50 km
25 miles

Sacile
Pordenone
Conegliano
Oderzo
Bassano del Grappa
Asolo
Montebelluna
Thiene
Castelfranco Veneto
Treviso
San Donà di Piave
Vicenza
Montecchio Maggiore
Mirano
Mestre
Verona
Soave
Padua
Venice
Parco Regionale dei Colli Euganei
Adriatic Sea

Venice & Tourism

BALANCING TOURISM AND LOCAL LIFE IN VENICE

'You hug us tightly,' says Paolo Lanapoppi in his essay, *Dear Tourist*. 'We're flattered, and some of us, many of us really, make our money from your presence. But now, at the start of the 21st century,' he concedes, 'something must be done.'

JAR066/SHUTTERSTOCK ©

He's not wrong. Pre-pandemic, life in the world's most beautiful city was verging on woeful due to the ever-rising tide of tourists – then estimated at 20 to 25 million per annum. Top of the list of grievances for the 53,000 remaining island inhabitants was a lack of affordable housing (Venice has Italy's highest Airbnb-to-population ratio), limited and low-wage employment, the loss of small businesses and underfunded infrastructure and public services.

Such was the situation, Unesco threatened to add Venice to its Endangered Heritage Sites list and art historian Salvatore Settis penned *If Venice Dies* warning that Western civilisation's prime achievements faced ruin if historic cities like Venice succumbed to mass tourism. But despite the alarm, the question remained: what exactly should be done to protect the city from the glare of global admiration and the increasing environmental damage caused by cruise ships and *acqua alta* (high water) floods?

The fact is Venice has made a handsome living off tourism for centuries. When Venice lost ground to the Ottomans in 1453 and trade moved west to the Atlantic in the 16th century, the city turned on the charm. Instead of shipping and commerce, it attracted visitors with dazzling art, world-class music and cultured courtesans. It was an essential stop on the European Grand Tour as it remains today thanks to the annual six-month-long Biennale.

But the mass tourism of recent decades was no match for the city's geographic realities (namely a land surface of just 2 sq km and medieval alleys barely 2m wide). The more tourists Venice attracted, the more residents were pushed out. Many Venetians found the situation intolerable but felt trapped. Grassroots organisations emerged, such

From left Cruise ship leaving Venice; gondolas crowing a canal; glasswork, Murano

as Venessia and We Are Here Venice, to raise awareness of the issues locals faced and lobby politicians. But as long as tourism dominated, other alternatives appeared impossible.

Then, in March 2020, Covid-19 happened and instead of Venice dying, tourism itself expired. Overnight, visitors vanished. Resident Gioielle Romanelli recalls an apocalyptic air of desertion and Claudio Scarpa, director of the hotel association, estimated the cost at more than €1 billion.

> Venice was an essential stop on the European Grand Tour as it remains today thanks to the annual six-month-long Biennale.

But, although the pandemic has been agonising, it has created space for a new conversation about tourism. Suddenly dreams of attracting arts foundations, business incubators and digital nomads seem not only feasible but essential if the living city is to survive. Empty Airbnbs have replenished housing stocks, while the improved health of the lagoon highlighted the environmental cost of large cruise ships. Subsequently, in July 2021 the national government banned ships over 25,000 tonnes from docking in Venice.

Travellers, too, have a role to play in Venice's revival. The city has always needed considerate visitors. Staying longer in officially registered accommodation, eating in local restaurants, buying products made by local artisans and exploring the city's hidden corners and magical lagoon, will all contribute to a healthier and happier city.

⊙ Local Connections

The Real Venice
Join **Luisella Romeo** (see venice.it), who'll take you to the city's gold beaters, silk weavers and honey harvesters.

Bar Hops
Keep up with food blogger **Monica Cesarato** (monica cesarato.com) on her riotous *cicheti* tours.

Local Stays
Try community-focused, home-sharing platform Fairbnb. Or choose locally owned accommodation like **B&B San Marco** (realvenice.it), **Hotel Flora** and **Cima Rosa**.

Authentic Experiences
Explore **Venezia Autentica** (veneziaautentica.com), which promotes local shops, restaurants and craft studios.

Lagoon Literacy
Cross-disciplinary centre **Ocean Space** hosts lagoon-inspired exhibitions and events.

SPATULETAIL/SHUTTERSTOCK ©

Forward-Thinking Padua

EPIC HISTORY ON A HUMAN SCALE

In *The Origins of Modern Science*, Herbert Butterfield, Vice-Chancellor of Cambridge University, named Padua the seat of the Scientific Revolution. Because Padua's embrace of humanist philosophy enabled the Renaissance and, thus, science to flourish.

Consider the fact, without enlightened Paduan jurists like Lovato dei Lovati (1241–1309), the Renaissance may never have happened. It was they who revived the moral philosophising of the ancient world. Recognising the similarities between medieval tyrants and the capricious Greek gods, they contemplated the potential agency of common men and the role of individuals in society.

Nowhere was this new notion of humanism better portrayed than in Giotto's stunning fresco cycle in the **Cappella degli Scrovegni**. Where before medieval churchgoers had been accustomed to blank stares from enthroned saints, Giotto introduced biblical figures as human characters in recognisable settings. This changed how people saw themselves: no longer lowly vassals, but as vessels for the divine, however flawed.

Giotto's naturalism reflected the Aristotelian philosophy of pursuing knowledge through natural observation which was favoured at Padua University, where anatomical dissection was codified in the statutes. Here Andreas Vesalius first taught medical students to believe what they saw rather than seeing what they believed. His magnus opus, *The Fabric of the Human Body* (1543), illustrated by Titian's student Jan van Calcer, established the field of modern anatomy and attracted scientists and artists to the university's anatomy theatre. Mantegna's *Dead Christ* (c 1480) is clearly informed by detailed anatomical knowledge; and, Marcantonio della Torre (a Paduan anatomy professor) instructed Leonardo da Vinci, the most influential artist-anatomist of all time. Thus, Padua's medical school enabled the evolution of Renaissance art.

From left *Marriage at Cana* fresco by Giotto, Cappella degli Scrovegni; Palazzo Bò; Basilica di Sant'Antonio

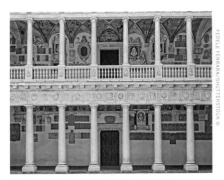

The humanity of da Vinci's paintings emerges from Padua's people-centered traditions, encapsulated in the motto: Universa Universis Patavina Libertas (Paduan Freedom is Universal for Everyone). It echoes the institution's fearless beginnings – it was established in 1222 by scholars rather than 'ex privilegio' (by special decree) – and its refusal to constrain the teachings of its faculty, or to ban students on the basis of race or creed.

It is, therefore, poignant to notice the brass *stolpersteine* (stumbling stones) set in the cobblestones on the threshold of Palazzo Bò. They commemorate six of the 200 Jews who were expelled from the university following the Nazi racial laws of 1938. While part of the Italian Social Republic (a German puppet state), Padua was also a hotbed of anti-Fascist resistance. University rector Concetto Marchesi called students to arms in his inaugural speech in 1943. Likewise, Placido Cortese, friar of the Basilica of St Anthony, helped hundreds escape. He, too, is remembered with a *Stolpersteine* in Piazza del Santo and is in line to be beatified.

> The humanity of Leonardo da Vinci's paintings emerges from Padua's people-centered traditions.

Padua humanist traditions prove that individuals can and do make a difference. It is a place where history doesn't weigh on the present, but rather invigorates it. Students still fill the piazzas with quick-witted conversation; rusty bikes clatter over the cobbles in the Jewish ghetto; and pilgrims still come in their droves to touch the tomb of St Anthony.

🏛 Living History

Palazzo Bò (unipd.it) The heart of Padua's history-making university, which you can visit on a tour that will turn your head with alumni that include Erasmus, Copernicus and Galileo.

Basilica di Sant'Antonio An epic, art-filled basilica, 'Il Santo' is the soul of Padua and the repository of St Anthony's 'incorrupt' tongue.

Orto Botanico The world's first botanical garden and the birthplace of modern pharmacology.

Sotto il Salone An 800-year-old shopping mall under the arches of the Palazzo della Ragione. Stop by **Il Tira Bouchon** for a prosecco and *spunci* (snack).

Prato della Valle The largest square in Italy, featuring an elliptical garden lined with 78 statues of Paduan VIPs. It's a favourite local hang-out.

24 Verona Beyond Romeo & JULIET

CULTURE | WINE | WALKING TOURS

While there's no evidence that Shakespeare ever visited Verona or that his young lovers resided here, his famous tale has created an enduring cult of romance around the city. To get beyond the clichés and avoid the crowds leaving lovelorn graffiti at Casa di Julietta, follow these tips and you'll find the real romance of this mini Rome.

PAOLO TRALLI/SHUTTERSTOCK ©

🗺 How to

Getting here/around
Verona is a main stop on the Italian rail network. Once in town, it's best to walk.

When to go Anytime, but: July and August for opera; September for the grape harvest; December for the Christmas mar-

kets; and, February for Carnevale.

Top tip Get discounts on many attractions with the **Verona Card** (verona touristoffice.it).

Top table Taste the magic of four hot-shot chefs at **Locanda 4 Cuochi** (locanda4cuochi.it).

MARIA VONOTNA/SHUTTERSTOCK ©

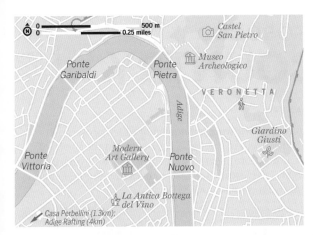

Top left View from Castel San Pietro
Bottom left Roman ruins seen from a riverside bar

Different perspectives There's more to Verona than picturesque ruins and lovelorn couples. For a new view, visit the superb **Modern Art Gallery** (gam.comune.verona.it) bequeathed by Jewish scholar Achille Forti. Or, indulge in world-class Michelin dining at **Casa Perbellini** or thrilling **white-water rafting** (adigerafting.it) down the river Adige. And, if you want to know where Verona's teen lovers really go, it's up to the hilltop terraces of **Castel San Pietro** (funicolarediverona.it) for spectacular sunset views.

Little Jerusalem Veronetta, on the right bank of the river Adige, is the 'other' Verona. This is the authentic part of the city although there's still plenty to see: a Renaissance garden, **Giardini Giusti**, a Roman theatre and a stunning **archaeological museum** (Regaste Redentore 2). It was also a popular place with the Knights Templar thanks to a rumour that Verona was founded by Noah's son. **Hierusalem Tours** (veronaminor hierusalem.it) run free walks to secret frescoed chapels and fascinating reliquaries.

Bittersweet flavours Verona's outsized reputation for opera often eclipses its ancient tradition of viticulture. Vineyards have been cultivated here since Etruscan times and the range of local wines is incredibly diverse: from homemade Valpolicella Classico to the epic Amarone (meaning 'the great bitter'), from crisp white Custoza to the sweet red Recioto. If there's one place you should visit in Verona, make it **La Antica Bottega del Vino** (bottegavini.it).

✅ Local Favourites

Colorificio Dolci (dolcicolor.it) Since 1910, this unique colour factory has used traditional techniques to process natural, organic and inorganic pigments vital in the fields of art, restoration and gilding. Tours on request.

Sala Morone (san bernardinoverona.it) The 'Sistine Chapel' of Verona painted by Domenico Morone, Andrea Mantegna's most talented pupil.

Caffè Tubino A tiny, historic cafe selling high-quality coffee blends.

Veronetta The Verona neighbourhood least touched by tourism.

Restaurant La Borsa (ristoranteborsa.it) The homemade tortellini at this restaurant just outside Verona is considered a cultural treasure.

Recommended by Lorella & Valeria, *certified Verona guides (veronatours.com)*

25 Prosecco **COUNTRY**

WINE TASTING | FOOD | ROAD TRIP

The Veneto is home to the worldwide phenomenon called prosecco. It comes from the rolling hillsides north of the Piave river between the towns of Valdobbiadene, Conegliano and Vittorio Veneto. There are over 100 wineries, but don't miss these highlights, as recommended by tour leader, sommelier and blogger Romena Bugnerotto (rominvenice.com).

PAVEL REZAC/SHUTTERSTOCK ©

🗺 Trip Notes

Getting around A car is essential. Conegliano, the regional hub, is accessible by train from Venice and Treviso.

When to go Anytime, except early January, the last two weeks of August and Sundays when wineries close. Lunch hour (noon to 2pm) is also sacred.

La Strada del Prosecco 'The Prosecco Road' is Italy's oldest wine route, with wineries listed at coneglianovaldobbiadene.it. Tours can be arranged with **Visit Prosecco** (visitproseccoitaly.com).

🍷 Tasting Tips

A good prosecco has a straw-like yellow colour touched with a greenish tinge. Its bubbles should be tiny, numerous and long-lasting in your glass. On the nose, it smells of white fruits and freshly mown grass, while in the mouth it is crisp and aromatic. Drink it young when it is full of fizz.

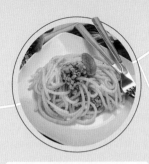

05 Sleep among the vines at **La Vigna di Sarah** (lavignadisarah. it), a prosecco vineyard near Vittorio Veneto. It runs excellent food and wine tours, cooking classes, hiking trips and more. wine, too.

Vittorio Veneto

04 No-frills **Forno di Refrontolo** (alforno.it) serves real traditional food. Enjoy true Veneto dishes combined with the most exciting prosecco of the region.

Refrontolo

03 Producing prosecco since 1964, **Toffoli** (proseccotoffoli.it) follows modern techniques to create an intense apple, pear and lemon nose. Try the Passito di Refrontolo dessert wine, too.

01 Cheese is a natural partner for prosecco, and **Perenzin** (perperenzin.it) is the 'cheese king'. Book for lunch or visit the fascinating laboratories, then stock up in the shop.

Conegliano

02 Servo Suo is the award-winning prosecco produced by the Faganello family at **Colsaliz** (colsaliz.it) in Refrontolo. Enjoy the view with a glass of their intense-tasting wine.

N

| 0 | | 4 km |
| 0 | | 2 miles |

Listings

BEST OF THE REST

Mighty Venetian Masterpieces

Basilica di San Marco

Venice's architectural wonder where East meets West under golden mosaic domes.

Gallerie dell'Accademia

Watch Venetian painters set the world ablaze with censorship-defying art.

Palazzo Ducale

The doge's palatial home decor is the world's prettiest propaganda.

Scuola Grande di San Rocco

Tintoretto upstages Veronese with action-packed scenes of angelic rescue squads.

Teatro La Fenice

'The Phoenix' is Venice's shamelessly beautiful theatre. It has been one of the world's top opera houses since 1792.

Veneto Feasts

Antiche Carampane   €€€

Fresh fish is the thing here. Francesco serves up masterful versions of recherché dishes like *cassopipa* (spaghetti with spiced shellfish).

Locanda Cipriani   €€€

Still owned by the famous family, this six-room inn on Torcello once catered to the likes of Ernest Hemingway and Truman Capote.

Riviera   €€€

The finest lagoon-foraged food is served at tables overlooking the Giudecca Canal. The multi-course menu is an education.

Al Covo   €€€

Promoting the unique produce of the Venetian lagoon, Covo's *fritto misto* (fried mixed fish) has become a cult, though everything on its menu is delicious.

Toni del Spin   €€

A reference point in Treviso since 1880, Toni serves silky plates of risotto with white asparagus and tagliatelle with duck *ragù*.

Da Nane della Giulia   €

Be transported to another era in Padua's oldest tavern where you can sample Padovan chicken in red grappa with pancetta.

 Cafes with Character

Caffè Florian

This 1720 cafe is a living museum. The jewel-like rooms provide a gilt-edged cocoon for eating fine patisserie in view of San Marco.

Caffè Pedrocchi

Padua's ornate Viennese-style cafe is a relic of olde worlde Europe. Austro-Hungarian troops fired on rabble-rousing students here in 1848.

Pasticceria Flego

The gold standard for Veronese pastry, Flego produces an irresistible array of pastries and the best Pandoro – Verona's signature cake.

YINGKO/SHUTTERSTOCK ©

Caffè Florian

Café Carducci

A 1920s-style Veronese bistro serving exquisitely sweet salami and punchy local cheeses.

Pasticceria Sorarù

A historic Vincenza pastry shop lined with gilded shelves and outdoor seating offering views of Palladio's elegant Basilica Palladiana.

Visionary Vineyards

Allegrini

The Allegrini family has been tending vines in Valpolicella since the 16th century. Wine tastings are held in the mannerist masterpiece, Villa della Torre.

1898 Cantina di Soave

This cooperative of 2000 Soave producers was once an official supplier to Italian royalty. Visit the cellars in Borgo Rocca Sveva.

Vignaioli Contra Soarda

Located in a volcanic valley, this vineyard produces award-winning wines from autochthonous grapes. Dine at its restaurant Pulierin.

Worth a Detour

Vicenza

Home to Europe's most influential architect, Andrea Palladio, honey-coloured Vicenza is a World Heritage Site. It is also full of lively *osterie,* such as Michelin-starred El Coq.

Treviso

Treviso with its canals and cobbled streets offers an authentic Veneto experience. Stay at Ai Bastioni, view modern art in a Habsburg prison, and eat ice cream at Gelateria Dassie.

Gysotheca e Museo Antonio Canova

Canova was Italy's virtuoso sculptor, his work sought after by patrons like the pope, Napoleon and George Washington. His atelier in Possagno reveals his genius.

Teatro Olimpico in Vicenza, designed by Andrea Palladio

Isola della Certosa

This Venetian island park has a mini marina and an excellent restaurant, Hostaria in Certosa. Venice Kayak also leads tours from here.

Artisan Finds

Chiarastella Cattana

A global go-to for exquisite Italian textiles in unique Venetian designs. Besides the linen there are clothes, carpets and Murano glass.

L'Isola

Backlit chalices and spotlit vases emit an otherworldly glow at this shrine to Murano modernist glass master, Carlo Moretti.

Pied à Terre

Purveyor of candy-coloured *furlane* (Venetian slippers) handmade with recycled bicycle tyre treads, ideal for gondola boarding.

Pinarello

Treviso's Pinarello handcraft the best road, track and cyclocross bikes, including 13 winners of the Tour de France.

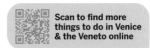
Scan to find more things to do in Venice & the Veneto online

26 Side Trip: A Bite of **BOLOGNA**

FOOD | PASTA | GASTRONOMY

Bologna is the gastronomic workhorse of what is arguably Italy's culinary capital, Emilia-Romagna, a gluttonous land of plenty whose kitchens have birthed rich and renown specialities like *ragù* (meat and tomato sauce), lasagna and tortellini. Loosen your belts – nobody gets out any lighter!

🗺 **How to**

Getting here/around
Bologna's Guglielmo Marconi Airport is well-connected with flights throughout Europe; Bologna Central station sits on Italy's high-speed rail line. The city centre is walkable – the world's most extensive portico network even offers protection from the elements – but local bus services are good, too.

When to go Spring (April/May) and Autumn (September/October) promise the best weather; overcrowding is not an issue.

Hop alert Explore Italy's craft beer scene at **Il Punto** (punto bologna.com).

Follow your Senses

Bologna's old food market, a squared grid of narrow lanes just off the southeast corner of Piazza Maggiore known as the **Quadrilatero**, has been slinging local specialities since the Middle Ages. Follow your senses as you navigate its cramped lanes, where artisanal food producers, speciality delis and market stalls teem with the best of Bologna: a parade of freshly shaped tortellini stuffed with ricotta, mountains of thinly sliced *mortadella* (pork cold cut), buckets of slow-cooked *ragù*.

Kitchen Confidential

For a deeper dive into local kitchens, **Le Cesarine** (cesarine.com), a national private cooking class network born in Bologna, offers wonderful opportunities to learn the city's signature dishes inside the homes of local culinarians. In Bologna that means learning

✕ **Bologna's Best**

I'll never forget the dishes my grandmother Ada prepared. *Tagliatelle* with classic Bolognese sauce: a warm hug! *Zuppa inglese* (Bolognese custard and sponge cake): the cure for my childish cries! Fried pork cutlet (*cotoletta*), sautéed with tomato sauce and peas: definitive!

By Elisa Rusconi, *owner and chef, Trattoria da Me, @trattoriadame*

Top left Food stalls, Bologna city centre.
Bottom left Zuppa inglese.
Above *Tagliatelle al ragù*

the art of *tagliatelle*, the city's traditional fresh egg pasta, which will then be smothered in the iconic meat sauce known as *ragù*. Sweet tooths need not worry – you'll whip up *zuppa inglese* as well, Bologna's signature dessert (hint: it's not soup and it's not English).

Sfogline Sisters

As you wander Bologna's marvellous medieval streets, pop in and see what's unravelling at appropriately named **Le Sfogline** (lesfogline. it), where Daniela and Monica make up the friendliest sister *sfoglina* (pasta maker) team in Bologna. A *sfgolina* is traditionally a woman who specialises in the hand-rolled pastas of the region (*tagliatelle*, tortellini, lasagna). Monica speaks English and will happily welcome you into her pasta fantasyland with open arms. Watch the masters at work before you walk out with a kilo of lasagna (it's impossible not to).

Foodies & Footie

At last count, Bologna's city centre was home to a head-spinning 700-plus restaurants and,

📖 A Culinary Chronicle

Two attributes have characterised Bologna since the Middle Ages: La Dotta ('the learned one') and La Grassa ('the fat one'). These two characteristics are deeply connected. Bologna is home to Europe's oldest university and is recognised as a gastronomic capital. The abundance and quality of food are part of the extraordinary welcome that foreigners found when dozens of nations mixed in the city. These same students and teachers were the ones who enriched the local culture, brought new tastes and different experiences, and spread the image of the city throughout the world.

By Massimo Montanari,
food historian, University of Bologna

Far left Handmade tortellini
Near left Meatballs with peas
Below *Tigelle e crescentine*

while you can't really go wrong at any of them, an insider culinary adventure awaits just outside the city's historic gates. At **Trattoria Bertozzi** (trattoria bertozzibologna.it), locals in the know, food experts from far and wide and Bologna FC superfans gather to indulge in authentic local specialities like *tagliatelle al ragù*, meatballs with peas, and *gramigna* pasta with saffron, guanciale and courgette. The antics of loud and brash partners Alessandro (kitchen) and Fabio (wine, socialising) only up the ante on this locals-in-the-know experience.

Head for the Hills

For a truly authentic Bolognese adventure, it's well-worth renting a car and heading into the surrounding hillsides, known as the *colli bolognesi*. Fiercely local trattorias pepper the landscape here, often with pastoral views across the surrounding countryside (and Bologna in the distance). At travel-worthy destination restaurants like **Nuova Roma** (ristorantenuovaroma. it), **Osteria dal Nonno** (osteriadalnonno.bologna. it) and **Trattoria Gilberto** (trattoriagilberto.it), locals devour platters of *mortadella*, prosciutto di Parma DOP, local *salume* and farmstead cheeses sandwiched between *crescentine* (fried squares of dough) and *tigelle* (baked round bread) – with nary a tourist in sight!

27 WEEKEND
in Motor Valley

SUPERCARS | DESIGN | MUSEUMS

Motor Valley, Emilia-Romagna's supercar sanctuary, is often heralded as the birthplace of speed. Indeed, Bologna, Modena and Maranello form an urban triad where unparalleled engineering and Italian design marry in the form of the world's most high-performance vehicles. Ferrari, Lamborghini, Maserati, Ducati and Pagani await. Get your motor running and head out on the highway!

D-VISIONS/SHUTTERSTOCK ©

🗺 How to

Getting here/around
Bologna's Guglielmo Marconi Airport is the main transport hub of the region, accommodating flights from throughout Europe and beyond. Post-arrival, renting your own wheels is – quite obviously – the best way to see Motor Valley.

When to go Spring (April/May) and Autumn (September/October) are perfect driving weather.

Rent a supercar GTRent (gtrent.com) and **Dolce V-Italy** (dolcev-italy.com) rent Ferraris and Lamborghinis in Bologna.

ANDRES CANEY/SHUTTERSTOCK ©

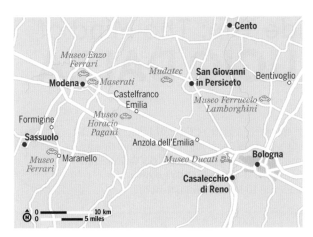

Top left Museo Enzo Ferrari, Modena
Bottom left Museo Ducati, Bologna

Lamborghinis, Ferraris and Maseratis, oh my! Dizzying displays of history, high-performance and stunning Italian design characterise the museums of Motor Valley. In Bologna, **Museo Ducati** (ducati.com) takes visitors on the top-end motorcycle brand's journey from vacuum tube and condenser beginnings to superbike. Ferrari offers a double dose of pilgrimage-worthy collections: the world-class **Museo Ferrari** (ferrari.com) at Maranello headquarters cradles the world's largest collection of Ferraris, while **Museo Enzo Ferrari** in Modena celebrates memorabilia of the founder. Lamborghini also splits inventories: **Mudatec** (lamborghini.com) in Sant'Agata Bolognese is the showcase gallery focusing on history and innovation, while Argelato's **Museo Ferruccio Lamborghini** (museolamborghini.com) is a mesmerising 9000 sq metres of family heirlooms: helicopters, tractors and legendary cars.

Under the bonnet Factory tours await car buffs looking for the Holy Grail of supercar fandom. Peeking behind the curtain on a production line tour at Lamborghini in Sant'Agata Bolognese is an absolutely hypnotic glimpse into a fantastically oiled machine. Deep dives into hand-built engines and the new MC20 production line dazzle at **Maserati** (maserati.com) in Modena. But at **Museo Horacio Pagani** (pagani.com) in San Cesario sul Panaro, which produces just 40 supercars per year, the stuff of motorsport dreams is made. Each piece of €1.3 to €2.5 million motorised fine art is astonishingly assembled *by hand* – no, really! Every one! – and seeing the action first-hand is as good as it gets for connoisseurs.

A Legend is Born

In Motor Valley, the history of the supercar was born. Over 100 years ago, the Maserati family chose to found their company because of the widespread culture linked to the construction of carriages (first horse-drawn and then motorised). With Enzo Ferrari, more than 30 years later, and then later still with Lamborghini, this tradition gave life to a real industry of companies and specialised artisans that, over time, contributed to creating a unique culture that is today linked to the renowned culinary tradition, art and beauty of the area.

By Horacio Pagani, *Founder & Chief Designer, Pagani Automobili,* @paganiautomobili

28 Side Trip: The Mind of
LUCIO DALLA

MUSIC | POP CULTURE | ART

Kid-in-a-candy-store spectacle awaits at Casa di Lucio Dalla, the Bologna home of one of Italy's most beloved and eccentric musicians. Hidden inside the 15th-century Palazzo Casa Fontana poi Gamberini, this *casa*-museum is a captivating off-the-radar attraction and a thrilling, frozen-in-time memorial to Dalla's fantastical life.

🗺 How to

Getting here/around
Fly to Bologna's Gugliel-mo Marconi Airport. Casa di Lucio Dalla is easily reached on foot once in town.

When to go Tours run Fridays only (adult/reduced €15/10); closed July and August.

Reservations Mandatory via **Fondazione Lucio Dalla** (fondazionelucio dalla.it) or **Bologna Welcome** (bolognawelcome.com).

Taste a lyric Gelato flavour 'Ma l'impresa eccezionale è essere normale' at **Cremeria D'Azeglio** is named from a Dalla lyric.

LUCA SCHILIRÒ/EDT SRL ©

Far left Exterior, Casa di Lucio Dalla **Bottom** Lucio Dalla **Near left** Interior, Casa di Lucio Dalla

Italian legend Despite over four decades of musical output (his extraordinary career wavered between jazz, folk and pop) and being held in the highest esteem of Italian singer-songwriter history, Lucio Dalla, who passed away in 2012, is little known outside of Italy. Within the country, though, his massive popularity cannot be understated nor his eccentric personality outdone. He is the soundtrack of multiple generations.

Cultural cavalcade Casa di Lucio Dalla includes an extraordinary collection of art, including numerous 18th-century Neapolitan nativity scenes and many eyebrow-raising works. The home, more or less untouched since his death, is also crammed with personal artefacts (awards, cigarette cases, pocket watches, musical instruments) and antiques the world over. A tour here is a journey into the mind of a musical genius – *then* you enter Dalla's Fool's Room.

Mesmerising man cave Dalla's 'Stanza dello Scemo' (Fool's Room) at the end of the tour through his Bologna home transports visitors deep into the singer-songwriter's esoteric psyche. A cursory glance focuses on the massive projection screen, the ridiculous toy train and recycled porn cinema seats; a deeper dive, however, reveals a collection of bric-a-brac, provocative art, model cars and carousels, imported furniture and a historic ceiling awash in brilliant frescoes.

🎧 Musical Tears

I adore songs like 'Meri Luis', 'Futura' and 'Le Rondini', but one song, not written by Lucio (but extraordinarily adapted) is very important to me: 'Ayrton'. Lucio had received the song from the author but it wasn't exactly a masterpiece. He said that he would record it anyway and that his version would make me cry. And that is exactly what happened. Once recorded, he brought me to his studio. The music started playing. All of a sudden I was overwhelmed by emotions – it brought tears to my eyes. And I heard Lucio saying, 'I knew it!'

By Gianni Salvioni, *Paris-based producer,* *@giannisalvioni1*

FLORENCE
& TUSCANY

ART | FOOD | WINE

**Experience
Florence
& Tuscany
online**

FLORENCE & TUSCANY
Trip Builder

With its lyrical landscapes, go-slow vibe and sensational *cucina contadina* (farmer's kitchen), the Tuscan experience is in perfect symbiosis with the land. Incredible frescoed churches, world-class art and unmatched Renaissance architecture in the capital Florence are the urban antidote to Tuscany's achingly romantic countryside.

The Apuane Alps

● Massa

● Viareggio

● Lucca

Pisa ●

Pontedera ●

Livorno ●

● Cecina

Ligurian Sea

Gorgona

Discover Etruscan legacy mysteries then stroll along the river Arno in **Pisa** (p176)
🕐 1 day

Capraia

Go dolphin- and whale-spotting on a sailing trip in the **Tuscan Archipelago** (p172)
🕐 1–2 days

Portoferraio

Elba

Golfo di Follonica

Pianosa

CORSICA
(FRANCE)

Tyrrhenian Sea

Montecristo

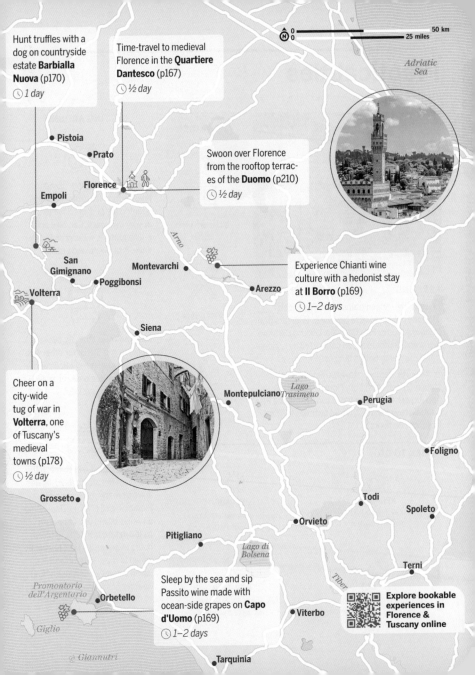

Hunt truffles with a dog on countryside estate **Barbialla Nuova** (p170)
🕐 *1 day*

Time-travel to medieval Florence in the **Quartiere Dantesco** (p167)
🕐 *½ day*

Swoon over Florence from the rooftop terraces of the **Duomo** (p210)
🕐 *½ day*

Experience Chianti wine culture with a hedonist stay at **Il Borro** (p169)
🕐 *1–2 days*

Cheer on a city-wide tug of war in **Volterra**, one of Tuscany's medieval towns (p178)
🕐 *½ day*

Sleep by the sea and sip Passito wine made with ocean-side grapes on **Capo d'Uomo** (p169)
🕐 *1–2 days*

Explore bookable experiences in Florence & Tuscany online

Pistoia

Prato

Florence

Empoli

San Gimignano

Poggibonsi

Volterra

Montevarchi

Arezzo

Arno

Siena

Montepulciano

Lago Trasimeno

Perugia

Foligno

Grosseto

Pitigliano

Todi

Spoleto

Orvieto

Lago di Bolsena

Terni

Promontorio dell'Argentario

Orbetello

Viterbo

Tiber

Giglio

Tarquinia

Giannutri

Adriatic Sea

0 ─ 50 km
0 ─ 25 miles

Practicalities

SALA DI ATTESA

V_E/SHUTTERSTOCK ©

ARRIVING

 Train High-speed trains reach Florence's Stazione di Santa Maria Novella in 1½ hours from Milan and Rome. Pisa Centrale, Livorno Centrale, Siena and Grosseto are all connected by regional trains – a cheap option but prone to delays.

 Airports Trams run to/from Florence's train station (22 minutes) from Florence Airport. From Pisa Airport, PisaMover trains run to Stazione Pisa Centrale (five minutes), linked by trains to/from Florence (1½ hours).

HOW MUCH FOR A

Museum visit
€10

Pici pasta
€15

Aperitivo
€8

WHEN TO GO

APR–JUN
Perfect weather for travelling; possibly crowded.

JUL–AUG
High summer; can be hot inland and too crowded on the coast.

SEP–OCT
With luck, still lovely travelling weather; crowds begin to dwindle.

NOV–MAR
Low season means no queues; not the best weather.

GETTING AROUND

Car and bicycle Undoubtedly the finest option for exploring scenic countryside and small hill towns at your own pace. Car, bike and e-bike rental is widespread in Florence, Pisa, Siena and Lucca.

Bus and train Intercity buses link Florence and Siena; for other Tuscan towns, including Lucca and Pisa, slower Regionale or speedier Intercity trains are best.

Ferries The best way to reach the islands of the archipelago, ferries leave from the main ports of Piombino and Livorno. Depending on which island you're headed to, it can take from one to three hours to arrive. It's best to check ahead to make sure timetables haven't changed because of bad weather or seasonal schedules.

EATING & DRINKING

Bistecca alla fiorentina The icon of Tuscan cuisine, Florence's chargrilled T-bone steak (pictured right) is smeared with olive oil, seared on the chargrill, seasoned and served from rare to well-cooked. Weighed before cooking, hence priced on menus per *l'etto* or 100g.

Soups Tuscany is well-known for its soups, an optimal meal choice for the colder months. Don't skip on the *ribollita* (meaning 'boiled twice'; pictured right), a cabbage, bean and bread soup boiled twice to stay true to its name.

Best tripe panino Trippaio Sergio Pollini (p180)

Must-try white truffles Le Lune (p170)

CONNECT & FIND YOUR WAY

Wi-fi Free wi-fi is widespread. In older hotel buildings – namely thick, stone-walled 15th-century *palazzi* – the connection in rooms can be poor.

Navigation Local tourist offices usually give out maps. Digital ones also work, but they can get confused in little streets and alleys of historical city centres (the same goes for car GPSs). Look out for ZTLs (limited traffic zones), which can lead to steep fines.

WHERE TO STAY

There are several options for where to rest your head in Tuscany, from chic city apartments to decades-old country houses, and each has its own unique vibe.

Place	Pro/Con
Florence	Boutique hotels and stylish B&Bs in historic *palazzi* (mansions); crowded in summer.
San Miniato	*Agriturismi* (farm stays) pepper surrounding hills; you'll need your own wheels.
Lucca	Small walled town with rich accommodation pickings; fills fast in summer and around the Lucca Comics & Games convention.
Chianti	Charming 'wine-country' villas and *agriturismi*; many only open April to September.
Elba	Best scenery of them all; transportation requires accurate planning.

SHOPPING

Most shops in big cities open continuously from morning to evening. In smaller towns and villages shops might close for lunch from around 2pm to 4pm.

MONEY

Be prepared for some places to only accept cash, and keep in mind that ATMs are abundant in cities, a rarity in the countryside. Florence sightseers can save money with a 72-hour **Firenzecard** (firenzecard.it).

29 MEDICI
Florence

RENAISSANCE | ART | HISTORY

With its beguiling tangle of medieval streets, Renaissance *palazzi* and fresco-laced churches, Florence evokes intriguing tales galore. But no story is more compelling than that of the Medicis – a flamboyant, powerful dynasty of bankers who assured Florence's enviable world-standing as cradle of the Renaissance.

🔖 How to

Getting around The authentic way is on foot; don sturdy shoes that you're sure can handle cobblestones.

When to go Spring and late-summer days mean less crowds and bewitching panoramas atop Florence's lookout towers, Palazzo Vecchio's Torre d'Adolfo included.

Top tip Don't miss the Medici walk, aka a stroll along the Corridoio Vasariano, a 1km-long covered passageway allowing the Medici to wander between their palaces (Uffizi and Palazzo Pitti) in privacy and comfort.

Sinner or Saint

Most artists are sinners, not saints. But Tuscan-born friar-painter Fra' Angelico (c 1395–1455) was a brilliant exception – as Cosimo the Elder, cleverly realised. The Medici patriarch's eye for artistic talent and burning desire to earn a place in heaven inspired him to rebuild a 13th-century Dominican monastery in San Marco in 1437 – today's **Museo di San Marco** – and commission the gifted friar to fresco it. Gorge on Fra' Angelico's *Annunciation* (c 1440) and his *Adoration of the Magi* in the cell used by Cosimo as a meditative retreat.

Staircase to Heaven

Inside **Biblioteca Medicea Laurenziana**, within the peaceful cloisters of the Basilica di San Lorenzo (itself one of Florence's

🏛 Gold & Frescoes

The Medicis commissioned art that stole your breathe and intimidated. Imagine you're a 15th-century visitor entering the **Chapel of the Magi** by candlelight. Revel in gold on frescoed walls and let the power wash over you.

By Alexandra Lawrence, *art lecturer and tour guide, exploreflorence.it*

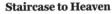

Top left *Adoration of the Magi.* **Bottom left** Fresco by Benozzo Gozzoli, Chapel of the Magi. **Above** *Annunciation.*

most harmonious examples of Renaissance architecture), swoon over the world's most beautiful library staircase, designed by Michelangelo in 1524 for the Medici library, home to over 11,000 manuscripts. The curvaceous sweep of stairs, cut in mellow Pietra Serena sandstone, fills the vestibule – a teeny ante-chamber designed in mannerist style as a dark and sober prelude to the light-flooded Reading Room beyond.

Chapels of Conceit

Nowhere is Medici conceit expressed so explicitly as in the **Cappelle Medicee** (Medici Chapels), burial place to 49 dynasty members. The ostentatious mausoleum drips in granite, marble and dazzling semiprecious stones. Michelangelo's most haunting sculptures are also here: *Dawn and Dusk* on the sarcophagus of Lorenzo II de' Medici (1492–1519); *Night and Day* on the sarcophagus

 ### The Medicis' Uffizi

Primavera (c 1480; Sandro Botticelli) Close-up it encompasses numerous aspects of Medici Florence: gardens, botanicals, mythology, poetry, love, neoplatonism, rebirth, dance.

Suleiman the Magnificent (c 1552–68; Cristofano Altissimo) Cultural exchange with the Islamic world was vital for art and scholarship under the Medicis. The sultan, with his magnificent turban, is hard to miss.

Tribuna (c 1581–83; Buontalenti) This octagonal room is considered the Western world's first museum and reflects Francesco I's interest in alchemy, art and esoteric spaces. Look up to admire some 6000 mother-of-pearl shells.

 By Molly McIlwrath, *Pistoia-based art history and Italian literature expert, tour guide, @vicolodeifuggiti*

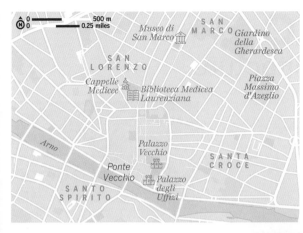

Left Botticelli's *Primavera*, Palazzo degli Uffizi **Below** Ceiling, Salone dei Cinquecento, Palazzo Vecchio

of Lorenzo il Magnifico's youngest son, Giuliano (1478–1516); and *Madonna and Child* on Lorenzo il Magnifico's own incongruously plain tomb.

Celebrating God Cosimo

Immerse yourself into the unabashed glitz of 15th-century Florence at **Palazzo Vecchio**, an imposing fortress-palace built between 1298 and 1314 to house the *signoria* (city government). From 1540 this was the ducal palace of Cosimo I (1519–74), brazenly portrayed as a god on the panelled ceiling in the Salone dei Cinquecento. Swirling battle scenes glorify Florentine victories over arch-rivals Pisa and Siena.

An Art Collection for Eternity

Feast on the world's greatest collection of Italian Renaissance art in the vast U-shaped **Palazzo degli Uffizi**, commissioned by Cosimo I in 1560 to bring all his government *uffizi* (offices) under one roof. The art collection, bequeathed to the city by the Medici family in 1743 on the condition it never leave Florence, contains some of Italy's best-known masterpieces.

DUOMO
Art & Architecture

01 Campanile

The 414-step climb up Giotto's graceful, 85m-tall bell tower rewards with heady views of the entire Duomo ensemble.

02 Brunelleschi's Dome

It took architect and engineer extraordi-naire Filippo Brunelleschi (1377–1446) 27 years to piece together all four-million ter-racotta bricks of Florence cathedral's iconic red dome.

03 The Last Judgement

Hell comes to life on one of the world's largest paintings – frescoed on the Duomo cupola by Giorgio Vasari and Federico Zuccari in 1572–79.

04 The Madonna with Glass Eyes

When bathed in sun-light on the Duomo's 14th-century facade, the spooky eyes of Arnolfo di Cambio's Madonna (Museo dell'Opera del Duomo) shone like human eyes.

05 Donatello's Mary Magdalene

Florentines venerated Donatello's wooden sculpture of a gaunt, desolate Mary Magda-lene in the 15th century

as a female expression of penance (Museo dell'Opera del Duomo).

06 Michelangelo's La Pietà

Michelangelo's sonnet, written while sculpting *La Pietà* (both Room 10, Museo dell'Opera del Duomo) in 1547–50, is as haunting as the artist's sculpture intended for his own funerary ensemble.

07 Baptistery

Babies born in the San Lorenzo parish have been baptised in this Romanesque, green-and-white marble striped baptistery since the 11th century.

08 Door of Paradise

Florentines 'read' Old Testament stories from top to bottom and from left to right on the baptistery's eastern door, Porta del Paradiso (1424–52), sculpted in gilded bronze by Lorenzo Ghiberti.

09 Pisano's South Door

Andrea Pisano's baptistery Porta Sud (1330–46), also safeguarded in the Museo dell'Opera del Duomo, illustrates the life of John the Baptist in exquisite bronze-carved detail.

30 DANTE'S
Commedia

ART | LITERATURE | CULTURE

▬▬▬▬ The impact Dante Alighieri and his *Divine Comedy* have had on Italian culture is indescribable. While there are many cities throughout Italy that carry traces of the life of *il Sommo Poeta* (the Supreme Poet), nowhere else does his spirit feel alive as it does in Florence. From churches to medieval streets, Dante's legacy continues on in his native city.

ZVONIMIR ATLETIC/SHUTTERSTOCK ©

🗺 How to

When to go Year-round. The warmer months will be more packed, as will weekends and public holidays.

Cost Admission fees at churches and museums average about €10, with reductions for students and families.

Food for thought If you need an energy boost during your explorations, stop at **All'Antico Vinaio** (Via dei Neri 65) to enjoy a Dante-inspired *schiacciata*, Tuscany's own focaccia.

NATALY REINCH/SHUTTERSTOCK ©

Far left Statue of Dante, Piazza Santa Croce **Bottom** Casa di Dante **Near left** Portrait of Dante with Divina Commedia by Domenico di Michelino, Santa Maria del Fiore (Duomo)

Alighieri's Florence

Around the city Piazza della Signoria, Orsanmichele, the Torre della Castagna and the Badia Fiorentina mark an area known as the **Quartiere Dantesco** (Dante Neighbourhood). It's the place most likely to still resemble the city Dante knew. This is where most of **Dante's Plaques** are located – 34 in total, quoting tercets from the *Commedia*. In this area you can also find Dante's family home, today a museum aptly named **Casa di Dante** (museocasadidante.it).

Churches It shouldn't be a surprise that several churches feature in the life of someone who wrote about heaven and hell. **Santa Croce** has Dante's famous towering statue and **Santa Maria del Fiore** (the Duomo) a fresco of Dante with his masterpiece that is present on every Italian schoolbook. But the two places Dante saw for himself back in the Middle Ages are the **Baptistery**, where he was baptised (he even mentions it in the XIX canto of the *Inferno*) and **Santa Margherita De' Cerchi**, where Dante married his wife Gemma Donati and met his lifelong muse, Beatrice Portinari.

Events The most iconic Dante-related event is a **Lectura Dantis**, a public reading of the *Commedia* (or a passage from it). The **Società Dantesca Italiana** (dantesca.it) is the best place to check if one is happening soon – it organises them more or less twice a year, even if not on fixed dates.

🥾 Dante's Trail

The cities and villages that have marked Dante's life after he was exiled from Florence in 1302 are connected by a relatively new hiking trail, the **Cammino di Dante** (camminodante. com) – 400km long and crossing all kinds of landscapes from Florence to Ravenna, the city where Dante is buried. Along the trail, curated by volunteers that also offer support and tips to hikers, you'll find seasonal events (especially during the warmer months) like conferences and performances, as well as panels summarising all 100 cantos of the *Commedia* to learn about the poem as you progress through each stop.

31 A Wine Lover's
ROAD TRIP

WINE | COUNTRYSIDE | ROAD TRIP

Wine is one of Tuscany's specialities, and if you're looking to sip on some grape juice, your only problem will be deciding which one – between Chianti, Passito, Brunello and more there's no shortage of options. All that separates you from tastings and cellar visits is a short drive through the countryside.

DIEGOMARIOTTINI/SHUTTERSTOCK ©

FLORENCE & TUSCANY EXPERIENCES

🗺 Trip Notes

Getting around The best way is to rent a car in the city closest to the wine area you want to visit. You'll need a designated driver, of course – or consider hiring a private driver service for this purpose.

When to go The loveliest months are the warmer ones, from mid-April to mid-October. Wine harvesting happens between September and October.

Top tip The tourist information offices in the main cities of Siena (terredisiena. it), Arezzo (arezzoturismo.it), Grosseto (provinciagrosseto.com) and Livorno (turismo.li) can provide detailed information about the area.

🎈 Extreme Pleasures

If you're looking for something a bit more extreme among the vineyards of Tuscany, head to **Avignonesi** (avignonesi.it), where you can book a hot-air balloon flight gliding above the countryside or a Ferrari drive (tastings included – *after* the drive, of course).

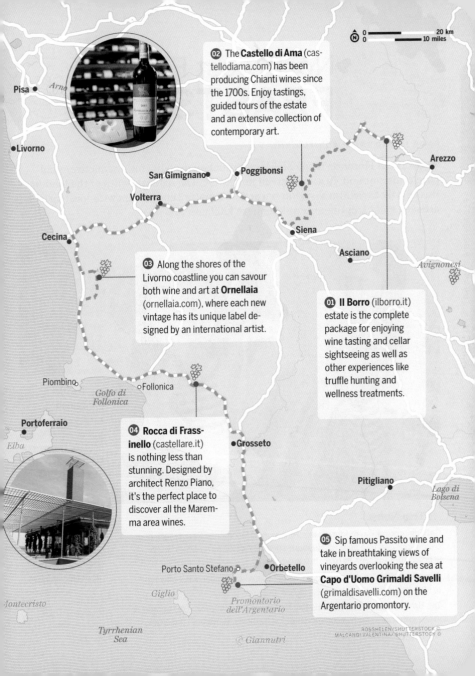

0 20 km
0 10 miles

Pisa

Arno

Livorno

02 The **Castello di Ama** (castellodiama.com) has been producing Chianti wines since the 1700s. Enjoy tastings, guided tours of the estate and an extensive collection of contemporary art.

San Gimignano

Poggibonsi

Arezzo

Volterra

Siena

Cecina

Asciano

Avignonesi

03 Along the shores of the Livorno coastline you can savour both wine and art at **Ornellaia** (ornellaia.com), where each new vintage has its unique label designed by an international artist.

01 **Il Borro** (ilborro.it) estate is the complete package for enjoying wine tasting and cellar sightseeing as well as other experiences like truffle hunting and wellness treatments.

Piombino

Golfo di Follonica

Follonica

Portoferraio

Elba

04 **Rocca di Frassinello** (castellare.it) is nothing less than stunning. Designed by architect Renzo Piano, it's the perfect place to discover all the Maremma area wines.

Grosseto

Pitigliano

Lago di Bolsena

05 Sip famous Passito wine and take in breathtaking views of vineyards overlooking the sea at **Capo d'Uomo Grimaldi Savelli** (grimaldisavelli.com) on the Argentario promontory.

Porto Santo Stefano

Orbetello

Giglio

Promontorio dell'Argentario

Montecristo

Tyrrhenian Sea

Giannutri

32 Northwest Farm **FEASTS**

FOOD | ROAD TRIP | AGRITURISMI

■■■ Ditch Florence, Siena and Pisa's grand-slam sights for a seductive, snail-pace cruise around Tuscany's green northwest. The natural riches of the land in this overtly agricultural region unearth fascinating encounters with local farmers, artisans and exceptional zero-kilometre kitchens.

FRANTIC00/SHUTTERSTOCK ©

🍴 Truffle Lunch

For a storm of white truffles in the Florentine hills, I suggest **Le Lune** (lelunefirenze. it), a farm restaurant in a plant nursery Petersham-style on Florence's Collina di San Domenico that serves white truffles, Chianina beef and other organic products from our farms.

By Guido Manfredi Rasponi, *organic farmer,* @barbialla

🗺 Trip Notes

Getting around Two or four wheels. Hire a car at Florence or Pisa airport, or create your own free-spirited, Hepburn-style Vespa tour by renting a Vespa scooter from **Toscana In Tour** (toscanaintour.it).

When to go Year-round works, but October to mid-December is the only time to hunt truffles.

Top tip Overnight in foodie towns San Miniato or Castelnuovo di Garfagnana, or in an *agriturismo* (farm accommodation) at Barbialla Nuova or Al Benefizio.

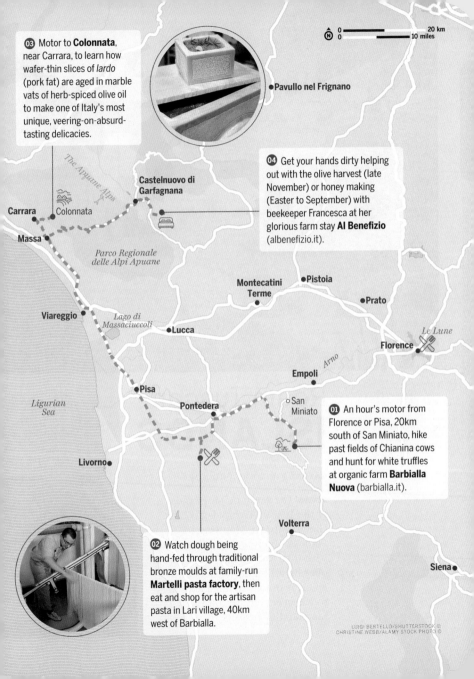

03 Motor to **Colonnata**, near Carrara, to learn how wafer-thin slices of *lardo* (pork fat) are aged in marble vats of herb-spiced olive oil to make one of Italy's most unique, veering-on-absurd-tasting delicacies.

04 Get your hands dirty helping out with the olive harvest (late November) or honey making (Easter to September) with beekeeper Francesca at her glorious farm stay **Al Benefizio** (albenefizio.it).

01 An hour's motor from Florence or Pisa, 20km south of San Miniato, hike past fields of Chianina cows and hunt for white truffles at organic farm **Barbialla Nuova** (barbialla.it).

02 Watch dough being hand-fed through traditional bronze moulds at family-run **Martelli pasta factory**, then eat and shop for the artisan pasta in Lari village, 40km west of Barbialla.

0 — 20 km
0 — 10 miles

N

Pavullo nel Frignano

The Apuane Alps

Castelnuovo di Garfagnana

Carrara • Colonnata

Massa

Parco Regionale delle Alpi Apuane

Montecatini Terme • Pistoia

• Prato

Viareggio

Lago di Massaciuccoli

• Lucca

Le Lune

Florence

Arno

Empoli

Pisa

Pontedera

San Miniato

Ligurian Sea

Livorno

Volterra

Siena

33 Roam Tuscan
ISLANDS

NATURE | ISLANDS | CULTURE

▬▬▬ The seven major islands of the Tuscan Archipelago (Elba, Giglio, Capraia, Montecristo, Pianosa, Giannutri and Gorgona), with their court of islets and reefs, offer breathtaking scenery and an array of nature-filled activities to whoever ventures off the mainland of Tuscany.

🗺 How to

Getting here The most common way to reach the islands is by ferry. Multiple companies sail out of Piombino, Livorno and Porto Santo Stefano, as well as Portoferraio on Elba (for the smaller islands). Travel times range from one to three hours; prices are from around €10 per

person (with reductions for children). It's always a good idea to check timetables beforehand since they can change according to season and weather.

When to go Summer months are the loveliest, but if you want to avoid extreme heat go in late spring or early autumn.

Out of the History Books

The Isle of Elba is the third-biggest island in Italy after Sicily and Sardinia and the largest in the Tuscan Archipelago. Its name might summon the spirit of Napoleon Bonaparte as it was the location chosen for the French emperor's (first) exile. His passage on the island can be easily traced, especially in the palaces that he used as residences – the **Palazzina dei Mulini** (Piazzale Napoleone) and the **Villa San Martino** (Via di San Martino), both in Portoferraio, Elba's main town. Not far from the *palazzina* is the **Spiaggia delle Viste**, where Napoleon escaped to return to France for his final 100 days.

🍴 Island Food

The archipelago's cuisine is rich in seafood, unique sweets and local wines. According to experts from the Parco Nazionale Arcipelago Toscano (islepark.it), **Rio nell'Elba** is the place to go to try typical dishes like *sburrita* (salted cod soup) and the raisin-and-pine-nut cake *schiaccia briaca*.

Natural Haven

There are heaps of outdoor activities to choose from once you disembark on Elba, starting

Top left Palazzina dei Mulini, Elba.
Bottom left *Schiaccia briaca*.
Above Villa San Martino, Elba.

with the many hiking trails for all expertise levels that lead to inland villages, sanctuaries and lighthouses. From Rio nell'Elba, for example, you can trek up to the **Hermitage of St Catherine**, which hosts a huge collection of flora as well as bee colonies. On the **'Granite Trail'**, beginning and ending in San Piero, you can discover the history of mining on Elba as well as enjoy stunning views of the other archipelago islands. For something a little more unconventional, try an excursion with donkeys (somareriadellelba.com), the island's ancient transportation mode, or dive in the waters that surround Elba for a wide variety of immersions for both amateurs and professionals, like the wreckage of the MS *Elviscot* off the shores of Pomonte. For more ideas check out visitelba.info.

Count's Domain

One of the most fascinating of the smaller archipelago islands is **Montecristo**, south of

☆ Animal Watching

The entire Tuscan Archipelago is also a national park protecting the unique environment of the islands. Because of this, there are few better places in Italy to catch sight of some fascinating fauna. You could dive in the waters around Giglio to see the red gorgon starfish, or climb to the top of Mt Serra on Elba to count birds of prey. The national park also falls within the Pelagos Sanctuary for Cetaceans and going out to sea to go dolphin- and whale-watching is an exciting adventure to add to any visit to these islands. You can check out details at the Elba-based **Marelibero association** (asdmarelibero.org).

Left Sealife around Elba
Below Pianosa

Elba. Its name brings to mind the 19th-century classic *The Count of Montecristo*, by French writer Alexandre Dumas, and the island does feature in the novel as the place where the protagonist obtains a fortune that allows him to set his revenge in motion. But it's not just its literary fame that makes this tiny island so unique – it's its elusiveness. As a natural reserve, access to Montecristo is highly regulated and only 2000 visitors per year can gain permission to visit the island (islepark.it/visitare-il-parco/montecristo). The waiting list is years long, but this secluded gem is worth the wait and planning.

Smaller Pleasures

The three smallest islands of the archipelago are Pianosa, Giannutri and Gorgona. You can explore **Pianosa** via land, with mountain bike and bus tours, or via sea paddling a kayak along its easternmost shoreline. **Giannutri** and **Gorgona** are perfect for hiking. Transport to Giannutri is available during the warm season, allowing you to roam the island and soak in its landscapes. Visits to Gorgona, on the other hand, are strictly regulated since the island is one of the last European penal colonies and is under the jurisdiction of the Penitentiary Police – hikers have to book in advance and walk a preplanned route with a guide (parcoarcipelago.info).

34 Pisa Beyond
MIRACLES

ARCHITECTURE | HISTORY | CULTURE

Just about the whole world knows Pisa for its leaning tower, located in the (evocatively but not accurately named) white-marbled Piazza dei Miracoli. But there's much more to this once merchant republic than its Unesco World Heritage Site – an array of art, science, history and architecture are waiting to be discovered.

How to

Getting here Pisa is easily reachable by train from most major Italian stations.

When to go To avoid the summer heat (and some of the major crowds), consider a visit in April, May or September.

Searching for snacks The chickpea-filled focaccia-like *cecina* is one of the staples of Pisa cuisine. You can find it all around the city; try **Il Montino** (Via Monte 1) or **Al Bagno di Nerone** (Largo Parlascio 26).

Uncovering antiquities

Like many Tuscan cities, Pisa was Etruscan before it was Roman. These mysterious people of unknown origin have left one of their most stunning burial sites right on the outskirts of Pisa – the striking **Tomb of the Etruscan Prince** (Via San Jacopo 183). Another unique Pisa feature is its **ring of walls**, the best preserved in Italy, with plenty of trails for visitors to follow (muradipisa.it).

Science hub Pisa saw the birth of several scientists, among whom the greatest are definitely mathematician Leonardo Fibonacci and

Top right Campo Santo, Piazza dei Miracoli **Bottom right** Lungarni

◎ The Miracles

The official name of **Piazza dei Miracoli** (Miracle Square) is Piazza del Duomo. Poet Gabriele D'Annunzio invented the more lyrical name in the early 1910s – inspired by the square's four medieval buildings (the Duomo, the Campanile, the Baptistery and the Monumental Cemetery) – and it stuck. The most famous of the buildings is the Campanile, the bell tower, also known as the **Leaning Tower of Pisa**.

astronomer Galileo Galilei. The former's famous Fibonacci Sequence is said to be immortalised in one of the lunettes above the entrance of the **Church of St Nicholas** (Via Santa Maria 2), where diameters and circumferences of the inlay work follow the first numbers. The latter's house can be found at Via Giuseppe Giusti 2, while both of their tombs are located inside the **Campo Santo** at Piazza dei Miracoli.

Living city To enjoy some local nightlife head for the **Lungarni**, the quays skirting the river Arno, where there's a multitude of bars and little restaurants you can stop by for an *aperitivo*. The same goes for **Piazza delle Vettovaglie** and **Piazza Garibaldi**, both beloved spots to start an evening.

35 MEDIEVAL
Town Crawl

CULTURE | ARCHITECTURE | ROAD TRIP

History has always felt real and present in Italy, and the medieval cities of Tuscany are no exception. With their towers and narrow cobbled streets, they offer breathtaking views from a past that is very much cherished and kept alive. All you need to do is choose which one you'd like to visit first.

ARKANTO/SHUTTERSTOCK ©

🗺 Trip Notes

Getting around Bigger cities are reachable by train; for smaller towns, the best option is renting a car (San Gimignano is also served by a dedicated bus line from Siena).

Nerd stop If you're travelling towards late October and are a pop culture fan, don't miss **Lucca Comics & Games**. One of the biggest conventions in the world, it's held in the picturesque setting of the Renaissance city of Lucca.

🏰 Straight for the Castle

If you want to indulge in medieval nobility, visit one of the many ancient castles Tuscany has to offer, such as **Nozzano Castello** (pictured), just outside Lucca; **Spedaletto**, a stop along the pilgrimage route from Canterbury to Rome; or one of the many more listed on **Castelli Toscani** (castelli toscani.com).

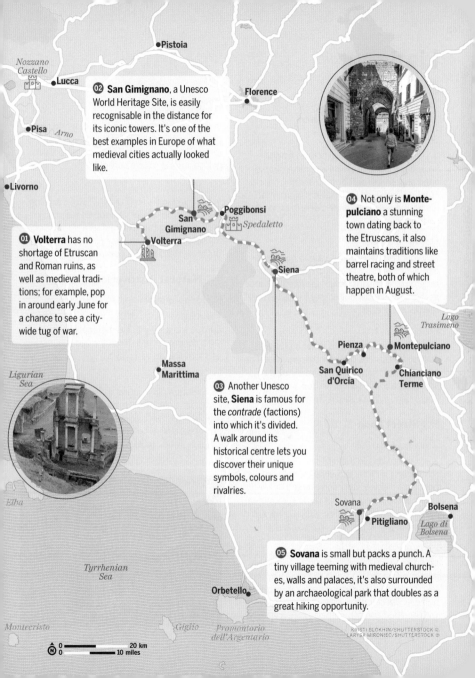

Pistoia

Nozzano Castello

Lucca

02 San Gimignano, a Unesco World Heritage Site, is easily recognisable in the distance for its iconic towers. It's one of the best examples in Europe of what medieval cities actually looked like.

Florence

Pisa *Arno*

Livorno

San Gimignano

Poggibonsi

Spedaletto

01 Volterra has no shortage of Etruscan and Roman ruins, as well as medieval traditions; for example, pop in around early June for a chance to see a city-wide tug of war.

Volterra

Siena

04 Not only is **Monte-pulciano** a stunning town dating back to the Etruscans, it also maintains traditions like barrel racing and street theatre, both of which happen in August.

Lago Trasimeno

Ligurian Sea

Massa Marittima

Pienza

Montepulciano

San Quirico d'Orcia

Chianciano Terme

03 Another Unesco site, **Siena** is famous for the *contrade* (factions) into which it's divided. A walk around its historical centre lets you discover their unique symbols, colours and rivalries.

Elba

Sovana

Bolsena

Lago di Bolsena

Pitigliano

05 Sovana is small but packs a punch. A tiny village teeming with medieval churches, walls and palaces, it's also surrounded by an archaeological park that doubles as a great hiking opportunity.

Tyrrhenian Sea

Orbetello

Montecristo

Giglio

Promontorio dell'Argentario

KRISTI BLOKHIN/SHUTTERSTOCK ©, LARYSA MIRONIEC/SHUTTERSTOCK ©

0 — 20 km
0 — 10 miles

Listings

BEST OF THE REST

Handmade in Florence

Benheart

In the finest of Florentine artisan tradition, shoe designer Ben crafts exquisite double-lined shoes with soft buffalo leather, hand-stitched and dyed with natural pigments. Find his boutiques in Florence's *centro storico* (historic centre).

Manifattura Tabacchi

Cut your own four-minute audio postcard – digital or vinyl – at Loudlift, a self-operating recording studio on an upcycled elevator at this 1930s tobacco factory turned experimental art centre.

Lorenzo Villoresi

Laurel, cypress, olive and other distinctive Tuscan fragrances blend with exotic essences from around the world to form exquisite scents at this artisan workshop, showroom and museum in a 15th-century *palazzo*.

🚚 Street Food

Trippaio Sergio Pollini   €

Join Florentines at the city's busiest *trippaio* (tripe cart) for a tripe *panino* (sandwich). Expect boiled cow's stomach bunged between bread and doused in *salsa verde* (pea-green sauce of smashed parsley, garlic, capers and anchovies).

Il Magnifico   €

Lorenzo Rossi is Siena's best baker, and his *panforte* (spiced fruit-and-nut cake), *ricciarelli* (sugar-dusted chewy almond biscuits) and *cavallucci* (chewy biscuits flavoured with aniseed and other spices) are a weekly purchase for most local households.

Gelateria Dondoli   €

In San Gimignano, former gelato world champion Sergio Dondoli is famed far and wide for his Crema di Santa Fina (saffron cream) gelato and Vernaccia sorbet.

I Salaioli   €€

In the handsome small town Pistoia, an easy train ride from Florence, foodies inevitably end up raiding this deli-restaurant for delectable salami wedges, cheese rounds and other titillating bites to take home.

🌿 Natural Discoveries

Parco Nazionale Arcipelago Toscano

The magical island of Elba pierces the heart of Europe's largest marine national park protecting a delicate ecosystem of seven islands and islets off the Tuscan coast.

Val d'Orcia

Picturesque agricultural valley in central Tuscany, protected as a Unesco World Heritage Site. Magnificent abbeys, flat chalk plains, pretty Renaissance towns and world-class wines only add to its natural appeal.

Val d'Orcia

Parco Regionale della Maremma

This spectacular regional park protects pine forests, marshy plains, pristine coastline and a maze of walking trails. Canoeing, horse riding and mountain- or e-biking are also wildly popular.

Apuane Alps

White marble, rather than snow, caps these dramatic mountain peaks around the mining town of Carrara and its famously foodie side-kick, the weeny village of Colonnata.

Traditional Tuscan

Il Leccio	€€

Watch the chef flit between stove and kitchen garden at this sensational trattoria in Brunello country, 10km southwest of Montalcino in Sant-Angelo in Colle.

Essenziale	€€€

Traditional Tuscan dishes provide the inspiration for the inventive, modern cuisine of brilliant young Florence chef Simone Cipriani. His alfresco summertime pop-ups and winter loft-style dining are equally unforgettable.

Sergio Falaschi	€

Forge your way to the back of this 1920s ceramic-tiled *macelleria* (butcher's shop) in Slow Food town San Miniato to feast on feisty dishes starring local Chianina beef, *mallegato* (blood sausage) and *cinta senese* (indigenous Tuscan pork from Siena).

Osteria dei Cavalieri	€€

Tripe, bone marrow stuffed with saffron-spiced rice, and handsome blue T-bone steaks are among the staunchly Tuscan favourites cooked up at this classic Pisa restaurant. End with lemon sorbet soaked in prosecco.

Il Castagnacciaio	€

An Elbese rite of passage when in Porto-ferraio. A lip-smacking plate of *torta di ceci* (chickpea pizza) followed by *castagnaccio*

Marble quarry, Apuane Alps

(chestnut cake) are *the* dishes to order at this frenetic eatery near the port.

Great Gardens

Il Giardino di Daniel Spoerri

Southern Tuscany squirrels away this eclectic sculpture garden – 16 hectares peppered with thought-provoking art installations by dozens of international artists.

Giardino Torrigiani

In Florence, trade the busy Boboli gardens for this clandestine oasis of centurion elegance – Europe's largest privately owned green space within a historic town centre.

Orto de' Pecci

Uncover sweet Tuscan peace, tranquillity, an organic farm, a medieval garden, a farm-to-table restaurant and an experimental vineyard in this urban garden in Siena.

Vignamaggio

Reserve a slot in advance at these cinematic formal gardens in Chianti, star of Kenneth Branagh's film adaptation of *Much Ado About Nothing*.

Scan to find more things to do in Florence & Tuscany online

NAPLES &
THE SOUTH

RUINS | OUTDOORS | FOOD

Experience
Naples &
the South
online

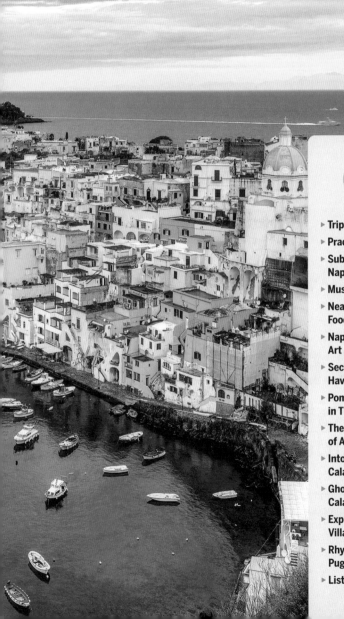

Caserta

Nola

Naples

Pozzuoli

Pompeii

Ischia

Sorrento

Capri
Town

Salerno

Avellino

Battipaglia

Potenza

Agropoli

Parco Nazionale
del Cilento e
Vallo di Diano

Parco Nazional
Dell'appennino
Lucano

Lagonegro

Golfo di
Policastro

Maratea

Scalea

Paola

Tropea

Golfo di
Gioia

Scilla

Messina

Sicily

Reggio di
Calabria

Amalfi Coast

*Golfo di
Salerno*

*Tyrrhenian
Sea*

Enjoy the slow life on
the tranquil island of
Procida (p197)
🕐 2 days

Admire ancient art
and baroque beauty in
Naples (p188)
🕐 2–3 days

Marvel at the ethereal
light of Capri's **Grotta
Azzurra** (p210)
🕐 1 day

Walk in the footsteps of
the ancients at **Pompeii**
(p198)
🕐 1 day

Marvel at the magnif-
icent Bronzi di Riace
in **Reggio di Calabria**
(p213)
🕐 1 day

NAPLES & THE SOUTH
Trip Builder

Take in cultural masterpieces, wild natural
beauty and sublime food in Italy's sun-baked south.
From Naples' historic streets to Pompeii's haunting
ruins, from spectacular Amalfi Coast seascapes to
Calabria's mountainous national parks, thrills await
at every turn.

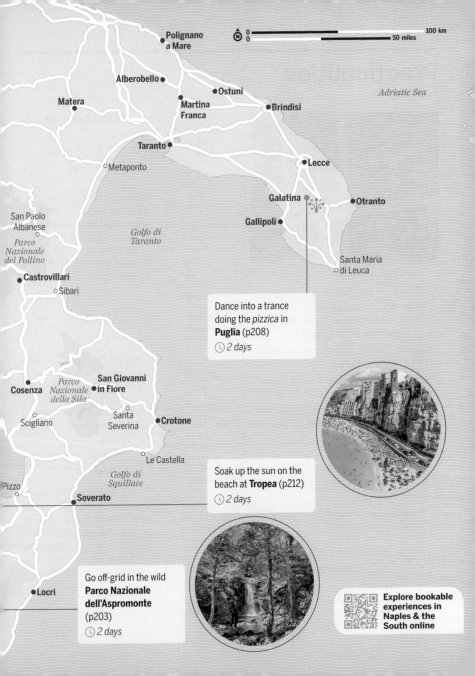

Polignano a Mare

Alberobello

Matera

Martina Franca

Ostuni

Brindisi

Adriatic Sea

Taranto

Metaponto

Lecce

Galatina

Otranto

San Paolo Albanese

Gallipoli

Parco Nazionale del Pollino

Golfo di Taranto

Santa Maria di Leuca

Castrovillari

Sibari

Dance into a trance doing the *pizzica* in **Puglia** (p208)
🕐 *2 days*

Cosenza

Parco Nazionale della Sila

San Giovanni in Fiore

Scigliano

Santa Severina

Crotone

Le Castella

Golfo di Squillace

Pizzo

Soverato

Soak up the sun on the beach at **Tropea** (p212)
🕐 *2 days*

Go off-grid in the wild **Parco Nazionale dell'Aspromonte** (p203)
🕐 *2 days*

Locri

Explore bookable experiences in Naples & the South online

0 —— 100 km
0 —— 50 miles
N

Practicalities

GIANNIS PAPANIKOS/SHUTTERSTOCK ©

ARRIVING

 Naples International Airport (Capodichino) Just 7km out of town and connected to the centre by the Alibus (€5).

 Stazione Centrale Naples' main train station. City buses depart from Piazza Garibaldi outside.

 Lamezia Terme Airport For Calabria. Buses run to regional cities and Lamezia Terme Centrale.

 Bari Karol Wojtyla Airport Puglia's main hub. Southeast, Brindisi airport is nearer the Salento.

HOW MUCH FOR A

Pizza margherita from €4

Gelato €2–5

Capri ferry ticket €22

GETTING AROUND

Buses Useful in Naples and for getting to/from the Amalfi Coast's main towns and villages. Elsewhere, you can get to most places by bus but services are scarce in remote inland areas and infrequent on Sundays.

Trains The Circumvesuviana train is the best way of getting from Naples to Pompeii and Sorrento. In Calabria, trains serve the main cities and towns on the Tyrrhenian and Ionian coasts.

Driving The best way of getting around inland areas and reaching small towns and villages, especially in Calabria's sparsely populated mountains. Roads can be narrow and bumpy, and parking can be a headache in towns and cities.

WHEN TO GO

APR–MAY

Sunny spring weather; ideal for hiking and many special events.

JUN–AUG

Scorching summer heat. Crowds on the coast, quieter in Naples.

SEP–OCT

Still warm enough for the beach; good for autumnal foraging.

NOV–MAR

Coldest, wettest time of year; possible snow in the mountains.

EATING & DRINKING

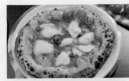

Pizza Keep it real in Naples, the birthplace of pizza, with a wood-fired pizza margherita or marinara. Try the pizzerias in the *centro storico* for an authentic Neapolitan experience.

Cheese and salami Campania is famous for its buffalo mozzarella while Puglia boasts superb *caciocavallo* (a semi-hard cheese). Calabria's headline act is *'nduja* (pictured right), a spreadable salami spiked with chillies.

Seafood Sample mussels *(cozze)*, octopus *(polpo)*, swordfish *(pesce spada)*, anchovies *(alici)* and tuna *(tonno)*.

Must-try pizza Pizzeria Gino Sorbillo (p211)

Best for tartufo gelato Bar Gelateria Ercole (p211)

CONNECT & FIND YOUR WAY

Wi-fi Free wi-fi is generally available in holiday accommodation but signal quality can be patchy, particularly in remote inland areas.

Navigation You'll find tourist offices in Naples and towns throughout the area. All can provide maps and local information. English is generally spoken in larger towns and major tourist areas but not always in smaller offices.

DISCOUNT CARDS

The **Campania Artecard** (campaniartecard.it) covers public transport and free and reduced price entry to cultural sites in Naples and Campania.

WHERE TO STAY

Accommodation is widely available across the region, ranging from luxury hotels to B&Bs, family-run *pensioni*, guesthouses and self-catering apartments. Prices skyrocket on the coast in July and August.

Place	Pro/Con
Naples	Options abound; the historic centre boasts atmosphere, Santa Lucia offers seafront style.
Lecce	Ideal base for the Salento with wonderful B&Bs, smart hotels and chic country retreats.
Parco Nazionale della Sila	Hotels, guesthouses and rustic B&Bs; main hubs are Camigliatello Silano and San Giovanni in Fiore.
Positano	Swish hotels and cheerful guesthouses; dreamy Amalfi Coast views; expensive.
Sorrento	From hotels to hostels, a wide choice. Books up fast in July and August.
Tropea	Top summer destination with everything from luxury resort hotels to B&Bs.

MONEY

Save money by stocking up on picnic provisions at delis and sticking to pizza when eating out. Save on accommodation costs by staying inland, in family-run B&Bs or country *agriturismi*. Avoid August.

36 Subterranean **NAPLES**

HISTORY | CATACOMBS | RUINS

Hidden beneath Naples' highly charged streets is a thrilling underworld of tunnels, Greek grottoes, early Christian tombs, catacombs and ancient ruins. Since the end of WWII, some 700 cavities have been discovered in the city's tufa-rock *sottosuolo* (underground) but experts reckon this is only the tip of the iceberg with another 2 million sq metres still to be unearthed.

FABIO MICHELE CAPELLI/SHUTTERSTOCK ©

🏛 **How to**

Getting here Take the metro to Dante for sites in the historic centre; for the catacombs, take bus R4 or 178 to Via Capodimonte.

Tours Visits to underground sites are by guided tour only, so book ahead if you want an English-speaking guide.

Cost Reckon on at least €9/5 per adult/child for a tour.

Clothes Even in hot weather, take a sweater as it gets cold down below.

SVETLANA JAFAROVA/SHUTTERSTOCK ©

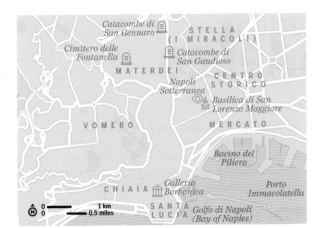

Top left Catacombe di San Gennaro
Bottom left Galleria Borbonica

Catacombs and cemeteries Naples' most famous catacombs run through the soft tufa rock beneath the Capodimonte hill. The **Catacombe di San Gennaro** are named after the city's patron saint who was buried in them from the 5th to 9th centuries. Frescoes and mosaics adorn the two-level complex whose dark tunnels contain around 3000 *hypogea* (tombs) as well as two underground churches.

Nearby, millions of human bones litter the ghoulish **Cimitero delle Fontanella** and the **Catacombe di San Gaudiosa**, Naples' second largest catacombs, extend beneath the Basilica di Santa Maria della Sanità.

Tunnels Venture under the Dickensian streets of the *centro storico* and you'll discover a rabbit warren of aqueducts, passages and cisterns. Originally dug by the Greeks to extract tufa rock for construction, this subterranean labyrinth was enlarged by the Romans and later used as an air-raid shelter in WWII. Nowadays, it's visitable through **Napoli Sotterranea**.

Another accessible tunnel system is the **Galleria Borbonica**, which was conceived in the mid-1800s to link Palazzo Reale with the sea. It was built into a 17th-century aqueduct system which itself incorporated 16th-century cisterns.

Buried cities One of Naples' finest medieval churches, the **Basilica di San Lorenzo Maggiore** (laneapolissotterrata.it) stands above a thrilling complex of underground ruins. Some of the most impressive survive from a 1st- to 2nd-century BCE *macellum* (market).

♡ A Message of Hope

Among the artworks in the Catacombe di San Gennaro, three stand out.

One, on the tomb of a mother and daughter, is the oldest existing image of San Gennaro. Another, a visitor favourite, shows the family Theotecnus 'like a 2000-year-old family photo'. The third, a beautiful mosaic depicting the African bishop Quodvultdeus, sends an important message of hope and acceptance.

Quodvultdeus was one of those Africans who arrived in Naples in the 5th century. They were persecuted in their own land so put to sea and eventually reached Naples where they were met with a great welcome.

By Vincenzo Porzio, *guide, Cooperativa La Paranza,* catacombedinapoli.it

37 Musical
NAPLES

NIGHTLIFE | CULTURE | PIAZZAS

Come to Naples for the pizza; stay for its eclectic and innovative underground music scene. You're spoiled for choice here for unforgettable musical experiences, whether it's dancing to house music at a beach club, catching a raging rap concert in the piazza, or wandering through a streetside singalong of 'O sole mio'. Here's our easy-listening guide to musical Naples.

ANGELAFOTO/GETTY IMAGES ©

How to

When to go Year-round, but especially from spring to autumn. Night shows start after 10pm.

Cost Musical events held at bars or in smaller piazzas are often free. Kick in for the band fees by buying a couple of rounds.

Lost in translation The Neapolitan music scene is all about diversity and originality. Even if you've never heard of the performers and can't understand the words, the energy is contagious.

MOHSINKHAWARPHOTOGRAPHY/GETTY IMAGES ©

Far left, bottom and near left Street musicians, Naples

Popular Music

Neapolitan folk You've definitely heard traditional Neapolitan *musica popolare* before; folk songs like 'Funiculì funiculà' are beloved worldwide. And they're still a huge part of modern Neapolitan identity, even if they were written over 100 years ago. Follow the accordions and tambourines to the historic city centre, or to the postcard towns dotting the coast, like **Sorrento** and **Massa Lubrense**, where you'll hear Neapolitan folk music at local festivals or in the piazzas.

Big acts Head to **La Casa della Musica** (new.palapartenope. it) to see international artists, as well as Neapolitan talents who've broken into the mainstream.

Piazza power Naples is hot – both when it comes to the weather and to passions – so some of the best music happens outdoors. **Piazza del Plebiscito** is Naples' quintessential piazza for live music, and you're bound to find someone playing in **Piazza Dante**, **Vomero**, **Via Benedetto Croce** or **Via Roma**, even if it's just a lone guitarist strumming Pino Daniele covers or a funky street band.

Let's dance Naples has an explosive house, trance and trap movement. Head to the Agnano, Flegrea and Fuorigrotta-Bagnoli areas, where you'll find *discoteche* like **Arenile di Bagnoli** (areniledibagnoli.it) on the beach. Hot DJ sets will get you on your feet.

 **Summer Music Festivals**

Pomigliano Jazz Festival
A fixture of the Neapolitan music festival scene since 1996, the late-summer Pomigliano Jazz Festival hosts world-class jazz acts. Musical and theatrical events are held in different spectacular outdoor spaces, like the Vesuvian Crater or the Roman Amphitheater in Avella. (pomiglianojazz. com)

Noisy Naples Fest
Arena Flegrea is home to this series of 'urban noise' concerts and theatrical performances. Local and internationally acclaimed acts. June and July. (noisynaplesfest.com)

Newroz
This musical festival showcases genres from hip-hop to indie to rock. It unfolds over several days in mid-July. (Via Mezzocannone 12)

38 Neapolitan
STREET FOOD

FOOD | TRADITION | PIZZA FRITTA

Neapolitan cuisine is adored throughout the world, but some of its most delicious dishes come from a cart and are eaten by hand. Here's a guide to Naples' best traditional street foods and where to get them. A stroll through the city's neighbourhoods has a whole other flavour when you've got *pizza fritta* in one hand and *taralli* in the other.

STESILVERS/SHUTTERSTOCK ©

📖 Trip Notes

Getting here Many of Naples' best street-food experiences are concentrated in the neighbouring areas of Spaccanapoli, Via dei Tribunali and San Gregorio Armeno. Also try Fuorigrotta and Via Toledo.

Walk You'll need to make room!

Cost No more than a few euro a pop.

Be prepared Queues at the popular stands or pizzerias like Da Michele and Sorbillo can run hours long, especially on weekends.

✕ Something Sweet

Dessert time! *Sfogliatella* (pictured) is the ultimate Neapolitan pastry, coming in two varieties: *riccia* (flaky) and *frolla* (smooth). Try both at **Antico Forno delle Sfogliatelle Calde Fratelli Attanasio**, or Galleria Umberto's historic **Sfogliatella Mary**. Cap things off at **Pasticceria Artigianale Salvatore Capparelli** with a *babà au rhum*, a rum-soaked cake.

05 Just 450m on to **Antica Pizza e Friggitoria di Matteo** (Via dei Tribunali 94) for *pizza fritta*. Deep-fried pizza pockets stuffed with ingredients like ricotta and *cicoli* (fatty pork cracklings).

04 Now you're just 350m away from some *taralli 'nzogna e pepe* (peppery ring-shaped crackers) at **Taralleria Napoletana** (Via San Biagio Dei Librai 3).

01 Start in **Montesanto**, and hit the **Pescheria Azzurra** (Via Porta-medina) fish market for a *cuoppo di pesce* – a paper cone heaped with crispy fried seafood.

03 Walk 800m east on Spaccanapoli to **Tandem d'asporto** (Via Mezzacannone 75) and snag another beloved Neapolitan street food: the *cuzzetiello* (a baguette filled with Neapolitan-style *ragù*).

02 Head 130m east to **Pigna-secca** street market; **Friggitoria Fiorenzano** (Via Pignasecca 48) serves delicious *zeppole* (fried dough) and *frittatine di pasta* (pasta croquettes).

0 — 200 m
0 — 0.1 miles

Piazza Cavour
Piazza Museo
Vico Cinquesanti
Vico Giganti
Via dei Tribunali
Via Enrico Pessina
Via San Biagio dei Librai (Spaccanapoli)
Vico S. Severino
Via Nilo
Via San Sebastiano
Via Benedetto Croce (Spaccanapoli)
Via G. Paladino
Via Mezzacannone
Via D. Capitelli
Piazza Gesù Nuovo
Via Santa Chiara
Via Portamedina
Via Pasquale Scura
Via S. Anna dei Lombardi
TOLEDO
Via Pignasecca

NAPLES
Metro Art

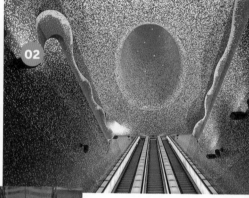

01 Walking, Waiting
Life-size images of passengers walking or waiting for the train, silkscreened onto mirrored panels.

02 Under the Sea
An unforgettable sea-floor-hued mosaic installation, complete with waves and a light show. (*Crater de luz/ Olas/Relative Light*, Toledo Station, Linea 1; and *Stazione*, Garibaldi Station, Linea 1)

03 Together Forever
Two staircases with colourful portraits of historic lovers, Dante and Beatrice. (*Dante e Beatrice*, Università Station, Linea 1)

04 Tribute
A mixed media tribute to the workers who built the train stations. (*Men at Work*, Toledo Station, Linea 1)

05 Fly High
This installation of people flying like birds brightens the dark subway tunnels. (*The Flying – Le tre finestre*, Toledo Station, Linea 1)

06 Minoan Dancers
A mosaic depicting a mountain landscape

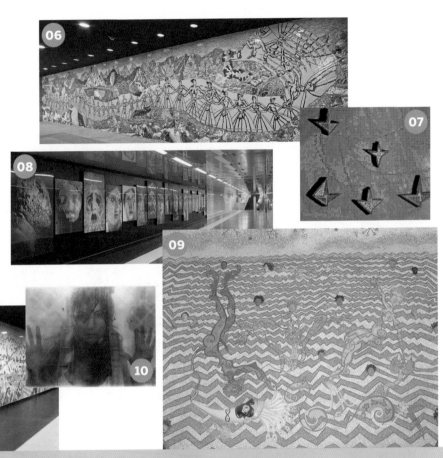

with female figures, evoking dancers from the Minoan period. (*Engiadina,* Toledo Station, Linea 1)

07 World Peace

Geometric shapes dancing against a blue background. (*Universo senza bombe, regno dei fiori,*

7 angeli rossi, Dante Station, Linea 1)

08 Mediterranean Origins

Eighteen black-and-white photographs of marble and mosaic faces examining the origins of Mediterranean culture. (*Anamnesi,* Museo Station, Linea 1)

09 Scugnizzi

Neapolitan street children, mythical creatures and Pulcinella frolic in the sea. (*Spulcinellando, Sguazzando, Scugnizzando,* Station Materdei, Linea 1, Station Atrium)

10 Dreams

Artist Betty Bee peers through a light box against clouds trapped in nets. (*Senza Titolo,* Quattro Giornate Station, Linea 1)

39 Secret Coastal **HAVENS**

VIEWS | CLIFFS | TURQUOISE SEAS

The Amalfi Coast, Ischia and Capri are on literally everyone's bucket list. But if you're looking for a real insider Amalfi Coast experience, consider heading to one of its many hidden beaches and Procida, its untapped island. Stroll medieval villages, visit natural reserves, and bask in (nearly) private turquoise sea paradises surrounded by dramatic cliffs. Here's a quick how-to guide.

ERI MORITA/GETTY IMAGES ©

🗺 **How to**

To the beach(es) A scooter or boat shuttle from Amalfi's Pennello port (€2) are your best bet; public transit (sitasudtrasporti.it) can be unreliable and parking difficult to find.

When to go Try May, June and September. The peak

summer months (July, August) are sweltering and crowded.

Cost The hidden beaches are free or have free areas; rent equipment from the *lidi*. Scooter rental costs €70 per day (positano.com).

Top tip Be prepared to hike long flights of steps.

PIEROPOMA/SHUTTERSTOCK ©

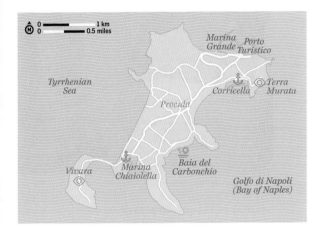

Top left Corricella, Procida **Bottom left** *Spaghetti ai ricci di mare*

Authentic Italian Island Life

Best-kept secret You won't find thumping nightlife and staged tourist traps on the colourful fishing island of **Procida**, as it's only opened up to tourists in recent years. What you will find is a truly authentic, truly relaxing, Italian island experience. Get there by ferry or hydrofoil; artsy Procida is less than an hour away from Naples and Pozzuoli.

Crystal waters Take a boat tour to admire the island's coastline and its surrounding waters. Swim, dive or snorkle in crystal-clear **Baia del Carbonchio**, or visit the tiny island of **Vivara**, a natural reserve connected to Procida by bridge to admire Mediterranean birds and flora.

Island architecture On the island, head up to the **Terra Murata**, Procida's walled medieval quarter, and see its many exquisite churches, like the **Abbazia San Michele Arcangelo**. Then visit the fishing bay of **Corricella**, where you'll find rows of charming colourful houses.

Giant lemons and fresh fish End your day with dinner at **Marina Chiaiolella**, with its many excellent restaurants and sweeping views of the gulf. Try Procida's famous *insalata di limone* – made with the soft white rind of Procida's giant lemons – and treat yourself to a plate of *spaghetti ai ricci di mare* (sea urchin spaghetti). Look out across the gulf as you sip your *limoncello* (lemon liqueur) and watch the sun sink into the sea.

Escape to Hidden Beaches

Fiordo di Furore An inlet beach crowned by an arched bridge. Find the steps leading down to this dreamy refuge from reality at SS163 km 23. Get there early: the sun disappears by lunchtime.

Spiaggia Santa Croce You can only reach this craggy corner of paradise by boat shuttle. There are two *lidi* with restaurants. Pebbly beach, glass-like water.

Il Duoglio The boat shuttle stops here, too, but if you're feeling vigorous, walk from the entry point on SS163 (Via Mauro Comite). It's 400 steps down, but the crystalline water and cliffside scenery are worth it.

Pompeii: Frozen in Time

ARCHAEOLOGICAL GIFT THAT KEEPS GIVING

With Mt Vesuvius brooding darkly on the horizon, Pompeii's sprawling ruins are an electrifying sight. Extensive and brilliantly preserved, they continue to be a source of significant finds which help shape our knowledge of life in the ancient city.

From left *Thermopolium*; fresco from *thermopolium*; charcoal inscription

ANDREAS SOLARO/AFP/GETTY IMAGES ©

Pompeii's tragic demise is one of the great dramas of ancient history. The story dates to the 1st century CE when Pompeii was a thriving port with a population of around 20,000 and all the trappings of a successful Roman city: amphitheatre, forum, basilica, temples and public fountains. Cramped housing blocks lined its busy streets alongside shops, bakeries, shrines, taverns and brothels.

The good life was short-lived, though, and in 62 CE a major earthquake struck, causing widespread damage. In fact, many buildings were still being rebuilt when, in 79 CE, Vesuvius blew its top. The eruption was devastating, causing a choking mix of ash and *lapilli* (burning pumice stone) to rain down on the city and deadly pyroclastic surges (waves of lethally hot gas and ash) to rip through the area killing everyone in their path. By the time the dust had settled, 2000 people had been killed and the city lay buried beneath 6m of solidified debris.

Excavations & the Great Pompeii Project

The city's underground remains were first discovered in 1594 but it wasn't until the mid-1700s that excavation work began in earnest. Initially, the main focus was on hunting for art treasures, but operations became more systematic in the 19th century under the directorship of archaeologist Giuseppe Fiorelli. He introduced processes to survey and preserve the site, as well as creating Pompeii's infamous body casts by pouring liquid plaster into the hollows left by decomposed bodies.

Fiorelli's scientific approach was recently updated for the 21st-century in the form of the Great Pompeii Project. Launched in 2012, this multimillion-euro programme as-

sembled an international team of specialists, including archae-ologists, anthropologists, volcanologists and palaeobotanists.

Their efforts have since borne spectacular fruit, resulting in a wave of new discoveries. In December 2020, for example, a richly decorated *thermopolium* (snack bar) was unveiled in the site's Regio V sector.

'There are about 90 *thermopolia* at Pompeii but this one is unique in its pictorial and advertising decoration,' explains Luana Toniolo, Pompeii's Director of Archaeological Operations. Its extraordinary frescoes depict a Nereid riding a seahorse and images of a rooster and ducks, animals that were probably cooked and served at the bar.

> By the time the dust had settled, 2000 people had been killed and the city lay buried beneath 6m of solidified debris.

Outside the main Pompeii site, excavations are ongoing at a villa in nearby Civita Giuliana. Several important finds have been unearthed there, most notably the remains of a horse and, in February 2021, a four-wheeled processional chariot.

Of recent finds, few have had the historical impact of the 2018 discovery of a charcoal inscription. This apparently innocuous graffiti seemed to confirm a theory that Vesuvius had actually erupted in October 79 CE (possibly on 24 October) and not on 24 August as had previously been thought. The inscription, which refers to a date 16 days before the '*calends*' of November (ie 17 October), provided the missing proof.

🏛 Site Highlights

You should absolutely see the **Teatri**. Then there are the **Case**. In recent years many houses have been opened, such as the **Casa degli Amanti**, the **Casa del Criptocorto**, the **Casa dei Ceii**.

There's also the **foro**, and the **Villa dei Misteri**, which is absolutely fundamental – it has the most beautiful paintings from antiquity.

Also very important is the **Antiquarium**. This opened in January [2021] and is a veritable Pompeii museum with many masterpieces and recent finds on show.'

By Luana Toniolo,
Director of Archae-ological Operations, Pompeii

40 The Tiles of AMALFI

ART | HISTORY | COLOURS

How could the Amalfi Coast possibly be made more beautiful? Only with colourful Vietri tiles. You'll find these hand-painted decorations splashed all over the region, especially the city of Vietri sul Mare, where the art form began. Admire them in villas and piazzas, on staircases and street corners, in their trademark colour palette: sea blue, forest green and lemon yellow.

ALESSANDRO TORTORA/SHUTTERSTOCK ©

🗺 **How to**

Getting here Public transit, or drive to Vietri sul Mare (40 minutes from Naples and Amalfi).

When to go Avoid tourist-packed August.

Take note Vietri tiles are inspired by the colours and hallmarks of Amalfi Coast life, like lemons,

donkeys and seascapes. Geometric patterns and floral motifs often decorate *riggiole* – the tiles covering walls, ceilings and floors.

By hand Don't fall for mass-produced fakes – real Vietri tiles are hand-painted, no two alike.

ROMAN BABAKIN/SHUTTERSTOCK ©

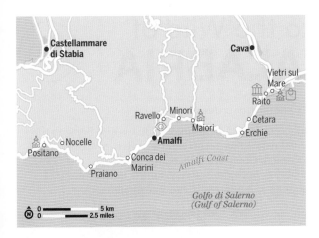

Top left Park at Villa Communale, Vietri sul Mare **Bottom left** Chiesa di Santa Maria Assunta, Positano

Beautiful Colours

Elegant villas The villas and hotels of the Amalfi Coast are a prime canvas for Vietri tiles, like **Hotel Villa Cimbrone** (hotelvillacimbrone.com) in Ravello. Visit its enchanting 19th-century gardens and enjoy its magical views of the sea, perfect for an aperitif.

Colourful cupolas The most emblematic Vietri-tiled structure in Vietri sul Mare is the cupola of the **Chiesa Parrocchiale di San Giovanni Battista**, completely covered in blue and yellow overlapping Vietri tiles called *ambrogette*. You'll see tiled cupolas in many of the Amalfi Coast's important churches, dominating the towns' panoramas. Particularly arresting are the cupolas of Positano's **Chiesa di Santa Maria Assunta** and Maiori's **Chiesa di Santa Maria a Mare**.

Handmade You'll find multi-generational ceramics makers' colourfully tiled shopfronts along Vietri sul Mare's Corso Umberto I, like **Ceramica Pinto** and **Ceramica Avossa**, where you can buy lovely household goods and decorations, from tiles to plates to lamps. The historic **Solimene Factory** (ceramicasolimene.it; Via Madonna degli Angeli 7) is also worth a visit. Its whimsical exterior, designed by Paolo Soleri in 1951, is entirely decorated with terracotta and Vietri tiles.

Rainbow waves All art forms must evolve; Vietri sul Mare's **Villa Comunale** (Via Enrico de Marinis) park overlooking the sea, with its trippy rainbow-swirled railings and colour-dotted steps, is a contemporary example of Vietri tile decoration. But it's no less breathtaking, especially at sunset.

A Historic Art Form

Vietri tiles have a very long history, dating back to the Middle Ages and the Renaissance, as well as a characteristic production method that utilises red clay and a double firing process.

Learn more at **Villa Guariglia** in Raito, a beautiful 16th-century estate with jewel-like interiors that today houses the **Museo della Ceramica Vietrese**. The museum has a permanent exhibit dedicated to Vietri tile production, as well as collections from various eras and a small section dedicated to *riggiole*.

It also hosts concerts and offers incredible views of the town. Free admission, closed Mondays.

Into the Wild of
CALABRIA

NATIONAL PARKS | NATURE | ANCIENT CULTURES

▬▬▬ Think Calabria, think beaches? Think again: Calabria is also home to three immensely biodiverse national parks offering an endless variety of sports and cultural experiences. Hike through Greek and Albanian villages amid the jaw-dropping scenery of the Calabrian Apennines; forage for the mushrooms that grow in the parks. Here's a guide to happy trails and safe foraging.

NELLA/SHUTTERSTOCK ©

🗺 **How to**

Getting here Public transport options exist, but driving is the most convenient option.

When to go Winter skiing, spring flowers, summer water sports, autumn foliage. Hiking, park-to-table wine and food experiences, and culture all year.

Cost Free admission.

Stay on track Inquire at the parks' Info Points about trail maps, eateries and guided tours. Download trails directly from apps or park sites. When hiking, watch for the red-and-white trail signs.

MARCO FINE/SHUTTERSTOCK ©

KARL ALLEN LUGMAYER/SHUTTERSTOCK ©

Far left Bosnian pines, Parco Nazionale del Pollino **Bottom** Mushrooms, Parco Nazionale della Sila **Near left** Fiumara Amendolea, Parco Nazionale Aspromonte

Great Hikes

Giant trees The three sub-ranges of the **Parco Nazionale della Sila** (parcosila.it) encompass bewildering arrays of wildlife. Take the CAI 313 - PNS 35 from **Caserma del Gariglione** in Sila Piccola through white birch forests to the Valle del Tacina, flooded with flowers in spring, and the Cascata del Piciaro. Or hike from **Camigliatello** in Sila Grande to the Giganti di Fallistro – massive secular larch pines. In Sila Greca, drive to Greek and Byzantine villages, like **Longobucco**. Meet its artisanal weavers.

Chase waterfalls The **Parco Nazionale dell'Aspromonte** (parcoaspromonte.gov.it) is renowned for its waterfalls and Greek heritage. The Sentiero dell'Inglese takes you through Greek Calabria and majestic waterways like the **Fiumara Amendolea**; nearby are ghost towns. The 140km **Sentiero del Brigante** (sentierodelbrigante.it) starts in Gambarie, passing through waterfalls and forests, while the 105 trail takes you to **Pietra Cappa**, Europe's tallest monolith.

Arbëreshë culture The **Parco Nazionale del Pollino** (parcopollino.it) is home to Bosnian pines, Italo-Albanian (Arbëreshë) communities and rugged mountains. Intermediate excursionists can take the 633 to **Castel Brancato** overlooking the Argentino river, passing through Byzantine monastic sites. Visit the Arbëreshë village **Civita**, where locals wear traditional dress (drive, or hike the Cammino Mariano Pollino). Sample Arbëreshë cuisine at **Kamastra**, then take the Ponte del Diavolo trail towards Gole del Raganello canyon.

🌿 Safe, Legal Foraging

Calabria's national parks are a wonderland of earthy edibles like asparagus (spring), berries (summer), and mushrooms, truffles, and chestnuts (autumn). However, foraging is prohibited in protected zones, so check park regulations before you snag those berries. Only licensed individuals may forage for mushrooms and truffles. You can apply for a mushroom foraging day permit through Calabria's city websites but your quickest – and safest – bet is to hire a guide.

Discover Pollino (discoverpollino.it) organises expert-led mushroom hikes and mushroom-themed dinners in both Pollino and Sila parks. **Visit Aspromonte** (visitaspromonte.it) arranges expeditions teaching how to identify mushrooms and plants.

42 GHOST
Towns of Calabria

RUINS | HISTORY | CLIFFS

▓▓▓▓ Calabria's Greek-speaking Aspromonte area is home to several *città fantasma* (ghost towns), once founded as Greek colonies and abandoned decades ago due to economic and natural disasters. Creepy or a fascinating testament to loss? Decide for yourself as you hike their mountain trails and wander their empty streets. See the objects they left behind; hear their stories in your mind.

POLONIO VIDEO/SHUTTERSTOCK ©

🗺 How to

Getting here No public transport to Roghudi Vecchio (tortuous road) or Africo Vecchio (park at Villaggio Carrà, then walk). Drive to Pentedattilo (park at the town entrance) or take the train to Melito di Porto Salvo, an 8km walk away.

When to go Year-round, but in summertime, Pentedattilo hosts events. Don't go during rainy weather.

Wear trekking shoes The paths are overgrown and bumpy.

MARCO BARONE/SHUTTERSTOCK ©

ANTONIO ARICO/SHUTTERSTOCK ©

Far left Pentedattilo **Bottom** Rocca del Drago **Near left** Roghudi Vecchio

Five-fingered salute Pentedattilo – the most celebrated Calabrian ghost town – is on the cliff of **Monte Calvario** in the Sant'Elia Valley. Its name comes from the archaic Greek word for 'five fingers', a nod to Monte Calvario's peculiar shape, reminiscent of a waving hand. You can hike the hills surrounding Pentedattilo, or freely explore many of its abandoned houses and buildings, inside and out. Look out for the **Chiesa dei Santi Pietro e Paolo**, the ruins of the castle, and the fresco of San Cristoforo at the base of Monte Calvario's 'thumb'.

More goats than people In contrast to Pentedattilo, Roghudi Vecchio and Africo Vecchio are completely abandoned, save for roaming livestock. The former pastoral village of **Roghudi Vecchio** is precariously perched on a cliff's razor edge between two rivers. Admire its buildings from the outside, though, as they're often unsafe to enter. You'll see the **Chiesetta di San Nicola** and a piazza, and just outside Roghudi Vecchio there are two notable geosites: the **Rocca del Drago** and the **Caldaie del Latte**.

Always sunny The name **Africo Vecchio** derives from a Greek word meaning 'exposed to the sun'. Some of its buildings, like the **Chiesa di San Salvatore** and the elementary school, are still recognisable and can be explored – outside only. Tour Africo Vecchio for a truly solitary, unforgettable experience.

⚜ Signs of Life

Most of Calabria's ghost towns are DOA, but since the mid-1990s, Pentedattilo has shown signs of life. While still mostly uninhabited, it now hosts festivals and shops.

Pentedattilo Film Festival (pentedattilofilm festival.net) For 'film artists who feel like ghosts'. Each August–September, this festival attracts scores of international talents.

Paleariza (paleariza.it) A nomadic festival celebrating Calabria's ancient Greek roots, making stops in Pentedattilo and Roghudi. Concerts, theatre, photography, gastronomy and more. August.

La Bottega del Bergamotto A museum/gift shop celebrating the bergamot, Calabria's quintessential citrus fruit.

43

Explore Ancient
VILLAGES

VILLAGES | ART | ANCIENT ARCHITECTURE

Locri, Stilo and Gerace are a cluster of villages on the Ionian coast that are famous for their Greek, Byzantine, Norman and medieval architecture. But while these villages have ancient roots, there's still modern life to be enjoyed. Explore castles, cathedrals and Greek ruins, then boutique-hop and dine at rustic *agriturismi* – all while enjoying impossibly picturesque views.

MICHELEMINATI/SHUTTERSTOCK ©

How to

Getting here Driving is the most convenient option, but you can also take the train to Locri or to Monasterace-Stilo (13km from town).

Getting around Explore on foot; you'll want to examine each balcony and doorknob.

When to go Year-round, but there are summer festivals like Stilo's **Palio di Ribusa** medieval fair re-enactment (August) and Gerace's **Borgo di Incanto** street art festival (26–28 July). Locri has a thriving beach culture.

POLONIO VIDEO/SHUTTERSTOCK ©

VADYM LAVRA/SHUTTERSTOCK ©

Far left Castello Normanno, Stilo
Bottom Gerace **Near left** Stilo

Architectural Treasures

Greek life The village of **Locri** on the Costa dei Gelsomini was one of Calabria's important Magna Graecia colonies; learn more at the **Museo e Parco Archeologico Nazionale di Locri**, where you can see its collection of impeccably preserved Greek artefacts and tour the ghostly remnants of Greek structures like the **Teatro Greco-Romano** or the **Santuario di Persefone**.

Byzantine temples Next up is **Stilo**, with its exquisite cobblestone alleyways and dramatic mountain backdrop. Admire its churches, like the baroque **Chiesa di San Francesco** or the **Chiesa Matrice**, and enjoy the views from the medieval city walls. Heading up towards **Monte Consolino**, you'll find Stilo's **laura** – lauritic worship cells inside the mountain's grottoes; the 12th-century **Castello Normanno**; and, finally, the **Cattolica di Stilo**, a stunning Greek-Byzantine frescoed temple overlooking the Vallata dello Stilaro.

Art and boutiques Beautiful **Gerace** is full of ancient architecture, like the Byzantine **Chiesa di Santa Maria del Mastro**, the gothic **Chiesa di San Francesco** or the **Castello Normanno** with its views of Parco Nazionale dell'Aspromonte. Visit the Byzantine-Romanesque-Norman **Basilica Concattedrale di Gerace** to see the tapestries of Jan Leyniers, or simply stroll Gerace's streets with their gorgeous doorways and mullioned windows. Browse boutiques and ceramic shops; cool off with one of Gerace's famous fresh fruit granitas.

Calabrian Cuisine

Round out your epic village experience with an epic feast. You'll have luck just about anywhere in this excellent foodie zone, but **Asquella** in Gerace takes top honours for authenticity, decadent eats and price.

This olive mill turned restaurant keeps its ambience and menu old school, serving homemade pastas like traditional *stroncatura* and *spaccatelle* with classic ingredients like aubergine and *'nduja*. Try the grilled meat specialities and sumptuous antipasto platters, heaped high with local *salumi*, cheeses, pickled vegetables and fried Calabrian delicacies like *grispelle* – fried potato doughnuts that practically melt in your mouth.

Rhythms of
PUGLIA

DANCE | MUSIC | SUMMER

You don't need to go clubbing to party the night away in Puglia. The Salento area of the region is home to the *pizzica*, a legendary folk dance whose frenzied rhythms provide the soundtrack to many popular summer celebrations. So follow the call of the beat and head south – a night of fiery Pugliese passion awaits.

GUIDO COZZI/ATLANTIDE PHOTOTRAVEL/GETTY IMAGES ©

🗺 **How to**

Getting here Regular **Trenitalia** (trenitalia. it) trains run to Lecce, the Salento's main city. Within the area, you can get around by Trenitalia or **Ferrovie del Sud Est** (fseonline.it) trains, and/or **STP** (stplecce.it) buses.

When to go Spring and summer when the festival season is in full swing.

Hear it Check out the **Orchestra Popolare La Notte della Taranta** (lanottedellataranta.it).

Cool off In the sea at **Porto Selvaggio** or **Porto Badisco**.

ANNA FEDOROVA_IT/SHUTTERSTOCK ©

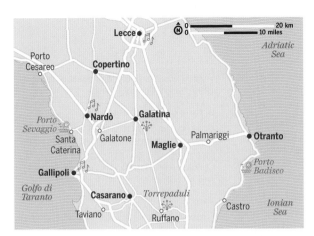

Top left Festa dei Santi Pietro e Paolo, Galatina **Bottom left** Tambourine, Avetrana

Origins The *pizzica* – one of several southern Italian folk dances classed as a *tarantella* – has its origins in a kind of musical exorcism that was used to treat victims of spider bites. The spider's venom was thought to induce a state of hysterical apathy for which the only known cure was to dance for hours and pray to St Paul and other saints.

Variations As performed today there are three *pizzica* variations. The *pizzica tarantata* reflects the traditional spider dance with participants dancing to free themselves of negative stresses. Then there's the *pizzica pizzica*, a seductive, fast-paced courtship dance. The *pizzica scherma* (sword dance) strikes a very different note as two opponents, usually men, perform a ritualised duel using their fingers in place of swords.

The traditional musical accompaniment is a tambourine, generally played at breakneck speed to echo the dancers' heartbeat.

How to experience it The most likely way you'll experience the *pizzica* is at a concert or during street festivities. As a spectator, you might dance along or just watch and admire the pros.

The town most readily associated with the *pizzica* is **Galatina**, where it's celebrated during the June Festa dei Santi Pietro e Paolo. It also features in a series of August concerts in **Lecce**, **Nardò**, **Gallipoli** and other Salento towns.

To witness the *pizzica scherma*, stop by **Torrepaduli** on 15 August for the Festa di San Rocco.

La Notte della Taranta

The *pizzica*'s great annual showcase is **La Notte della Taranta** (lanotte dellataranta.it), Italy's largest popular musical event. Concerts are held across the Salento in the run up to the festival's grand finale, the Concertone at Melpignano. This huge outdoor concert draws hundreds of thousands of spectators and a roll-call of Italian and international performers, including the Orchestra Popolare La Notte della Taranta – 'the *pizzica* ambassador to the world', according to Gabriella Della Monaca of the Fondazione La Notte della Taranta.

Pizzica and tambourine workshops also give visitors the chance to learn the ropes and have a twirl.

Listings

BEST OF THE REST

Ancient Treasures

Museo Archeologico Nazionale

Naples' premier museum showcases many priceless finds from Pompeii and other Vesuvius-hit sites. Chief among its treasures are a series of extraordinary mosaics and the epic *Toro Farnese* sculpture.

Herculaneum

A short train ride from Naples, Herculaneum is one of Italy's best under-the-radar archaeological sites. Its remarkably well-conserved ruins harbour a wealth of compelling artefacts.

Villa Jovis

The spectacularly sited ruins of the emperor Tiberius' Capri palace make for one of the island's great sights. Regular ferries serve Capri from Naples, Sorrento and the Amalfi Coast.

Palaces, Chapels & Cathedrals

Museo di Capidomonte

Caravaggio's *Flagellazione* is just one of the masterpieces on show at this palatial art museum in Naples' Capodimonte district. Look for works by Michelangelo, Raphael, Titian and Botticelli.

Cappella Sansevero

In the heart of Naples' *centro storico*, this baroque chapel houses one of the city's greatest art works: Giuseppe Sanmartino's astonishing *Cristo Velato* (Veiled Christ).

Reggia di Caserta

Southern Italy's Versailles, this vast baroque palace dominates Caserta, a half-hour train ride from Naples. The creation of Luigi Van-

vitelli, it was reputedly the largest building in 18th-century Europe.

Certosa e Museo di San Martino

Up in Naples' Vomero district, this charterhouse-museum represents the high-point (quite literally) of Neapolitan baroque. Check out its magnificent cloisters, impressive art collection and stunning bay views.

Duomo

Frescoes by Giovanni Lanfranco and Jusepe de Ribera, 4th-century mosaics and a thrice-yearly miracle make Naples' city-centre cathedral a must-see.

Cattedrale di Sant'Andrea

With its stripy facade and mix of architectural styles, Amalfi's signature cathedral provides the perfect holiday snap as it stands atop a staircase overlooking the town's central piazza.

Gardens, Grottoes & Views

Grotta Azzurra

A spectacular sea cave illuminated by an otherworldly blue light, the Blue Grotto is one of Capri's biggest draws.

Villa Jovis

Villa Cimbrone

For the ultimate Amalfi Coast photo, make for this dreamy villa in Ravello. Search out the Belvedere of Infinity in the gardens and snap sublime views of the vertiginous coastline.

Sentiero degli Dei

The Amalfi Coast's most famous walking trail, the Path of the Gods offers fine walking and dreamy vistas as it wends its way from Bomerano to Nocelle, above Positano.

Mt Vesuvius

Hike to the summit crater of Naples' great slumbering volcano, source of so much destruction over the ages.

Local Flavours

Concettina Ai Tre Santi   €

Scrupulously sourced artisanal ingredients pair with flawless bases at this pizza hotspot in Naples' Sanità district.

Pizzeria Gino Sorbillo   €

A legendary pizzeria in the heart of Naples' historic centre. Expect fast service and classic wood-fired Neapolitan pizzas.

Da Ettore   €€

This homey Naples trattoria has an epic reputation for its classical regional cooking which includes one of the best *spaghetti alle vongole* (spaghetti with clams) in town.

La Palette   €€

Seasonal island ingredients are skilfully worked into creative dishes at this panoramic Capri restaurant.

Donna Rosa   €€€

Once a humble trattoria, family-run Donna Rosa is now an Amalfi Coast classic serving excellent local cuisine in Montepertuso high above Positano.

Ravello

Cafes & Cocktails

L'Antiquario

Impeccable cocktails headline at this sultry, speakeasy-style cocktail bar in Naples' up-market Chiaia district. Regular live jazz-centric tunes add to the smooth atmosphere.

Caffè Gambrinus

White-jacketed baristas serve superlative coffees under the chandeliers at Naples' oldest and most venerable cafe. Everyone has sipped here from Oscar Wilde to Bill Clinton.

D'Anton

A Sorrento cocktail bar doubling as an interior-design boutique, D'Anton lets you sip Negronis as you debate buying the sofa you're sitting on.

La Pansa

This marbled and mirrored cafe has been an Amalfi landmark for generations. Stop by for a classic Italian breakfast of freshly made *cornetti* and frothy cappuccino.

Tartufo & Caciocavallo

Bar Gelateria Ercole   €

Pizzo Calabro is famous for its *tartufo* (hazelnut gelato truffles), and this historic bar makes some of the town's best. Also serves great brioche and *torrone* (nougat). In Piazza della Repubblica.

La Locanda di Alia €€€

Family-run restaurant in Castrovillari that serves delicious cuisine using seasonal ingredients cultivated in Parco Nazionale del Pollino like Podolica veal, Mormanno beans and Castrovillari onions. Idyllic rustic setting.

Il Brillo Parlante €€

A homey eatery in Parco Nazionale della Sila (San Giovanni in Fiore) on Lago Arvo. Enjoy rustic specialities like grilled *caciocavallo* cheese, roasted porcini, panini and steaks. Local, seasonal ingredients.

La Cascina 1899 €€€

A rustic yet elegant restaurant in a sprawling 19th-century farmhouse. Renowned for its homemade condiments and baked goods, which you can buy at the site's shop. Just outside of Roccella Ionica.

~~~ Sea & Sand

Spiaggia dell'Arcomagno

Secluded beach cove with crystal-clear water that takes its name from its arched rock formation. Just north of San Nicola Arcella's main beach; follow the mountain path. Dazzling at sunset.

Spiaggia della Rotonda

Beautiful white-sand beach with Tropea's ancient quarter as its backdrop and the enchanting, dome-shaped Grotta di San Leonardo on the right. Explore the grotto's depths; bask in Tropea's perfect turquoise sea.

Spiaggia di Grotticelle

Its clear blue waters are a paradise for divers and snorkellers. Cradled by the Capo Vaticano promontory and Santa Maria beach. Incredible view of the Aeolian Islands.

Scogliera di Capo Bruzzano

Beach on the southern Ionian coast, known for the striking scattering of rocks on its shore that form rectangular 'pools' of different sizes. Just outside of Africo Nuovo.

Isola di Dino

For unspoiled beauty, the Isola di Dino is a lush island near Praia di Mare. Don't miss its breathtaking *grotta azzurra* – a partially submerged cave whose blue waters seem to glow.

Art & Craft

Museo della Liquirizia 'Giorgio Amarelli'

Visit this historic factory-and-museum complex to learn how Rossano's Amarelli family makes its famous licorice. Pick up licorice-laced products like chocolate and beer at the shop. Just 1.4km from Lido Sant'Angelo.

Tessitura Artistica a Mano di Mario Celestino

Since 1930, the Celestino family in Longobucco has been weaving traditionally loomed textiles. Stock up on blankets, tapestries and linens at their historic workshop. Near the Santuario di Santa Maria Assunta.

LIANEM/SHUTTERSTOCK ©

Isola di Dino

Mulinum

A modern flour mill dedicated to preserving ancient grains and milling techniques. Tour the sprawling mill; buy its artisanal flour, baked goods and pizza. Just outside of San Floro.

 Cultural Riches

Museo Archeologico Nazionale di Reggio Calabria

See the world-famous Bronzi di Riace sculptures, as well as prehistoric relics and collections from the Magna Graecia period in Calabria. Across from Piazza de Nava.

MAB Cosenza – Museo all'Aperto Bilotti

Open-air museum along Corso Mazzini in Cosenza, home to important sculptures and contemporary art installations by masters like Salvador Dalí and Amedeo Modigliani.

Museo Diocesano e del Codex

Home to the sacred text of the Rossano Gospels, one of the oldest surviving illuminated manuscripts of the New Testament. Located in the rooms behind the Cathedral of Rossano Calabro.

Chiesa di Piedigrotta

A 19th-century church carved into a grotto from sedimentary rock, filled with unbelievably intricate statues and frescoes. In Pizzo Calabro, on a lovely beach at the bottom of stone staircases.

Castello Aragonese di Le Castella

An imposing 15th-century fortress with ancient Greek origins on a small islet in the Capo Rizzuto marine protected area. Cross the drawbridge to visit the ancient village.

Chiesa di Piedigrotta, Pizzo Calabro

 Natural Wonders

Le Grotte di Zungri

Just outside of Capo Vaticano, a unique geosite consisting of ancient cave dwellings carved into sandstone. See areas allocated for the shelter of livestock, wine production and the storage of grain.

Botte Donato

The highest peak (1928m) in the Sila Grande sub-range of Parco Nazionale della Sila, between Lago Argo and Lago Cecita; popular for skiing in winter and trekking year-round.

Grotta del Romito

A limestone cave in the Lao Valley of Parco Nazionale del Pollino. Home to several ancient burial sites as well as a perfectly preserved Upper Palaeolithic rock engraving of an aurochs.

 Scan to find more things to do in Naples & the South online

45

Escape to Seismic
SICILY

HISTORY | ADVENTURE | FOOD

Welcome to Sicily, Italy's island of the south: hot, dry, wracked by earthquake and eruption. Here 25 centuries of Mediterranean history and culture have converged to leave a legacy of splendid civilisations set amid a stunning diversity of landscapes shaped by Europe's most active stratovolcano.

K. ROY ZERLOCH/SHUTTERSTOCK ©

NATURSPORTS/SHUTTERSTOCK ©

📖 How to

Getting around You can cover more ground with a car, but the network of buses, trains and hydrofoils is efficient.

When to go April to June for volcano hiking and Greek theatre; September and October for balmy beach days and fewer tourists.

Top tip Epic Sicilian festivals include the **Sciacca Carnevale** (sciaccarnevale.it), Catania's **Festa di Sant'Agata** (festa disantagata.it), **Ortigia Sound System** (ortigia soundsystem.com) and **Taormina Arte** (taoarte.it).

STEFANO_VALERI/SHUTTERSTOCK ©

The classicists Afloat in the centre of the Mediterranean, commanding the narrow straits between mainland Italy and Cap Bon in Tunisia, Sicily is a lesson in geopolitics. When the great city-states of Greece began flexing their muscles, it was only natural they would land in Sicily. In 736 BC, the Corinthians built honey-coloured Syracuse, where tragedies are still performed in a ruined **Greek Theatre** (indafondazione.org). Their temples, too, litter the island – the most beautiful at Segesta, Selinunte and in Agrigento's **Valle dei Templi** (parcovalledeitempli.it) – while their finest art is housed in Palermo's **Archaeological Museum** (regione.sicilia.it/bbccaa/salinas).

Roman country style Naturally, the growing Greek power in Sicily created uncomfortable tensions with the Carthaginians in Tunisia, while Rome greedily eyed the island's rich

🍴 Cook with Royalty

Food, history and literature combine in this cooking course (butera28.it) conducted by Duchess Nicoletta Polo Lanza Tomasi in a Palermo palace once home to the author of *The Leopard*. A morning at the market is followed by the creation of a four-course lunch and a palace tour.

Top left Mt Etna as seen from the Greek theatre in Taormina
Bottom left Temple ruins Selinunte
Above Valle dei Templi, Agrigento

resources. The Punic Wars (264–146 BC) between them placed Sicily firmly within the Roman Empire. For a vision of rare Roman country style, visit **Villa Romana del Casale** (villaromanadelcasale.it) to admire the world's finest mosaics. Then, dine like an emperor at **Al Fogher** (alfogher.sicilia. restaurant). This southeastern corner of the island is Sicily at its most seductive so be sure to dip in and out of nearby Noto, Ragusa, Modica and Scicli. You can walk the

cobbles with **A Porte Aperte** (facebook.com/ aporteaperte), dine at Michelin-starred **Accursio** (accursioristorante.it) and eat gelato at century-old **Caffè Sicilia** (caffesicilia.it).

A' muntagna 'The mountain' as Etna (3324m) is known locally, is Europe's tallest active volcano and its smoking peak is a heart-stirring sight. The main access is Rifugio Sapienza where the **Etna funicular** (funiviaetna.com) will whisk you to the summit. But for surreal treks through scarred

🍇 Volcanic Wine

Etna's lava flows bring destruction, but they also enrich the soil, making the slopes perfect for growing grapes. Standout wineries:

Cantina Frank Cornelissen (frankcornelissen.it) Thrilling natural wines made from old, ungrafted vines.

Planeta Feudo di Mezzo (planeta.it) An acclaimed estate serving tastings with a traditional lunch.

Monaci delle Terre Nere (monacidelleterrenere. it) One of Sicily's most beautiful boutique hotels, set in a winery.

Vini Calcagno (vinicalcagno.it) A fifth-generation, family-run estate noted for its refined rosé.

Cantina Malopasso (cantinamalopasso.it) Small-batch wines made from unusual native varieties.

Left Mosaic floor, Villa Romana del Casale **Below** Lipari

lava flows join geologist Ernesto Magri at **Etna Guided Tours** (facebook.com/EtnaGuidedTours). Etna's epic power can also be seen in Catania, the regional capital, which was submerged in lava in 1669. The city rebuilt itself in the mountain's image with fanciful lava-and-limestone churches and *palazzi*. The finest ring Piazza del Duomo. At the southern end of the piazza, a fountain marks where the river Amenano once ran, now replaced by Catania's theatrical fish market, **La Pescheria** (Via Pardo). Lunch at the excellent **Fratelli Vittorio** (Via Dusmet 1) then stop at **Nonna Vincenza's** (dolcinonnavincenza.it) for the best *cannoli* in town.

Elemental islands Etna is part of a volcanic chain that stretches north encompassing the volcanic archipelago of the **Aeolian Islands**. These islands were created by successive explosions – first Panarea, Filicudi and Alicudi, then Lipari, Salina and Vulcano, and finally the still-boiling Stromboli. Lipari, the main island, is the liveliest and offers stunning diving in cobalt-blue waters, but hiking Salina's tranquil vineyards or catching sunsets on Stromboli's fiery slopes make for unforgettable memories, too. Hole up at **Al Salvatore di Lipari** (facebook.com/bbalsalvatore), **Hotel Signum** (hotelsignum.it), **Casa del Sole** (casadelsole stromboli.it) or **La Canna** (lacannahotel.it).

SARDINIA

OUTDOORS | BEACHES | FOOD

Experience Sardinia online

TRAVELWILD/SHUTTERSTOCK ©

SARDINIA
Trip Builder

With its stunning beaches, exhilarating landscapes and prehistoric relics, Sardinia is a glorious world apart. Outdoor enthusiasts will love its crystalline seas and spectacular interior, while history buffs can explore mysterious ruins, and food lovers can feast on hearty island food.

0 50 km
0 25 miles

Corsica (FRANCE)
Bouches de Bonifacio

Golfo dell' Asinara

Arzachena

Tempio Pausania

Golfo di Olbia

Porto Torres

Olbia

Sassari

San Teodoro

Ozieri

Siniscola

Tyrrhenian Sea

Alghero

Bosa

Nuoro

Dorgali

Macomer

Abbasanta

Parco Nazionale del Golfo di Orosei e del Gennargentu

Baunei

Golfo di Oristano

Oristano

Sadali

Tortolì

Terralba

Mandas

Guspini

Villacidro

Monastir

Villaputzu

Iglesias

Cagliari

San Pietro

Carbonia

Golfo di Cagliari

Villasimius

Sant' Antioco

Teulada

Pula

Feast on Catalan-style cuisine in medieval **Alghero** (p224)
⏱ 2 days

Enjoy secluded bays and frost-white beaches on the **Sinis Peninsula** (p223)
⏱ 2 days

Sunbathe on the dreamy beaches of **San Teodoro** (p223)
⏱ 2 days

Hike, bike or boat around the **Golfo di Orosei** (p230)
⏱ 2 days

Delve into mysterious prehistory at the **Nuraghe su Nuraxi** (p226)
⏱ ½ day

Admire sweeping city views from the hilltop ramparts of **Cagliari** (p233)
⏱ 2 days

Explore bookable experiences in Sardinia online

ARTMEDIAFACTORY/SHUTTERSTOCK ©
VALERIOMEI/SHUTTERSTOCK ©

Practicalities

ARRIVING

 Cagliari Elmas Airport Trains take 10 minutes to Cagliari.

Aeroporto di Olbia Costa Smeralda Buses run to Olbia, 10 minutes away.

Alghero Airport Buses take you to Alghero in 25 minutes.

CONNECT

Free wi-fi is available in most hostels, B&Bs and hotels, as well as many cafes and restaurants. Signal quality varies.

MONEY

Take cash if exploring remoter areas as credit cards might not be accepted and you may find ATMs scarce.

WHERE TO STAY

Place	Pro/Con
Cagliari	B&Bs, guesthouses, boutique hotels in the main transport hub.
Alghero	Ideal base for the island's northwest with campsites, B&Bs and seafront hotels.
Cala Gonone	*Agriturismi* and hotels offer sea views for beach lovers and outdoor enthusiasts.
Arzachena	Rustic B&Bs reveal another side to the Costa Smeralda.

EATING & DRINKING

Island meal Kick off with *culurgiones* (stuffed ravioli served with tomato sauce) before a main course of *porceddu* (slow-roasted pork; pictured top left). For dessert try a honey-drenched *seadas* (a pastry filled with ricotta; pictured bottom left).

Wine Try aromatic Vermentino whites from Gallura and robust Cannonau reds from Oliena.

Best revisited typical cuisine Luigi Pomata (p233)

Must-try liqueur *Mirto* (p224)

GETTING AROUND

Driving The best way to explore the island. Traffic is worst in July and August, especially on coastal roads.

Buses The best form of public transport, serving most cities, towns and villages.

Trains Slow and connections are limited to the main cities.

 APR–JUN
Spring sunshine and blooming flowers; ideal for outdoor activities.

 JUL–AUG
Hot beach weather; crowds and high-season prices.

 SEP–OCT
Still sunny but cooler; great for hiking and cycling.

 NOV– MAR
Cold and rain; many coastal businesses are closed.

46 Paradise **BEACHES**

SWIMMING | SNORKELLING | SUMMER

Sandy dunes, stretches of rice-like quartz pebbles and secluded rocky bays are only some of the features of Sardinia's rugged coastline. Like its wild inland, the beaches are diverse and perfect for a wide range of activities for everyone from adventure-seeking travellers to families with kids. You can try adrenaline-charged watersports, boat excursions or just simply relaxing in the sunshine.

EVA BOCEK/SHUTTERSTOCK ©

🗺 **How to**

Getting here The closest airport for Stintino is Alghero-Fertilia; for Palau/La Maddalena, Aeroporto di Olbia Costa Smeralda; for the Sinis Peninsula, Cagliari-Elmas.

When to go July and August are peak summer but jam-packed; June and

September are sunny but less crowded.

Cost Boat tours around La Maddalena Archipelago, €700 to €1200. Asinara day tours, €60 to €70.

Boat tours Futurismo Asinara (futurismoasinara.com); **Delfino Bianco di Paolo Orecchioni** (noleggiobarchepalau.it).

KRISTYNA HENKEOVA/SHUTTERSTOCK ©

Top left Cala Domestica **Bottom** Hiker near Cala Goloritzé, Golfo di Orosei **Near left** Arcipelago di La Maddalena

Choose Your Beach

Relaxing shores Sardinia's sandy beaches are perfect for lying on a towel and sunbathing. Northeast, head to **San Teodoro** for beaches such as La Cinta with its sugar-like sand and translucent waters and Cala Brandinchi, surrounded by pinewoods and nicknamed Tahiti for its Caribbean look. Southeast, inside a military zone is the hidden gem of **Cala Murtas**, open only in summer and surrounded by a wild landscape ideal for trekking, cycling and birdwatching. Northwest, **La Pelosa** is hemmed with juniper-clothed dunes, white sand and emerald waters.

Intimate coves Nestled in the Golfo di Orosei near Baunei, **Cala Goloritzé** is a must for adrenaline seekers. It's easy to reach by boat from Cala Gonone, or to get there by foot you'll need to follow a trekking route of about an hour. On the southwestern coast, **Cala Domestica**, 2km from Buggerru, is a secluded bay of golden-amber hues framed by Mediterranean scrub-dotted limestone cliffs and sandy dunes.

Boat excursions When the mainland gets too crowded, join a day trip from Stintino to **Parco Nazionale dell'Asinara** for an unforgettable ecotourism experience trekking in unspoiled nature, spotting local wildlife and snorkelling. From the northern town of Palau, you can book a private excursion on a *gommone* (inflatable) or sailboat to discover **Arcipelago di La Maddalena**. Counting some 60 small islands, it's a treasure trove of hidden inlets such as Cala Corsara and Cala Soraya, and famous shores like Budelli pink beach.

🛥️ Expert Tips

Some of the best destinations are inside a Parco Marino (Marine Protected Area) because they offer an all-round experience. The **Sinis Peninsula** boasts great beaches like Is Arutas, popular for its rice-like sand, archaeological ruins such as Tharros, and Cabras' Museo Civico, which hosts the Giants of Mont'e Prama nuraghic findings and the wreck of an ancient Roman ship discovered nearby.

On the western coast, waters are colder because of the mistral wind and dangerous when the sea is rough. Among the most dangerous beaches are Is Arenas and Tresnuraghes.

By Giulio Garau, *former Italian Navy deep diver and expert on the Sardinian coastline*

Sardinia's
KITCHEN

FOOD | WINE | TRADITION

▬▬▬ Sardinia's long history of foreign invasions has made for a wonderfully diverse cuisine. Explore Tunisian and Ligurian flavours in Carloforte, Catalan-inspired dishes in Alghero, and recipes from farming and fishing villages such as Cabras' *bottarga* (mullet roe) and Ogliastra's succulent *culurgiones* (potato dumplings with pecorino and mint).

🍽 How to

Cost First courses €10 to €25, mains €20 to €35. Day food tours €60 to €80.

Pair the wine With fish, top white wines are Contini's Karmis, Pedra Majore's I Graniti, and Depperu's Ruinas. With meat, try Cannonau red wines Orgosa from Orgosolo, Mamuthone from Mamoiada and Argiolas' Turriga.

Food tours Tasting Sardinia (tastingsardinia. com); **Sardinia To Do** (sardiniatodo.com).

After dinner Try *mirto*, a wild myrtle berry liqueur.

Map showing locations: Sassari, Alghero, Bosa, Macomer, Mamoiada, Nuoro, Dorgali, Siniscola, Seneghe, Parco Nazionale del Golfo di Orosei e del Gennargentu, Cabras, Oristano, Tortolì, Ogliastra, Villaputzu, Iglesias, San Pietro, Carloforte, Carbonia, Cagliari, Villasimius, Golfo di Cagliari, Sant' Antioco — with scale 0–50 km / 0–25 miles

---

Local markets Every town has its daily civic market and weekly farmers markets selling local produce and ready meals. Cagliari's **Mercato Civico di San Benedetto** is a great place to pick up food, oil and wine. Hit the ground-floor fish market for a perfect snack of deep-fried small fish.

Festivals Visit Seneghe in December for **Prentzas Apertas** (open oil mills) where locals open their traditional homes and welcome walk-ins. Alongside olive oil, you'll also find great honey and sweets such as almond-based *sospiri*. In November, Mamoiada celebrates **Cortes Apertas**. Here,

Top right *Culurgiones*
Bottom right *Bottarga*

🏔 Agriturismo Life

The rooms of **Agriturismo Canales**, 5km from Dorgali, overlook forest-cloaked mountains and the Cedrino river, where you can kayak your way to Su Gologone karst spring. The *agriturismo* (farm stay) hosts go out of their way to make guests feel at home, suggesting excursions and cooking memorable meals featuring ingredients from the farm.

visitors can enjoy inexpensive homemade meals including spit-roasted *porceddu* (suckling pig), paper-thin *carasau* bread, and *papassini* cakes made with *sapa* (grape syrup).

Tours and tastings

Cagliari-based chef Luigi Pomata suggests 'stopping at Sardinian wine cellars for aperitif and tastings, a great chance to get to know the local community and products.' Joining a food tour is another immersive way to get an authentic taste of Sardinian life and culinary traditions across the island, from Cagliari to the wild Barbagia region. Options include pasta-making classes ending with a family meal; active food tours exploring archaeological sites and wilderness; and gourmet tours sampling regional treats like the shell-shaped *malloreddus* pasta, stretched-curd *casizolu* cheese and olive oil.

Ancient Rock Puzzles

SARDINIA'S PREHISTORY WRITTEN IN STONE

The crumbling towers and strange rock formations that litter Sardinia's rugged landscape offer a priceless window into its prehistoric past and first great civilisation, which emerged at the end of the 4th millennium BCE in the late Neolithic period.

From left Monte d'Accoddi; Nuraghe di Santa Cristina; Giant of Mont'e Prama, Cagliari Archaeological Museum

Ozieri Culture

Most of what we know about the Ozieri culture comes from findings unearthed in and around the northern town of Ozieri. In fact, the culture was first identified after fragments of pottery and figurines were discovered in the Grotta di San Michele in Ozieri – hence you'll sometimes see it called the 'San Michele culture'.

Excavations have since uncovered evidence of Ozieri hut villages across Sardinia, allowing scholars to build up a picture of a peaceful pastoral society. The Ozieri crafted tools from obsidian and produced refined Greek-style ceramics.

They were also great tomb-diggers, carving *domus de janas* (cave tombs) and constructing *dolmens* (chambered tombs) across the island. However, the most striking remnant of the period is the temple of Monte d'Accoddi in the province of Sassari. First built in the 4th millennium BCE, this extraordinary structure resembles more a Mesopotamian ziggurat than a megalithic monument.

Nuraghi

Sardinia's best known archaeological treasures are its mysterious Bronze Age *nuraghi* (stone towers). There are reckoned to be about 7000 of these truncated conical structures on the island, probably twice that many if you count those still underground. Most date to the period between 1800 and 500 BCE but debate still rages about their function.

'Some consider them militarised buildings in which community leaders lived. Others hypothesise that they were used for the rites of cults tied to celestial deities and

the apparent movement of the sun,' explains Pierluigi Montalbano, a Sardinian archaeology expert.

Early *nuraghi* were simple, free-standing towers with internal chambers. But over time they became increasingly complex as elaborate rooms and labyrinthine passageways were added. Many were also incorporated into walled compounds, such as the fortified village that grew up around the Nuraghe Su Nuraxi.

Nuraghic building techniques were also employed in other signature structures. Chief among these were collective tombs known as *tombe di giganti* and sacred wells called *pozzi sacri*. Archaeologists have uncovered around 40 well temples across Sardinia including a fine example at the Nuraghe di Santa Cristina northeast of Oristano.

> The most striking remnant of the period is the temple of Monte d'Accoddi in the province of Sassari.

Further light is shed on nuraghic religious practices by the hundreds of *bronzetti* (bronze figurines) that populate the island's archaeological museums. Scholars reckon these primitive carvings were used as temple votive offerings.

Research into Sardinia's nuraghic culture is an ongoing process and one that continues to throw up astonishing finds such as the Giants of Mont'e Prama. Discovered on the Sinis Peninsula, these date to the 8th or 9th century BCE, and are among the oldest anthropomorphic statues ever found in the Mediterranean.

🏛 Top Sites

For the Copper Age we have the altar of **Monte d'Accoddi** in Sassari and the enclosure-tower of **Monte Baranta** in Olmedo.

For the nuraghic age, the most important [sites] are the **Nuraghe Arrubiu di Orroli**, which consists of five towers surrounding a central one and a rampart with 14 towers; the **Nuraghe Santu Antine di Torralba**, formed by three lateral towers joined by 40m corridors surrounding a central tower; and the **Nuraghe di Barumini** [Nuraghe Su Nuraxi] with four two-storey towers built around a central three-storey tower.

By Pierluigi Montalbano, *President of the Associazione Culturale Honebu*

48 ECLECTIC
Festivals

TRADITION | FOOD | MUSIC

▬▬ Every city, town and village across Sardinia has its own festival, each revealing the island's soul and traditions. Most have a religious base, but many can be dated to pagan times when the new harvest was welcomed with all kinds of rituals. There are big eye-catching festivals as well as more intimate ones where you'll see virtually no tourists. Join the crowd as passers-by are always welcome.

LORENZА6Z/SHUTTERSTOCK ©

🗺 How to

Getting around Trains and ARST buses reach main cities and some smaller towns, but to get around it's best to rent a car at the airport.

Planning ahead Book hotels well in advance as places can get very busy.

Cost Sant'Efisio tickets €15 to €30; Time in Jazz evening concerts €10 to €23; Sartiglia tickets €10 to €40.

Festivals Sant'Efisio (facebook.com/sant efisio); **Time in Jazz** (timeinjazz.it); **Sartiglia** (sartiglia.info); **Mamu-thones** (mamuthones.it).

FVPHOTOGRAPHY/SHUTTERSTOCK ©

Top left Festa di Sant'Efisio, Cagliari
Bottom left *Torrone* from Tonara

Join the Party

Tradition On 1 May, more than 3000 people showcase the quintessence of Sardinian handicraft parading in traditional costumes along the rose-petal-carpeted streets of Cagliari. Decorated bulls, horse riders and the sound of *launeddas* folk instruments complete the scenic annual tribute to Christian martyr **Sant'Efisio**, who was killed in Nora, some 40km away, under Diocletian. Book your grandstand seat for a complete view of the procession. Be sure to taste local foods sold at the stalls lined up along the streets.

Jazz With settings like wind-sculpted granite rocks and archaeological ruins, music festivals have been giving a new rhythm to Sardinian summers. Founded by trumpet virtuoso Paolo Fresu in his town Berchidda and held in August, **Time In Jazz** hosts Italian and international artists in an array of events including book presentations, documentaries, food and kids activities. 'The festival is important for what it conveys: good music, hospitality, paying attention to the local resources,' explains Fresu. Wander the surrounding woods and visit local towns for an all-round experience.

Food *Sagre* food fairs take place across Sardinia all year long. Some of the most popular celebrate Tonara's *torrone* (nougat) in April, *su succu* (a saffron and cheese pasta) in Busachi in September, and famous *bottarga* (mullet roe) in Cabras in August. Different town, different product, but what they all have in common is plenty of free tasting, street stalls selling all manner of dishes made with the star of the show, and a glimpse of local life.

Best of the Rest

Sa Sartiglia
For Carnevale, watch Oristano's masked riders darting to catch the Star symbol of the race and perform equestrian vaulting in squads of three. Watch from the grandstands or join the street crowds for an authentic local experience.

Mamuthones
During Carnevale celebrations in Mamoiada, locals dressed as *mamuthones* – wearing wooden masks, black sheepskin and 30kg of bells on their shoulders – dance their way through the streets mingling with the crowds.

S'Ardia
Every 6 July, Sedilo's horse riders engage in one of Sardinia's most reckless races as a tribute to St Constantine. Wait under the sun for the riders to reach the rural sanctuary or join local devotees' parade to the steep bucolic venue.

49 The Wild EAST

HIKING | CYCLING | SCENERY

Eastern Sardinia's soaring coastline, plunging gorges and wild, mountainous interior beg exploration on foot or by bike. From gentle walks to tough multi-day treks, from winding rides along corkscrewing roads to rugged off-road descents, routes run the gamut, offering challenges to everyone from weekend amblers to hardcore adrenaline junkies.

How to

Getting here The nearest airport is Aeroporto di Olbia Costa Smeralda. Convenient bases in the area include Dorgali, Oliena, Orosei and Cala Gonone; all can be reached by ARST bus from Nuoro.

When to go Spring (April to June) and autumn (September to October) are best.

Guided walks A half-day guided hike will typically cost €40 to €50.

Cycling Bike Tour Sardinia (biketoursardinia.com).

Hiking Midway up Sardinia's east coast, there's superb hiking in and around the **Golfo di Orosei**. You can enjoy stunning coastal scenery on trails from Cala Gonone to Cala Luna and from Piana del Golgo to Cala Goloritzé. Inland, popular half-day hikes lead to the nuraghic village of **Tiscali** and deep into the mighty gorge of **Gola Su Gorropu**. For more experienced trekkers, local guide Corrado Conca recommends the multi-day Grande Traversata del Gennargentu (GTG) or Grande Traversata del Supramonte (GTS), both of which take in some of

Top right Selvaggio Blu
Bottom right Trail to Cala Luna

ⓘ Phone Tip

It's very important to realise that there isn't always a phone signal, so if you're relying on a smartphone for GPS you should know that you'll often have to use it offline.

By Corrado Conca,
*hiking guide,
corradoconca.it*

Sardinia's most spectacular mountain country.

The most celebrated of Sardinia's great hikes is the **Selvaggio Blu**, an epic seven-day, 45km trek along the Golfo di Orosei's coast involving some scrambling, abseiling and navigation.

Cycling Road cycling is big in Sardinia, especially in spring and autumn when the traffic thins and temperatures are pleasantly mild. For a taste, the SS125 road provides a challenging workout as it corkscrews through the rugged mountain terrain between Dorgali and Santa Maria Navarrese offering inspiring views at every turn.

Mountain biking There are some wonderful cross-country routes in the remote Piana del Golgo (Baunei) and Valle di Lanaitto (Oliena).

Listings

BEST OF THE REST

Ancient Ruins

Pozzo Sacro di Santa Cristina

Sardinia's best-kept nuraghic sacred well is a water temple near Santa Cristina Nuraghe in Paulilatino, 25km east of Oristano. Every March and September equinox around noon the sunrays reflect right on the bottom of the well through its staircase.

Tharros

Located on the southernmost end of the Sinis Peninsula, Tharros was founded by the Phoenicians around the 7th century BCE on the site of a nuraghic settlement. Standing against a backdrop of turquoise sea, its giant pillars make for the perfect postcard picture.

Nora

First Phoenician city in Sardinia and later an important Roman hub, Nora has the remains of a temple, necropolis, forum, aqueduct and baths. Southwest of Cagliari near Pula.

Nuraghe Santu Antine

In Torralba, this elaborate example of nuraghic engineering is believed to have been the seat of the tribal chief. The frescoed necropolis of Sant'Andrea Priu is only a 14km drive away and worth a stop.

Hiking, Grottoes & Views

Su Gorropu Gorge

To descend one of Europe's deepest canyons, there are different trekking routes depending on the difficulty level. Located between Urzulei and Orgosolo in Nuoro province. Local guides available.

Bue Marino Grottoes

Once home to monk seals that locals used to call *bue marino*, hence the name Sea Oxen Grottoes, these mesmerising sea caves in the Golfo di Orosei can be reached by boat from Cala Gonone, Arbatax and Santa Maria Navarrese.

Trenino Verde (Green Train)

Old narrow-gauge railways running across five different routes offer slow travel experiences and coast-to-inland itineraries through traditional towns and unspoiled natural views.

Art & Craft

Sounding Stones

In the colourful town of San Sperate, some 20km from Cagliari, the open-air museum of late sculptor Pinuccio Sciola displays his famous sound-making stones. Email associazionepsmuseum@gmail.com to book your visit.

Byssus Sea Silk

Visit the Byssus museum-lab in Sant'Antioco to see where local artist Chiara Vigo

Tharros

weaves the strands obtained from the Mediterranean shell *Pinna nobilis* to create the precious thread to be embroidered into decorative golden patterns.

 Cultural Riches

Museo delle Maschere del Mediterraneo

Museum devoted to the *mamuthones* and *issohadores*, ancient masquerades from Mamoiada, and to the masks used in many Sardinian towns and festivals. Located 16km south of Nuoro.

Casa di Grazia Deledda

The house where Grazia Deledda, Sardinian recipient of the Nobel Prize for Literature, was born and raised in Nuoro is now a museum. In a small church at the foot of Mt Ortobene, 700m from the museum, is the writer's tomb.

Cagliari's Old Quarter

Access Castello, Cagliari's medieval quarter, through one of the original gates and wander the maze of narrow alleys. Historical sites include 13th-century Cattedrale di Santa Maria, the Royal Palace and St Remy Bastion for great views of the city.

 Traditional Restaurants

Luigi Pomata   €€€

In the namesake Cagliari restaurant of the renowned chef, you'll find an elegant minimalist decor and a menu of expertly prepared modern takes on traditional fish and seafood-based dishes. Dine outside in warm weather.

Su Carduleu   €€€

Chef Roberto Serra serves a modern interpretation of authentic Sardinian dishes such as fresh pasta, sheep offal and Mediterranean sea anemone. Located in Abbasanta, 40km from Oristano. It's popular – book ahead.

Cattedrale di Santa Maria, Castello, Cagliari

Sa Cardiga e su Schironi   €€€

This high-end restaurant with marine-style decor dishes out mouth-wateringly fresh seafood including snapper carpaccio on potato cream, fresh *tagliatelle* on mullet ragout with a sprinkle of *bottarga*, and grilled catch of the day. Near Maddalena beach in Capoterra, southwest of Cagliari.

 Recharge

Sardegna Grand Hotel Terme

Soak up the serenity with your pick of treatments including hydrotherapy, mud wraps and a spring-fed plunge pool. Located in Fordongianus next to the ruins of ancient Roman baths.

Antiche Terme di Sardara

Well-equipped spa sanctuary and fitness centre in a lush natural park with a great on-site restaurant. Located in Sardara, 40km from Oristano, 60km from Cagliari. Complimentary private parking.

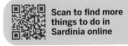

Scan to find more things to do in Sardinia online

Practicalities

ARRIVING

236

GETTING AROUND

238

SAFE TRAVEL

240

MONEY

241

RESPONSIBLE TRAVEL

242

ACCOMMODATION

244

ESSENTIALS

246

LANGUAGE

248

Right Ballaro Market, Palermo

EASY STEPS FROM THE AIRPORT TO THE CITY CENTRE

Rome's Fiumicino Airport (officially Aeroporto Leonardo da Vinci) is Italy's main intercontinental airport, catering to over 40 million passengers and 70 countries annually. Located on the coast some 40km west of central Rome, the airport has two terminals in operation at the time of writing: T1 (mostly Alitalia and Sky-Team partners) and T3 (the biggest and busiest). Milan and Venice are also home to widely used airports.

AT THE AIRPORT

SIM card kiosks such as TIM (tim. it) and Vodafone (vodafone.it) are located in the T3 arrivals hall at Fiumicino, but you can just as easily (and perhaps more calmly) pick one up in the city centre.

Foreign exchange booths operate in the arrivals hall of Fiumicino, but you won't get the most bang for your buck in any of them. The best rates will always come straight from the ATMs in both terminals.

Free wi-fi is available – connect to Airport Free Wi-Fi then follow the prompts.

ATMs are located in the arrivals hall (avoid Euronet due to high fees and unwelcoming exchange rates).

Charging stations can be found near baggage-claim belts 3 and 11, and near Semplicemente Roma cafes in baggage claim and arrivals.

CUSTOMS REGULATIONS

Duty free For goods from outside the EU, limits include 200 cigarettes and 1L of spirits above 22% strength (or 2L below 22%).

Art and antiques Goods under 50 years old (or by living artists) must be self-certified by the purchaser at an Export Office; older works need a certificate of free circulation, which takes between 15 and 40 days to obtain.

GETTING TO THE CITY CENTRE

Authorised taxis from Fiumicino Airport head to Rome's city centre (set fare €48) in about 45 to 60 minutes (be aware that this set fare is good for destinations within the Aurelian Walls only). Set fares include up to four passengers and luggage.

Buses to Rome's Stazione Centrale (€4.50 to €10) take an hour and operate between 6.05am and midnight. Popular companies include Cotral (cotralspa.it), SIT Bus Shuttle (sitbusshuttle.com), TAM (tambus.it) and Terravision (terravision. eu). Shuttles between the airport and Rome hotels are also an option.

Leonardo Express trains offer the fastest and easiest ride to the city centre, zipping to Stazione Termini (€14) in 32 minutes and running every 15 minutes from 6.23am to 11.23pm. Slower FL1 trains to Trastevere, Ostiense and Tiburtina stations operate from 5.57am to 10.42pm (€8).

HOW MUCH FOR A

Taxi
€48
45–60min

Terravision bus
€10
1hr

Leonardo Express
€14
32min

TAXI
Metered city taxis are white (ignore everyone else); credit card machines are required by law. Free Now (free-now.com) is the go-to taxi app.

RIDE-SHARE
Uber Black is available as an executive-level option in Rome (and Milan) only. You're out of luck elsewhere in Italy.

DISCOUNT CITY CARDS Roma Pass (romapass.it) and the 72-hour Omnia (omniavaticanrome.org) include unlimited travel on the city's public transport network for their duration. Purchase the former online or at Roma Pass network museums and sites, tourist Infopoints and select subway ticket offices (48/72-hour €32/52); the latter, which includes Vatican City, is sold online (24/72-hour €55/113).

OTHER POINTS OF ENTRY

Milan's Aeroporto Malpensa and Venice's Marco Polo Airport are also well served by nonstop flights from around the world. Low-cost carriers fly from a growing number of European cities to more than two dozen Italian destinations, typically landing in smaller airports such as Rome's Ciampino Airport and Bologna's Guglielmo Marconi Airport.

Regular trains on two western lines connect Italy with France (one along the coast and the other from Turin into the French Alps). Trains from Milan head north into Switzerland and on towards the Benelux countries. Further east, two main lines head for the main cities in central and eastern Europe. Those crossing the Brenner Pass go to Innsbruck, Stuttgart and Munich. Those crossing at Tarvisio proceed to Vienna, Salzburg and Prague.

Passenger and car ferries sail from numerous Italian cities (including Trieste, Ancona, Bari, Genoa, Venice, Brindisi, Savona, Salerno and Palermo, among others) to a wealth of countries such as Greece, Albania, Croatia, Spain, Morocco, Malta, Montenegro and Tunisia.

Roadways link Italy with Austria, France, Slovenia and Switzerland.

TRANSPORT TIPS TO HELP YOU GET AROUND

Italy's long and narrow figure makes it especially suitable for train travel; a well-connected, high-speed network helps ensure this is the most popular mode of transport in the country. There's something to be said for having your own wheels as well, though; this gives you the freedom to explore outside the main cities and take to the countryside. Andiamo!

CAR

Italy's national automobile association, the Automobile Club d'Italia (aci.it) is a driver's best resource. Travellers holding driver's licences from non-EU countries should obtain an International Driving Permit (IDP) through their national automobile association.

BICYCLE

Cycling is a great way to get around (and thwart the ZTLs in city centres!). Bike-friendly cities include Turin (175km of bike paths), Ferrara (largest number of bikes per capita) and Lucca (car-free biking paradise). Theft isn't uncommon, so invest in a heavy-duty lock.

CAR RENTAL PER DAY

from €30

Petrol approx €1.50/litre

Motorway tolls €9/100km

PLANE Italy's flag carrier, Alitalia (alitalia.com), flies domestically. Several low-cost airlines also operate in the country, including Milan-based Neos (neosair.it), Blue Panorama (blue-panorama.com), Ryanair (ryanair.com), easyJet (easyjet.com) and Volotea (volotea.com).

BUS Bus companies provide everything from local buses to fast, reliable intercity connections. Routes are heavily regionalised, but Italybus (italybus.it), SAIS Autolinee (saisautolinee.it) and SAIS Trasporti (saistrasporti.it) offer some national routes.

DRIVING ESSENTIALS

Drive on the right; the steering wheel is on the left.

Speed limit 130km/h; 50km/h in urban areas unless otherwise posted.

Blood alcohol limit 0.05% (0% for drivers under 21).

Give way to the left at intersections and roundabouts.

Zone Traffico Limitato (ZTLs) restrict traffic in city centres.

Most Italian cities and towns enforce restricted traffic areas known as a Zona Traffico Limitato (ZTL; Limited Traffic Zone) and driving into them – despite where your GPS tells you to go or the location of your hotel – results in big fines. ZTLs are always clearly marked but not always in English. Never drive into an Italian city centre without inquiring about the ZTL; passes are often available for purchase – ask your hotel.

TRAIN The biggest service provider is state-run Trenitalia (trenitalia.com), followed by private company Italo (italotreno.it) and Lombardy's regional Trenord (trenord.it). From slowest to fastest, Trenitalia's services are Regionale, Espresso, Intercity/Intercity Night, Frecciabianca, Frecciargento and Frecciarossa. The longest high-speed route is Turin to Reggio Calabria, 1387km covered in 10 hours and 50 minutes.

FERRY *Navi* (large ferries) sail to Sicily and Sardinia, while *traghetti* (smaller ferries) and *aliscafi* (hydrofoils) serve smaller islands. Most ferries carry vehicles; hydrofoils do not. Direct Ferries (directferries.co.uk) lets you search routes, compare prices and book.

TAXIS & RIDE-SHARES Calling a taxi means the meter starts rolling from wherever they are coming from – not when you enter the vehicle. Uber is generally banned (Uber Black exists in Rome and Milan only), so, while convenient, taxi fares add up quickly.

KNOW YOUR CARBON FOOTPRINT A flight from Milan to Naples would emit about 216kg of carbon dioxide per passenger. A car would emit 174kg for the same distance. A train would emit about 46kg. There are a number of carbon calculators online. We use Resurgence at resurgence.org/resources/carbon-calculator.html.

ROAD DISTANCE CHART (KMS)

	Amalfi	Bologna	Florence	Milan	Naples	Reggio di Calabria	Rome	Turin	Valtellina
Bologna	625								
Florence	531	109							
Milan	824	216	303						
Naples	62	576	573	772					
Reggio di Calabria	462	1049	946	1246	491				
Rome	278	376	273	573	226	700			
Turin	941	332	420	145	889	1363	689		
Valtellina	949	341	428	131	897	1371	698	261	
Venice	777	154	256	270	725	1199	526	401	337

ITALY GETTING AROUND

DANGERS, ANNOYANCES & SAFETY

Italy is generally a very safe country for travellers, but always keep your wits about you as you would at home. Petty theft and scams, natural disasters and some pesky mosquitoes (though non-disease carrying) can certainly interrupt your Italian dream.

MOSQUITOES
Hot and muggy lowlands (especially in the Veneto and Tuscany), coastal towns and islands are perfect breeding grounds for mosquitoes, including the beastly tiger incarnation. Between March and November, take appropriate precautions.

EARTHQUAKES Due to its position where the African and Eurasian tectonic plates converge, seismic risk in Italy is very high, with the central Apennines bearing the brunt of the risk. Rome, Florence and Bologna are in the danger zone. Be aware of your surroundings and move away from potential falling objects if you feel a shake.

VOLCANOES Italy has the world's largest number of volcano-risk-exposed inhabitants. Sicily's Mt Etna, Mt Vesuvius near Naples and Mt Stromboli on Stromboli are all persistently lively. If caught near an eruption, use a dust respirator mask and goggles to protect yourself from inhaling volcanic ash. Italy's Protezione Civile (protezionecivile.gov.it) monitors threat levels.

TRAVEL SCAMS Italy-specific travel scams: restaurants overcharging in heavily touristed zones (always ask for an itemised receipt: *'Il conto dettagliato'*); offers of free coats from women posing as fashion house representatives in Rome; and imposters posing as fiscal police (Guardia di Finanza) who demand restaurant receipts in the street (always ask for a badge; call 113 if in doubt).

Immuni (immuni.italia.it) is Italy's official contract-tracing app. The EU Digital COVID Certificate ('green pass') is required for access to events, restaurants, museums, long-distance travel and more. Proof of vaccination from some non-EU countries is recognised. Check your government's advice before travelling.

LIGEIA/SHUTTERSTOCK ©

THEFT & FRAUD Pickpockets and thieves are very active in touristy areas and on crowded public transport. In case of theft or loss, report the incident to the police within 24 hours and ask for a statement.

DRUGS
If caught with a deal-able quantity of drugs, you risk prison sentences up to 22 years. Cannabis possession for personal use is decriminalised, but possession of other drugs is punishable by administrative sanctions.

QUICK TIPS TO HELP YOU MANAGE YOUR MONEY

TAXES & REFUNDS A 22% value-added tax known as IVA (Imposta sul Valore Aggiunta) is included in the price of most goods and services. Non-EU residents who spend more than €154.95 in one shop at a single time can claim a refund when leaving the EU (the refund only applies to purchases from stores that display a 'Tax Free' sign). For more info, see taxrefund.it.

CREDIT CARDS
Major cards are widely accepted (Amex less so) in most places but some accommodation, restaurants and attractions are cash only.

MONEY CHANGERS
ATMs offer better rates for getting Euros, but exchange offices *(cambio)*, post offices and some banks exchange money.

CURRENCY

Euro

HOW MUCH FOR A

Espresso
€1.10

Negroni
€7

Midrange meal
€13–23

SAVING MONEY Italy generally offers good value but there are ways to save more.

City tourist cards Offer substantial discounts on local attractions and tours – and sometimes free transport.

Bus passes Purchase multi-ticket passes instead of pay-as-you-go on board.

Bars/cafes Always take coffee/brioche at the bar to avoid table service charges.

ATMs
ATMs *(banco-mat)* are widely available, accepting cards tied into the Visa/MasterCard/Cirrus/Maestro systems. Avoid Euronet ATMs, which charge inflated fees and exchange rates.

BARGAINING
Gentle haggling is common in street markets (though not food markets). Haggling in stores is generally unacceptable, though good-humoured bargaining at smaller shops in the south is not unusual if making multiple purchases.

PAYING THE BILL In a restaurant, you must ask for the bill (*'Il conto, per favore?'*), though it's not uncommon to simply walk up to the register and ask to pay. For your own protection as well as discouraging tax avoidance, do not let a restaurant drop a piece of paper with nothing but a scribbled total – ask for an itemised bill (*'Il conto dettagliato.'*). Overcharging in very touristy areas unfortunately happens – sometimes even making international headlines! – so pay attention while dining out.

TIPPING Italians do not generally tip.

Restaurants The *coperto* (cover) is already included in restaurant bills and includes service and bread.

Bars No.

Taxis Absolutely not.

Hotels Foreigners might; Italians not so much.

RESPONSIBLE TRAVEL

Tips to leave a lighter footprint, support local and have a positive impact on local communities.

ON THE ROAD

Calculate your carbon. There are a number of online calculators. Try resurgence.org/resources/carbon-calculator.html.

Eat seasonally. Truffles, tomatoes, porcini, artichokes (pictured right), asparagus, courgette flowers – Italy boasts some of the best produce and ingredients in the world. Eating seasonally ensures it's always fresh and local.

Immerse yourself. Travel slowly and delve into local life.

Bring your own. Put together a handy ecofriendly travel kit with reusable bags, cups and cutlery, water bottle, steriliser and the like.

Eat pizza! SP.accio (spaccio. sanpatrignano.org) pizzeria in the therapeutic rehabilitation community of San Patrignano near Rimini is run by (and supports) members of the community.

Support clean economy tourism. Staying in cooperative-run estates in Calabria and Sicily confiscated from the mafia. Libera il G(i)usto di Viaggiare (ilgiustodi viaggiare.it) and AddioPizzo Travel (addiopizzotravel.it) specialise in ethical anti-mafia travel.

RIMMA BONDARENKO/SHUTTERSTOCK ©

GIVE BACK

Visit national parks and protected areas (parks.it) and support organisations conserving wildlife and biodiversity.

Support social enterprises. Check out Legacoopsociali (legacoopsociali.it) and Federsolidarietà (federsolidarieta. confcooperative.it) for ideas.

Clean up the coastline. Annual beach clean-up initiatives, known as Spiaggia e Fondali Puliti, are organised by Italy's best-known conservation group Legambiente (legambiente.it).

Work on an organic farm. World Wide Opportunities on Organic Farms (wwoof.it) provides a list of farms seeking volunteers for a membership fee of €35.

Join short-term community projects covering the environment, archaeology and arts. Concordia International Volunteer Projects (concordiavolun teers.org.uk) lists opportunities.

Help revive towns and villages unaccustomed to tourism. According to Legambiente, there are over 2500 'dying villages' in less well-trodden regions like Umbria, Calabria and Molise.

DOS & DON'TS

Don't touch frescoes or other works of art – natural oils in your fingers contribute to their deterioration.

Don't picnic on or at historic steps, fountains, museums, ruins or monuments.

Do dress to impress – appearances matter in Italy.

Don't touch produce with bare hands – plastic gloves are provided.

LEAVE A SMALL FOOTPRINT

Forgo flights and ride the rails! Italy is particularly suited to travel by train. And its charming towns and villages are best seen on foot and by bicycle.

Get a real rural experience. Italy's network of *agriturismi* (agriturismo.it) offers affordable, authentic experiences in incomparable settings, often with meals sourced on site.

Avoid cruise ships. Though they are now banned from Venice's historic centre, cruise ship pollution remains a serious issue.

Say no to digital pollution. Travelling long distances for one Instagram shot of Burano leaves a large footprint.

ITALY POSITIVE-IMPACT TRAVEL

SUPPORT LOCAL

Shop local By souvenirs (like Amalfi Coast ceramics, pictured left) from local businesses, especially in small towns where tourist cash goes a long way.

Eat local Be on the lookout for members of Italy's Slow Food (slowfood.it) movement and products advertised as 'Km0'.

Buy direct Seek out gifts and souvenirs like Murano glass or Tuscan olive oil directly from artists, artisans and independent shops. Look for the 'Made in Italy' campaign for locally produced goods.

CLIMATE CHANGE & TRAVEL

It's impossible to ignore the impact we have when travelling, and the importance of making changes where we can. Lonely Planet urges all travellers to engage with their travel carbon footprint. There are many carbon calculators online that allow travellers to estimate the carbon emissions generated by their journey; try resurgence.org/resources/carbon-calculator.html. Many airlines and booking sites offer travellers the option of offsetting the impact of greenhouse gas emissions by contributing to climate-friendly initiatives around the world. We continue to offset the carbon footprint of all Lonely Planet staff travel, while recognising this is a mitigation more than a solution.

RESOURCES

aitr.org
borghiautenticitaliditalia.it
legambienteturismo.it
fondazioneuniverde.it

UNIQUE & LOCAL WAYS TO STAY

There's a surplus of traditional lodging choices in Italy, including plentiful hostels, guesthouses and hotels, but the country also affords no shortage of unique options. Sleeping in a sasso (cave dwelling), trullo (conical stone hut) or an ancient monastery are highlights, and a weekend farm stay combines the best of Italy.

HOW MUCH FOR A

Campsite
€5-25

Agriturismo
€40-80

Designer hotel
from €200

ANDREA IZZOTTI/SHUTTERSTOCK ©

CONVENTS & MONASTERIES
Italy's convents and monasteries count as some of the country's most divine and memorable lodging options. Many working convents and monasteries let out cells or rooms as a modest revenue-making exercise and happily take in tourists, while others only take in pilgrims or people who are on a spiritual retreat (both popular in Assisi, for example). Elsewhere, such as Umbria's Eremito (eremito.com), ancient religious institutions have been converted into luxury lodging while preserving much of the original architecture and ethos. Double rooms hover in the €70 range.

MOUNTAIN HUTS
Italy's user-friendly *rifugi* (mountain huts) in the Alps, Apennines and other mountains are usually only open from June to late September. Offerings range from rudimentary shelters (known as *bivacchi*) to hostel-like Alpine lodges with heating, electricity and often hot meals. Club Alpino Italiano (cai.it) keeps an updated *rifugi* directory.

SHAITH/SHUTTERSTOCK ©

FARM STAYS
Live out bucolic dreams at one of Italy's growing number of *agriturismi* and *masserie* (farm stays). Perfect for families, relaxation and cultural immersion, *agriturismi* range from rustic farmhouses to luxe country estates. While long a booming industry in Tuscany and Umbria, farm stays have spread across the country, with options from Trentino-Alto Adige to Sicily.

Two of Italy's most unique and atmospheric accommodation types are found in the south and are well worth a visit.

SASSI In otherworldly Matera in Basilicata, ancient *sassi* (cave dwellings) have found new life as boutique hotels (pictured). These limestone caves, considered potentially part of the third-longest continuously inhabited human settlements on earth, were once denounced as a national shame. In the 1950s, Prime Minister Alcide De Gasperi didn't mince words when he considered the appalling living conditions and abject poverty of the cave dwellers, who were eventually moved out. Decades later, preserving the extraordinary uniqueness of the *sassi* earned Matera Unesco World Heritage status and sleeping in the caves is one of Italy's most exceptional overnight experiences.

TRULLI Next door in Italy's heel, the characteristic whitewashed conical houses of Puglia, known as *trulli*, are another remarkable accommodation option. Often jokingly referred to as Smurf houses, these dry-stone huts were originally constructed as field shelters and storage structures, and are found scattered about the countryside. Like Matera's *sassi*, the *trulli* are now a Unesco-listed World Heritage Site in Alberobello, where these unique architectural treasures make up entire neighbourhoods of the village.

BOOKING Accommodation rates fluctuate enormously depending on the season, with Easter, summer and the Christmas period being the typical peak tourist times. Seasonality also varies according to location. Expect to pay most in the mountains during the ski season (December to March) or on the coast in summer (July and August). Conversely, summer in the parched cities can equal low season; in August, many city hotels charge as little as half price. Visitors may be charged an extra €1 to €7 per person per night as a 'tourist tax' or 'room occupancy tax'.

Lonely Planet (lonelyplanet.com/hotels) Find independent reviews, as well as recommendations on the best places to stay – and then book them online.

Agriturismo.it (agriturismo.it) Farm-stay bookings across Italy.

Campeggi.com (campeggi.com) Campground bookings nationwide.

Essential Italy (essentialitaly.co.uk) Italian holiday villas, apartments and hotels.

Monastery Stays (monasterystays.com) Monasteries and convents.

In Italia (initalia.it) Good resource for hotels and *pensioni*.

BBItalia.it (bbitalia.it) B&B listings throughout Italy.

Bed-and-Breakfast.it (bed-and-breakfast.it) B&B listings throughout Italy.

B&Bs A bed and brioche is Italy's most common lodging choice, ranging from restored farmhouses and city *palazzi* (mansions) to seaside bungalows and rooms in family houses. Double prices cast a wide net (€60 to €140).

ESSENTIAL NUTS & BOLTS

HOLIDAYS
Public holidays total 11 annually. Most Italians take their yearly holiday in August – many businesses close for at least part of this month.

DRESS CODE
Cover shoulders, torso and thighs when visiting churches and dress smartly when eating out – Italians don't appreciate beach attire in restaurants.

SMOKING
Smoking is banned in enclosed public spaces, which includes restaurants, bars, shops and public transport.

FAST FACTS

Time Zone
UTC+1

Country Code
39

Electricity
220V-230V/
50Hz

GOOD TO KNOW

Italy isn't exactly app-friendly – calling for a restaurant reservation or taxi is still the norm.

The legal drinking age to be served alcohol in a restaurant or bar in Italy is 16.

Pack your pills as over-the-counter medicines are expensive in Italy.

Visas are not generally required for stays up to 90 days. Some nationalities require a Schengen visa.

Besides in museums, galleries, department stores and train stations, there are few public toilets in Italy.

ACCESSIBLE TRAVEL

Cobblestone streets and pavements blocked by cars and scooters make getting around difficult for wheelchair users.

If travelling by train, arrange assistance through SalaBlu (salabluonline.rfi.it).

Many urban buses are wheelchair-accessible; however, some of the stops may not be – ask before you board.

Some taxis are equipped to carry passengers in wheelchairs; ask for a taxi for a sedia a rotelle (wheelchair).

Village for All (villageforall.net/en) performs on-site audits of tourist facilities

A list of accessible beaches is available from Fondazione Cesare Serono (fondazioneserono.org).

Accessible Italy (accessibleitaly.com) is a useful resource.

Download Lonely Planet's free Accessible Travel guide from shop.lonelyplanet.com/categories/accessible-travel.com

GREETINGS

Greet strangers in public with a *'buongiorno'* (good morning), *'buonasera'* (good evening) or *'salve'* (hello).

EMERGENCY NUMBERS

If you need emergency services, dial 118 (ambulance), 112 or 113 (police) and 115 (fire).

TABLE MANNERS

Eat pasta with a fork, not a spoon; it's OK to eat pizza with your hands.

FAMILY TRAVEL

At state-run museums and sites, admission is free for under-18s.

Infants under 36 months of age travel free of charge on Italo trains; on Trenitalia, under 48 months travel for free without a seat (with a seat, there's a 50% discount).

Some restaurants offer a *menu bambino* (child's menu), but it's not common – Italian kids eat what adults eat! Order a half portion (*'mezzo porzione'*).

When in doubt: gelato!

ITALIAN MENUS

Menus are divided into the following sections: *antipasti* (something to nibble on, like an appetiser), *primo* (first course, always pasta), *secondo* (second course, usually meat or fish), *contorni* (side dishes, usually vegetables) and *dolce* (dessert).

POLICE

The Italian police are divided into three main bodies: the *polizia di stato* (civil police), who wear navy-blue jackets; the *carabinieri* (military police), in black uniforms with a red stripe; and the grey-clad *guardia di finanza* (fiscal police), responsible for fighting tax evasion and drug smuggling.

LGBTIQ+ TRAVELLERS

Same-sex relationships are legal, but Italy is fairly conservative in its attitudes – discretion remains wise.

Overt displays of affection by LGBTIQ+ couples can attract a negative response, especially in smaller towns.

Displays of affection in more gay-friendly cities (Bologna, Florence, Milan, Naples and Rome, among others) and some coastal towns and resorts (Torre del Lago in Tuscany, Taormina in Sicily and Gallipoli in Puglia) will draw distinctly less attention.

Head to Gay.it (gay.it) for LGBTIQ+ news, features and gossip.

Left Milano Pride

Standard Italian is taught and spoken throughout Italy. Regional dialects are an important part of identity in many parts of the country, but you'll have no trouble being understood anywhere if you stick to standard Italian. The sounds used in spoken Italian can all be found in English. If you read our pronunciation guides as if they were English, you'll be understood. The stressed syllables are indicated with italics. Note that *ai* is pronounced as in 'aisle', *ay* as in 'say', *ow* as in 'how', *dz* as the 'ds' in 'lids', and that *r* is a strong and rolled sound.

TIME & NUMBERS

What time is it?	*Che ora è?*	ke o·ra e
It's (two) o'clock.	*Sono le (due).*	so·no le (doo·e)
Half past (one).	*(L'una) e mezza.*	(loo·na) e me·dza

in the morning	*di mattina*	dee ma·tee·na
in the afternoon	*di pomeriggio*	dee po·me·ree·jo
in the evening	*di sera*	dee se·ra
yesterday	*ieri*	ye·ree
today	*oggi*	o·jee
tomorrow	*domani*	do·ma·nee

1	*uno*	oo·no		**6**	*sei*	say
2	*due*	doo·e		**7**	*sette*	se·te
3	*tre*	tre		**8**	*otto*	o·to
4	*quattro*	kwa·tro		**9**	*nove*	no·ve
5	*cinque*	cheen·kwe		**10**	*dieci*	dye·chee

BASICS

Hello.	*Buongiorno.*	bwon·jor·no
Goodbye.	*Arrivederci.*	a·ree·ve·der·chee
Yes./No.	*Sì./No.*	see/no
Please.	*Per favore.*	per fa·vo·re
Thank you.	*Grazie.*	gra·tsye
You're welcome.	*Prego.*	pre·go
Excuse me.	*Mi scusi. (pol)*	mee skoo·zee
	Scusami. (inf)	skoo·za·mee

What's your name?
Come si chiama? (pol) — ko·me see kya·ma
Come ti chiami? (inf) — ko·me tee kya·mee

My name is ...
Mi chiamo ... — mee kya·mo ...

Do you speak English?
Parla/Parli — par·la/par·lee
inglese? (pol/inf) — een·gle·ze

I don't understand.
Non capisco. — non ka·pee·sko

EMERGENCIES

Help!	*Aiuto!*	a·yoo·to
Leave me alone!	*Lasciami in pace!*	la·sha·mee een pa·che
Call the police!	*Chiami la polizia!*	kya·mee la po·lee·tsee·a
I'm lost.	*Mi sono perso/a. (m/f)*	mee so·no per·so/a

Index

000 Map pages

MARGHERITA RAGG

Born and raised in Milan, Margherita loves exploring the city by bike, and hanging out with her cat Tappo. She is the co-creator of The Crowded Planet travel blog, and is in the process of launching a new Milan-focused website.

@the_crowded_planet

My favourite experience is riding my bike along the Navigli. Naviglio Martesana is great for a sunset ride, while Naviglio di Bereguardo is my go-to for a nature escape.

KEVIN RAUB

Bologna-based Kevin Raub has co-authored nearly 100 Lonely Planet guides. When at home, he is likely savouring irresponsibly hoppy craft beers and managing the adventures of his future travelling offspring, Austin Zeno Superstar.

@RaubontheRoad

My favourite experience is arriving in Bologna and realising everything you knew about Italy's second most famous dish was wrong. But the truth is a gourmand's revelation!

EVA SANDOVAL

Eva writes about food and travel for publications like *Condé Nast Traveller*, *BBC Future* and *Fodor's Travel Guides*. She divides her time between Italy and the US, eating and writing as much as she can in both countries.

@ieatmypigeon

My favourite experience is bingeing on street food in Naples. There's nothing in the world that a *cuoppo di pesce* can't cure.

NICOLA WILLIAMS

Lonely Planet's Tuscany expert for more than a decade, Nicola lives a scenic flit through the Mont Blanc Tunnel from Italy. When not trail running or wild swimming in the Alps, she writes for Lonely Planet, the *Telegraph*, *Guardian* and BBC.

@tripalong

My favourite experience is Tuscany's Northwest Farm Feasts. To tramp through woods in search of your own aromatic white truffle, and later eat it, is gourmet gold.

THIS BOOK

Design development
Lauren Egan, Tina Garcia, Fergal Condon

Content development
Anne Mason

Cartography development
Wayne Murphy, Katerina Pavkova

Production development
Mario D'Arco, Dan Moore, Sandie Kestell, Virginia Moreno, Juan Winata

Series development leadership
Liz Heynes, Darren O'Connell, Piers Pickard, Chris Zeiher

Commissioning Editors
Michelle Bennett, Rosie Nicholson, Sandie Kestell

Product Editor
James Appleton

Book Designer
Virginia Moreno

Cartographers
Anthony Phelan, Corey Hutchison

Assisting Editors
Gabrielle Stefanos

Cover Researcher
Lauren Egan

Thanks Ronan Abayawickrema, Gwen Cotter, Lauren Egan, Clare Healy, Karen Henderson, Alison Killilea, Anne Mason, John Taufa

ITALY OUR WRITERS

Our Writers

ANGELA CORRIAS

Sardinia-born Angela is a Rome-based travel journalist and blogger. Passionate about culture and lesser-visited destinations, she is writing a book about her travels and life in Afghanistan.

@angelacorrias

My favourite experience is strolling Rome's off-the-beaten-path streets and neighbourhoods to find hidden gems and underground historical sites.

ERICA FIRPO

Erica is a Rome-based travel journalist, cultural anthropologist and podcast host of *Ciao Bella*, focusing on 21st-century Italy and its creators. She is a contributor to *Washington Post, Fathom, Conde Nast Traveller* and more.

@ericafirpo

My favourite experience is a street art stroll from Testaccio to Ostiense while munching on a *trapizzino*.

DUNCAN GARWOOD

Rome-based Duncan is a guidebook author and travel writer specialising in Italy and the Mediterranean. He's worked on more than 70 Lonely Planet titles and written for newspapers, magazines and websites.

@DuncanGarwood

My favourite experience is feasting on *porchetta* and other local specialities after a long day's walk in the woods of the Castelli Romani.

BENEDETTA GEDDO

Benedetta has lived in France, Ireland, Poland and the US before returning to her native Italy where she is now based. Her work, ranging from travel to pop culture to politics, has been published in Italian and international media.

@beegeddo

My favourite experience is the Festival of Festivals in Asti. Eating and drinking outdoors when summer is almost over feels quintessentially Italian to me.

PAULA HARDY

Paula is a travel journalist who loves modern-medieval cities like Venice and Marrakesh, between which she divides her time. She's authored over 25 Italian Lonely Planet guides and contributes to the *Telegraph, Guardian* and *New York Times*.

@paulahardy

My favourite experiences are madcap Biennale openings, kayaking in the surreal quiet of the lagoon and *aperitivo* with friends on a sunny *fondamente* (canalside).

STEPHANIE ONG

A hankering to see the world took Melbourne-born Stephanie to Milan, where she's based. She's written travel guides and coffee-table books for Lonely Planet and Le Cool Publishing. When she's not writing, she's eating well and complaining about tax – like every good Italian.

My favourite experience is standing in front of *The Last Supper*. No matter how many times I've seen it, the experience always seems astonishingly new.